RICHARD
HUGHES
NOVELIST

RICHARD HUGHES
NOVELIST

RICHARD POOLE

POETRY WALES PRESS
1986

POETRY WALES PRESS
56 PARCAU AVENUE, BRIDGEND, MID GLAMORGAN

British Library Cataloguing in Publication Data

Poole, Richard
1. Hughes, Richard, 1900-1976 —
Criticism and interpretation
I. Title
823'.912   PR 6015.U35Z
ISBN 0-907476-52-X

Cover design: Jeane Rees
Cover Photograph: Julian Shepherd

Published with the financial assistance of the Welsh Arts Council

Typeset in Baskerville by Afal, Cardiff
Printed by Antony Rowe Ltd., Chippenham

Contents

This book is for Lucy McEntee,
Penny Minney,
and Robert and Sheila Hughes

Foreword

I first met Richard Hughes at Coleg Harlech, the Welsh Residential College for Adults, in September 1973. The occasion was a week-end course organized by the English Language Section of Yr Academi Gymreig, the Welsh Academy. After I had chaired a talk given by Hughes on the future of the novel, Hughes asked me whether I'd mind if he attended, on the following morning, a lecture I was giving on his work. I said I wouldn't. So, next day, each of us found himself undergoing a unique experience: I talking about the work of an author present in my audience, and Hughes listening to a lecture on his novels. Certainly he didn"t make it difficult for me: whenever I looked towards where he sat at the back of the room, I saw him sitting hunched forwards, staring at the back of the chair in front of him. He never looked directly at me. When, afterwards, I asked him what the experience of being lectured about was like, he replied that it was a very strange experience. Why? — because many of the things I had found in his books were not things he had consciously put there. Immediately we were launched upon the mutually fascinating question of the kinds of meaning that novels contain, and debating the validity of interpretation. There was no sense of constraint between us; it seemed easy and natural to talk about his work with him. These initial encounters proved the first of a number which took place at irregular intervals during the next two and a half years — mostly at Môr Edrin, his home, but on one occasion at the flat my wife Sandra and I rented in Harlech. I had already published an essay on *A High Wind in Jamaica,* and was flattered to discover that Hughes had read it and thought highly of it. So I subsequently sent him drafts of my next two essays on his work. These he read carefully and courteously; he would suggest that I develop this point, or expand that, but he would never take issue with me on the rightness or wrongness of my interpretations. Towards the end of 1975 I sent him a draft of an essay on *The Human Predicament.* His reply of January 23rd 1976 — less than three months before his death — makes a distinction between two orders of symbolism which harks back to the very first conversation we had at Coleg Harlech, and is entirely characteristic of his theoretical thinking:

> You know that I rate questioning above answering as the writer's
> proper function: conscious symbolism tends to serve the latter
> category, unconscious symbolism the former. Again conscious
> symbolism tends to be merely simple, to strike a single note of
> meaning, whereas unconscious symbolism tends to be multiple — to
> convey a whole polyphony of meanings. And this thought brings us on
> to the two distinct headings under which the 'meaning' of any piece of
> writing has to be considered: there is its causal meaning, the state
> duced the writer to write it, and its effective meaning — the state of
> mind which reading it induces in a reader, which may be very different
> and yet is surely an equally valid subject for the critic to consider.
> Resonances woken in the reader's mind by symbolisms of which the
> writer may be totally unconscious can play an important part in
> 'meaning' of this latter kind — even if the reader remains unconscious
> of them too!

My first visit to Môr Edrin occurred shortly after a review I'd written of
The Wooden Shepherdess had appeared in *The Anglo-Welsh Review*. After we
had dined, Hughes took me off into his book-lined study where a fire blazed
before his worn leather-upholstered furniture — a sofa and an armchair.

"I read your review of *Shepherdess*," he said.

"Oh yes . . .?" I replied somewhat tentatively: "What did you think of it?"
The review had mixed praise and criticism, with the former
predominating. I wondered apprehensively if this was to be a case of the
critic getting some of his own medicine.

But, to my surprise, rather than pointing out my woeful lack of
perspicacity, Hughes proceeded to express a qualified dissatisfaction with
the book. "It was a transitional piece," he told me: "I wrote it too quickly."
Too quickly! And he'd spent twelve years on it!

At the time I took this comment at face value: was it not, after all,
delivered in a suitably grave voice? Now, reflecting upon his words, I
wonder if an irony lurked there. For Hughes was an extremely complex
man.

I cannot claim to have 'known' Hughes — whatever 'knowing' a person
means, if such a thing is possible (he himself believed it wasn't) — but I can
at least describe him as, in these last few years, he appeared to me. He struck
me above all as a quiet man. In a group, he invariably gave the impression of
being engaged in a deep reflectiveness, as if his deepest life was going on
inwardly. But, in response to the voicing of some ill-considered opinion, he
would snap out of his contemplativeness to fire a verbal arrow into the
proffered target with devastating effect. He was, then, a companion in

whose presence it was wise to weigh your words. And yet there was nothing of the stand-offish about him, nothing of the self-preening complacency of The Famous Man of Letters. Though dignified, he was a modest and even a humble man. He never gave me the impression of one who has achieved, after many years and much experience, an eyrie from which to look down upon an absurd world and, confidently and authoritatively, to pronounce upon human follies and issue judgements pregnant with 'wisdom'. He struck me as a man who, conscious of how time treats human vanities and self-importances, had schooled ego until it had dwindled to a pinpoint. I imagine him to have been, then, a man still searching, still open to influence: that outer quietude masked — like the still surface of a lake the many fish swimming beneath it — an inner restlessness.

I say this tentatively, conscious that Hughes was a man of many personas. "You only knew Diccon in his latest transformation — the grizzled Tolstoyan sage," Amabel Williams-Ellis once told me. Was there an irreducible Richard Hughes beneath this and other 'selves'? If there was, I have not discovered it. Hughes himself was much preoccupied with the question of identity, and his later theoretical pronouncements insist upon the need for human beings to recognize and respect one another's 'personhood'. But he was not a philosopher, and he nowhere seeks to define personality in the sort of terms that might satisfy a philosopher. 'Personhood', perhaps, is a matter for faith rather than something susceptible of analytical proof — an assumption indispensable to a civilized existence. For if we must prove analytically that 'persons' exist before we are prepared to respect them, then (he might have said) we are indeed lost. As perhaps we are. . . But if each of us contains no irreducible psychological 'essence', if we are only a series of transitive personae held together by a fallible memory, if (to borrow Hughes's own metaphor for T.E. Lawrence) the onion man is composed only of layer upon layer of flesh: then the septuagenarian Hughes, the self-deprecating Tolstoyan, was as authentic a version of the man as any other I might have encountered at an earlier point along his life-line.

*

I have divided this book into two parts. The first, which is biographical, is less than half as long as the second, which is critical. In Part One I have sought to compete neither with Penny Hughes's delightful Memoir of her father (*Richard Hughes: Author, Father*) nor with the work of Hughes's authorized biographer, Richard Perceval Graves. Rather, my purpose has been to sketch in enough of the life to show what sort of a writer Hughes was, to outline the ideas he held at various times about the craft of writing, to describe the circumstances in which his works were written, and — tentatively — to identify some of those areas of personal experience which fed his creativity.

I have no single, dominant thesis to propound. I do not believe that thesis-ridden works do a service to their subjects. I have approached Hughes's life's-work as one might a tapestry whose inwoven patterns and motifs are irregular and yet unitary. I have sought, by identifying and attempting to keep in play as many significant threads as possible, to explore as much of the tapestry as I could in the space at my disposal. I am aware that I cannot have been exhaustive; aware, too, that this particular tapestry is unfinished, and ends abruptly and arbitrarily at an edge rudely sheared. In pursuing a polysemous approach to Hughes's writing, I am conscious of having been influenced by his own creative technique. If any convictions have guided my pen more than others, they are: that Hughes is a poetic novelist; and that he is a novelist of ideas. I am not a member of any of those contemporary schools of critical thought which deny that literary works are the products of individual and unique minds possessed of intentions which are relevant to the understanding of those works (though I recognise, as does Hughes himself in the extract I have quoted, that the authorial 'subject', even where it is not obviously a persona, is unlikely to be a wholly conscious and self-conscious entity).

To acknowledge the formal influence of the writer whose work I have set out to discuss is not, perhaps, inappropriate at the beginning of a book which has for me something of the character of a debt repaid. Hughes was a man I liked; and his books have never ceased to give me pleasure and food for thought.

*

My subsidiary debts are many. I could not have written this book without the patient and enthusiastic support of Lucy McEntee. The late Mrs. Frances Hughes, the late Lady Williams-Ellis, Penny Minney (née Hughes), Robert and Sheila Hughes, and Rose and Joe Basketts all offered me valuable help and/or hospitality. Ieuan Hughes supplied me with a fine anecdote. Michael Bakewell most kindly gave me permission to quote from his radio script 'Richard Hughes — A Life Sentence', and I am grateful for the words of those contributors individually identified in my text.

My thanks also to Alfred Holt and Co., who gave me permission to quote from documents relating to the voyage of *S.S. Phemius* in 1932. For bibliographical aid I am indebted to Peter Thomas and John Jenkins.

Martin Eckley, Linda Tomos and Marian Jones, the librarians of Coleg Harlech, have been indefatigable in searching out obscure material for me, and I bow to them. I am grateful also to the librarians of William Brown Library, Liverpool; the Central Library, Bradford; and the Brotherton Library in the University of Leeds; in all of which institutions I was made welcome.

No one but myself is responsible for my style and opinions, but George Wray, Jim Fletcher, and my wife Sandra, who read and criticized this book in draft, have undoubtedly saved my readers from some of my direr perpetrations.

Last but not least, I must acknowledge my debt to Cary Archard and Mick Felton of Poetry Wales Press, who have encouraged me throughout this project.

Richard Poole
Llandanwg, December 1985

PART ONE:

A Life, and Letters

"Part of Diccon's originality consists
in having defeated the mediocrity of
contemporary life."
— Lance Sieveking

Chapter One: Childhood and University

Recalling his early childhood in later life, Richard Hughes wove a tapestry dominated by three motifs: the person of his mother, his intense sensuous awareness of natural objects, and the fact of death.

As a small child, his senses were vividly alive. He could distinguish people by their smell — just as his dog Rory could. Motorcars passing even as much as a field's width away would set the two of them sneezing their separate heads off. The neglected regions of the garden tugged invitingly at him; he penetrated shrubberies, haunted a rotting summerhouse, roamed woods where the vegetable smells he most liked hung for the taking on the air:

> The cool smell of the north side of a beech-tree trunk . . . . The ground under hazel-bushes . . . . A flint newly kicked out of the damp earth. The smell of a twig where a bat has been hanging, or of a hare's form . . .[1]

Not just his nose was keen: his fingers, ears, eyes all communicated a world of sensual joy — or pain:

> *All* sound was bell-music; the sight of any friend was a vision of angels. Even English summer heat was a blast furnace; a wasp's sting, the martyr's worst pangs. Each experience of sight or sound or touch, each scent, each sweat or shiver, each slipperiness or stickiness or wetness, existed of itself and for its own sake . . .[2]

When Hughes came to write his first novel, it would be the vivid realm of childhood he would evoke — albeit on the island of Jamaica rather than on the island of England. And that realm would contain danger as well as ease, terror as well as pleasure, and mortality amidst the astonishing fecundities of animal and vegetable nature . . .

Born at Caterham, Surrey, on the nineteenth of April, 1900 — so that his age lagged always only a few months behind the century's — Richard

Arthur Warren Hughes shared his middle names with a brother, Arthur Warren Collingwood Hughes. This brother died, aged thirteen months, when Richard was eight days old. Their father Arthur Hughes (born 1861) was employed in the Public Record Office. *His* father, also Arthur Hughes (born 1836), was the third son of William Hughes (born 1803), a Barrister-at-Law whose brothers Sir Frederick and Sir William Collingwood Hughes had been, respectively, the seventh and eighth baronets of East Bergholt. The first baronet, Captain Sir Richard Hughes, a Commander of the dockyard at Portsmouth, had been raised to the peerage on the seventeenth of July, 1773. The Hughes family had thrown up naval men and clerics, but, before Richard Arthur Warren, none for whom writing counted for as much as — or more than — God or the sea. Debrett *does*, however, mention Sir Richard Hughes the second baronet: "who was 2nd in Cmd. under Lord Howe in the memorable relief of Gibralter, and who captured the *Solitaire*, and beat the French in a sea fight off Barbados in 1782." This Sir Richard was so good a French scholar that he translated *The Spectator* into that language — thus providing at least one Hughes who combined a vivid physical life with a taste for literature. When Richard Arthur Warren's father chose his son's forenames, he placed before his own, Arthur, quite the most resonant that his family had passed down through the years. The third, Warren, was the maiden name of Richard's mother, Louise Grace Warren, whom he married in 1897. Arthur Hughes survived two of his children, but died when the third was five years old.

The thirteen-month son I have already recorded. A daughter, Grace Margaret Lilias, born in 1898, survived till 1902 — three times as long. Richard Hughes remembered this sister:

> I think those who knew us felt that death had chosen selfishly in taking my sister rather than me. Everyone liked her. She used to sit perfectly still for hours, till the pigeons came and ate crumbs from her hand; but I would hide in the bushes till the birds were within a foot of her, and then roll out with a loud "boo" to scare them. This I thought very funny; but nobody else did.[3]

He remembered his father, but not his father's voice: for a course of treatment for cancer of the throat which Mr. Hughes underwent in Germany had involved the cauterizing of his vocal cords. So, by the time his daughter died, the father could only whisper. Then he too died — of pneumonia, suddenly.

When Richard was told of his father's death, he wept tears of despair. Instead of taking tea in the drawing-room with his two aunts, he had it in the kitchen with Cook. Even the raspberry jam tasted of salt. Waking in the night, it seemed to him that he must have dreamt his father's death: surely it was too appalling to be true. He crept to his mother's room to find, not the reassurance he sought, but a reiteration of the brutal fact. Morning came; the house woke up to its grief. And then

> midmorning, and I suddenly wanted to ask Father something so scampered up to his room and flung open the door — to find the death-room darkened with drawn blinds, heavy with the scent of his favourite narcissus; and under the stiff folds of the sheet what looked like a not very skilful wax copy of my father.
>
> How on earth could I have *forgotten* — I, who loved him so much?[4]

Hughes felt that at this moment he understood not only death but guilt. Death he understood as well as an adult understands it, but guilt even better:

> for how can any adult sense of guilt (so condoned and qualified with excuses) compare at all in horror with the searing, excuseless guilt of a guilty child? Luckily not: for grown-ups couldn't stand it. They are so much less tough than children, who are tough with the toughness of a grain that has not yet sprouted.[5]

This is the perception of a man whose childhood is intensely alive in him. Yet Hughes does not sink regressively into his past self, cede it the field. No sooner do grown-ups drop in the scales of the comparison than, with a jerk, the balance comes level again: children's toughness is something untested as yet by life. The double-mindedness of the whole is pure Richard Hughes.

Arthur Hughes's early death left his family poorly-off. In a household crammed with aunts — "a grey synod" — Mrs. Hughes supported her only surviving child by writing novelettes for magazine publication. Dick, as his mother called him (he seems himself to have adopted the nickname 'Diccon' at a later date), was fundamentally a happy child. When his happiness became too intense to bear, it bubbled out of him in verse. He would secrete himself among the laurel bushes until the words snaking about in his mind had uncoiled themselves into sense. Then, trying hard not to forget what he had composed, he would carry the finished product to his mother, who would record it in a notebook. This before he could read or write. So, at the age of six, he composed these lines:[6]

> Fair maiden, fair maiden,
>   Come spin for me:
> Come spin till you're laden,
>   Though hard it may be.

> 'Tis an honour and glory
>   To be a king's maid,
> Though (I'll not tell a story)
>   You won't be well paid.

I once asked Hughes if the title of this poem, 'Invocation to the Muse', was his own, and original. He replied firmly that it was. Few writers, one imagines, have possessed the audacity, not only to summon the Muse at so tender an age, but to warn her that she's going to get little for her pains.

At the age of seven he composed 'Explanation, on Coming Home Late'.[7]

> We went down to the river's brink
> To of those clear waters drink,
> Where the fishes, gold and red,
> Ever quickly past us sped,
>
> And the pebbles, red and blue,
> Which we saw the green weeds through
> At the bottom shining lay:
> It was their shining made us stay.

I'm inclined to think that, his extravagantly split infinitive notwithstanding (has it not, in fact, considerable charm?), Hughes never wrote a more attractive poem than this. Certainly he wrote more ambitious poems, but 'Explanation' is a splendid achievement for a seven year old. It is indeed explanatory, not excusatory. Its visual lucidity, childlike without being childish, suggests an unclouded innocence; and its last line possesses an utterly unselfconscious wistfulness which must, one thinks, quite disarm the irate parent for whom, in witty anticipation of a late homecoming, it has been prepared.

Hughes's mother not only delighted in her son's oral compositions, she fed his imagination by telling him stories. On one occasion, he recalled, his attention was straying from the story of Heracles and the giant Atlas which she was recounting when his imagination was transfixed by the phrase: "He holds up Heaven on his shoulders!"

> Before my inward eye, there flashed a vivid picture: the Cyclopean figure of the giant, his enormous hams based on half the desert plains of Africa — the clouds floating lightly round the straining muscles of his back — his mile-thick neck, bending like a willow under that unthinkable weight — the limitless blue vault which sprang from this single pillar. For I was given to seeing things like that, in pictures.[8]

The language in which his childhood act of imagining is expressed here is plainly that of the mature, consummate artist. For all that, the passage makes explicit what is implicit in "Explanation, on Coming Home Late": not only was Hughes the boy gifted with spontaneous vibrant powers of visualization, he possessed also an ability to translate mental images into language. Other stories Mrs. Hughes told her son concerned her childhood in Jamaica. She had lived there till she was ten. She spoke of the wild landscape, its exotic flora and fauna, and of her adventures on the island. Dick never forgot, among other things, her account of how to set tree-snares to catch uncircumspect birds.

After his father's death, his godfather Charles Johnson became the most important male figure in Hughes's life. Johnson, like Arthur Hughes, worked in the Public Record Office. He was an authority on Mediaeval Latin, and on the Domesday Book. The writer Lance Sieveking believed that Hughes's "invariably gentle" voice had been acquired from his godfather, who talked "in exactly that very gentle, rather flat tone, pronouncing certain words in a way peculiar to himself, and occasionally making a startling statement in the very same quiet, ordinary tone."[9]

Between 1904 and 1908 Hughes attended a Kindergarten half a mile from his home in Caterham. He began Latin there, but it was not until he moved on to the Dene Preparatory School that school-work became a serious matter. There at the age of ten he started Greek and encountered the scholarship system, which he later described as "a perfect instrument for ruining the intelligence of any child who is suspected of having one".[10] He was a slow worker, taking much longer to do his homework than any of his classmates. He would usually give the whole of a weekend over to the writing of his weekly essay — which sometimes amounted to three or four thousand words.

Of his childhood holidays, two stand out in importance. While staying in Essex at the age of eight, he came across a derelict duck-punt on the mudflats.

> I stepped a willow-pole (of all timber!) for mast, in a bit of old iron. A sack ripped open served for a squaresail — two ropes I controlled with my hands, two I trimmed with my bare toes, and I steered (perceptibly) with a board tucked under my arm. No Americas Cup contestant certainly: but the rapture of spanking along at a round knot and a half! Sliding over the mud in a few inches of water, and jeering at the proper yachts stuck fast till the next tide! Vermin that I was, I used to hail them and offer them a tow.[11]

A lifelong enthusiasm for wind and sea had begun. Then, when he was eleven, his mother took him to Barmouth for a holiday. It was his first visit to

Wales, and seminal. He scrambled about the empty slopes of Cader Idris; he learnt by heart the first verse of 'Mae Hên Wlad fy Nhadau' (Land of My Fathers). Returning to Caterham, he felt homesick for the place he'd just left. "I determined then and there to live in Wales as soon as I was able."[12] The homesickness was atavistic indeed: Hughes's ancestors had, after all, emigrated to England in the time of the Tudors. *And* embraced with apparent zeal the lifestyle of English gentry. But Richard now, making use of researches pursued by his grandfather Arthur Hughes (who died in 1909), and encouraged by his godfather, investigated his Welsh ancestry. He found that the charges on the quarterings of Hughes of East Bergholt's shield represented, respectively: Hughes; Elystan Glodrydd; Beli Mawr; Tudor Trevor; Gwaeth Voyd Vawr; Ynyr King of Gwent; Ithell Felyn of Yale; and Llewellyn Aur Dorchog; an impeccable, if remote, Cambrian kin. Later he told his daughter Penny that he had discovered he was descended both from the goddess Venus and from Regan, King Lear's wolfish daughter; and that for a long time he had closely observed his aunts with a view to ascertaining whether Venus or Regan predominated in them. Inconclusively, it would appear . . .

In 1913 he won a scholarship to Charterhouse: a relief to his mother, who couldn't afford to pay for an expensive secondary education for her son, and a surprise to his schoolmaster. Perhaps as a reward he was given a bicycle and allowed, for the first time, to go off on his own on a cycle-tour of the New Forest. Each night he wrote a postcard home to say where he was.

When he arrived at the school, Robert Graves was just ending a tempestuous career there. But Hughes was in time to record the singular style in which Graves carried off two school boxing championships:

> He was a completely dark horse, and practically untaught, but he knocked the almost hypnotised school champions one after the other clean over the ropes — like the hero of a school story, except that he drank plenty of cherry brandy between the bouts.[13]

Hughes made few friends at Charterhouse, yet maintained that he had been very happy there — and that more emphatically in his earlier than in his later years. At the end, in fact, he found himself "pushed into" the position of head boy, and absolute monarch over six hundred others. Thus he was responsible for the task of beating his juniors — one that he carried out although he took little pleasure in it — thinking the business even ridiculous.

He was now working towards an Oxford scholarship. As the years went by, the study of Latin and Greek became not easier, but increasingly onerous. A period of very early rising (4 a.m.) gave way to a practice of working through the night one night per week: "The threat of a breakdown, however, and stringent doctor's orders, finally brought some relaxation."[14] Suddenly his chief interests were scientific and mathematical. His brain worked on dimensional geometry and practical calculus. He invented a sighting apparatus for the accurate dropping of bombs, and a perpetual lunar calendar. Then built a telescope "from inked cardboard tubes"

> powerful enough to show the rings of Saturn, to photograph the spots on the Sun, and to study the larger of the valleys and mountains of the Moon; or, for terrestrial purposes, one could read a book with it, if the light was good, a hundred yards off.[15]

Practical or not, it sounds as though he'd done just that.

He felt that the poetry he wrote during his adolescence didn't, in general, represent a great advance on his earliest efforts. There is, however, 'The Ballad of Benjamin Crocker'.[16] Benjamin is a pirate:

> Fierce was his scowl, and his skin tanned red,
> And a knotted silk kerchief covered his head
> That was scarred with ivory, steel and lead:
> He wore three knives, and a cutlass, too,
> To slit the gullets of men of thew:
> Or his thumbs could strangle a whole ship's crew . . .

The folk that voyage with "Bloody Ben" are "none of them squeamish sort of men", and are accustomed to pillage and kill to their hearts' content. Somewhere on the coast of Brazil, however, the crew gets too drunk to leave the beach, and Benjamin sets out alone. Coming across old Gal-gar-ul he snaps her bones "like a dry quill pen" — just as a matter of course. Then comes the poem's most suggestive stanza:

> He burnt the place, and he took away
> (Warm your guts with a soak of rum!)
> A small green flute for his child to play
> (Drink, till the New Jerusalum!)
> And a scented idol of smooth hard wood,
> And knotted strings, and a feather hood
> — Things he hardly understood.
> And horny knives, of a strange device,
> And things ill-gotten, above all price:
> Ear-rings, nose rings: gone in a trice:
> And slaked his thirst with a draught of rum.

Ben fails to notice the black beast that hobbles in Gal-gar-ul's shadow and follows him back to his ship.

Next day they found the Captain dead
In thick green bilge, without nose or lip,
His entrails plastered across his hip,
In a mess of blood where a foot might slip,
And an oozy track where the Thing had come.

It is all done with a swaggering relish and a quite amoral detachment. When Hughes returns to the theme in adulthood, however, it will be to find that a little girl is quite as effective in doing for a buccaneer as a three-legged obscure Thing.

In his last year at school he accepted an invitation from Charles Graves, a classmate, to visit his family home near Harlech. It is more than likely that he encountered Robert Graves at this time, for Graves, who had married earlier in the year, spent the summer of 1918 with his wife's family near Harlech. Hughes scouted the area until he located in the grounds of Maes-y-Neuadd (a Tudor mansion not far from Talsarnau that is now a hotel), a single-roomed half-ruined Cromwellian cottage called Ysgol Fach. This 'little school' had been a dame-school; now it housed leaf-mould. Hughes rented it from the Stuart-Wortleys (the family which in turn rented Maes-y-Neuadd) at the princely cost of fourpence a year, two pots of honey, and three days' work in the landlord's garden. (After one day's work, part of the rent was remitted because he did so much damage!) There was a large hole in the roof. This he attacked at first from below; then, when he could do no more, he enlisted the help of a child who positioned roof-slates in accordance with his directions: for the roof was too frail to bear his own weight. Clearing the leaf-mould, he uncovered a spring. This rose under the fireplace, meandered across the stone floor, and exited through the door. His furniture — acquired at the expense of the four pounds which was his entire fortune — consisted of "a really noble kitchen table, two backless oak chairs from somebody's wood-shed, and an iron spring mattress one end of which rested at night on the kitchen-table and the other on the windy window-sill".[17]

After only a few days' residence, he wrote 'Old Cat Care',[18] a poem celebrating the sense of untroubled freedom that living in the cottage gave him. It begins:

Green-eyed Care
May prowl and glare
And poke his snub, be-whiskered nose:
But Door fits tight
Against the Night:
Through criss-cross cracks no evil goes.

With the windows still unglazed and the spring still undrained, he invited, in his "pride", his first guest — the novelist Frank Penn Smith. Smith, a childhood friend of his grandmother, was en route from Nigeria to a German spa where he intended to take a course of treatment for rheumatism.

> My guest slept on that precarious 'bed' poised between wind and water while I roosted in a loft. It cured his rheumatism: in the end he never needed to go to the spa at all. Apparently only dampness is bad for rheumatism, and real running water under the bed is a positive cure.[19]

Hughes soon felt "firmly established" at Ysgol Fach. "I taught myself to cook, and refused ever again to regard as my home the house in England where I had been brought up."[20] He was to enjoy the cottage for three years.

At Charterhouse, as an army cadet, he had commenced military training. On leaving, he was sent to a training camp for young officers. His predicament there was precisely that of Augustine Penry-Herbert, the central character of his two post-war novels, whom Hughes makes exactly his own age. In *The Fox in the Attic* we find a description of Augustine directing a squad of boys in bayonet practice:

> Scowling as savagely as he could he jerked out the staccato commands "In! — Out!— On guard!" while the little boys struggled with their heavy rifles and bayonets to jab the swinging sacks of straw called 'Germans' piping as they did the officially-taught obscenities supposed to arouse blood-lust in them. (p.110)

The passage brings to mind one from Graves's *Goodbye To All That*: observing, on his return to France in January 1917, instructors at the Bull Ring seeking to instil into their reluctant trainees precisely the same newly-prescribed enthusiasms, Graves was glad to get to the front away from it.[21] Both Hughes and Augustine had every reason to expect their absurd play-acting to turn into the real thing. The terrible truth of the situation was this: young men could not expect to survive much beyond the age of nineteen. Their sisters might live out their lives, they would not. Hughes's Army service was cut short by an illness which required his hospitalization — then, abruptly, the war ended. It is not, I think, unreasonable to take Augustine's response of stupendous shock as his creator's own:

> No one had warned him he might after all find himself with his life to live out: with sixty years still to spend, perhaps, instead of the bare six months he thought was all he had in his pocket. Peace was a condition unknown to him and scarcely imaginable. The whole real-seeming world in which he had grown to manhood had melted around him. It

was not till Oxford he had even begun to build a new world — he, and his whole generation — from the foundations up. (*FA* p.111)

And it was to Oxford, to Oriel College, that Hughes went in the January of 1919.

He found it "a strange place in those days".[22] The university was more than half-full of ex-soldiers; some of his fellow-under-graduates were Brigadier-Generals. There was a young Greek who had been a Governor in the Aegean between the ages of nineteen and twenty-one, and who was still politically active. And there were numerous writers: Robert Graves came up two terms after Hughes; Robert Nichols, Aldous Huxley, L.A.G. Strong, Roy Campbell, Alan Porter, John Strachey and Edmund Blunden were also there. Hughes later wrote:

> Coming up to Oxford almost straight from school, it made me feel a sad failure that I should have reached the advanced age of nearly nineteen without having a book or two to my credit, or a year or two's fighting, like my friends.[23]

Through Graves, he met T.E. Lawrence, then a Fellow of All Souls — and was enormously impressed by him. One night, in the summer of 1921, Lawrence spent several hours telling Hughes, Hugh Lyon, and a few others the story of his life. Despite what he regarded as his "unusual powers of forgetting", Hughes claimed that he remembered everything Lawrence said — apart from the reason for this extended narrative. (Later, reading *Seven Pillars of Wisdom*, he would recognise incident after incident.) Contact with Lawrence aroused in him "the highest kind of numinous excitement"[24] he believed himself capable of feeling. This was Lawrence's "middle period", when what Hughes termed his "suicide inwards" had been "determined upon but not begun".[25] Reviewing Lawrence's *Letters* in 1938, he would recall:

> At that time you met plenty of people who were ready to tell you (all differently) what Lawrence was really like. They had seen through this layer or that, and underneath the "real" Lawrence was so-and-so. Well, you can do that with some men: peel off the skin, like the skin of an apple, and see the flesh of the fruit. But Lawrence was built more like an onion — where for every skin you peel off there is another underneath, for-ever-and-ever-Amen. There was no getting — then — at any "true" Lawrence.[26]

The completeness of Lawrence's later self-abnegation fascinated Hughes. The fact that Lawrence had achieved greatness seemed to him less remarkable than the fact that, having achieved the heights, Lawrence had wilfully renounced them.

> Other men, who have risen as high as he did, have either struggled higher or missed their hold and fallen. Lawrence neither struggled higher nor fell. He dived. He beat his way back into obscurity against greater opposition, both without and within, than he had faced when he beat his way to fame. To a level of obscurity lower than he had risen from.[27]

Lawrence's death in a casual motor-cycle accident was not, then, inappropriate.

It's not perhaps surprising that, with such men as Graves and Lawrence at Oxford, with W.B. Yeats for a time inhabitant of the town, and with John Masefield, Robert Bridges and A.E. Coppard living within walking distance, Hughes should find the University classroom less than magnetic. Later, he had no choice but to admit that his career there was "an uneasy and restless one, and a scholastic failure".[28] Despite soon abandoning the study of the Classics in favour of English Literature, he still seemed "temperamentally incapable"[29] of absorbing anything from his tutors. It was from his friends that he learnt: from Masefield in his gardener's cottage at Boar's Hill, and from Graves — who lived at Islip with his wife Nancy and their rapidly growing family.

Graves, who himself "studied fitfully for his degree in English Literature"[30] between 1919 and 1925, was, during the earlier part of that period, engaged in writing the poems that went into *Country Sentiment* (1920) and *The Pier-Glass* (1921), and on the essay *On English Poetry* (1922). In a seventieth-birthday tribute that he paid to Graves in 1965, Hughes wrote:

> there seemed more pith in some half-sentence he shot over his shoulder, darting from the scullery with frying-pan in one hand and poem in the other to still some urgent nursery howl, than in any interminable college lecture-room.[31]

On English Poetry was subtitled *Being an Irregular Approach to the Psychology of This Art, From Evidence Mainly Subjective.* Its limited but genuine originality lay in the fact that Graves was the first Englishman to attempt to describe the process of poetic composition by means of psychological conceptions — and by the ideas of Freud in particular. Graves defined poetry as "the unforeseen fusion in [the poet's] mind of apparently contradictory ideas",[32] but saved it from incoherence by insisting that, having awakened from the trance in which he has created his draft-poem, the poet must work on in a consciously critical spirit in order to render the finished product intelligible to a reader. Hughes's first collection, *Gipsy-Night and Other Poems,* came out in 1922 in advance of *On English Poetry*. Its author testifies to the importance that Graves's ideas had for him when, in a brief Preface, he refers to Graves's imminent book as "Probably the most important contribution to modern poetical theory". (If he knew of Eliot's 1919 essay, 'Tradition and the Individual Talent', he nowhere reveals that he did.) Declaring rather grandly that Graves's theory is grounded in a conception of "Man as a Neurotic Animal", he goes on to summarize it in a single sentence:

> Poetry is to the poet ... what dreams are to the ordinary man: a symbolical way, that is, of resolving those complexes which deadlock of emotion has produced.

But although Hughes felt that Graves's argument contained truth, he could allow it, in 1922, only the status of a partial truth. Why, we must wait till a later chapter to see.

Even before going up to Oxford, Hughes had embarked upon a pattern of vacational activity which might have been designed to counteract the constraining effects of a childhood spent in a household full of overprotective women, and of a public school education. Determined to rid himself of the taint of gentility, he would walk down to his cottage in North Wales — sleeping rough, and cultivating the company of "tramps, beggars and vagabonds" [33] The poem and stories he wrote between 1918 and 1922 — many of them at Ysgol Fach — reflect this penchant for inelegant living. He writes of tramping in 'A Song of the Walking Road', and in 'Vagrancy' [34]:

> Down to a beechen hollow winds the track
> And tunnels past my twilit bivouac:
> Two spiring wisps of smoke go singly up
> And scarcely tremble in the leafy air.

of night-time landscapes and obscure travels in 'Weald', 'Dream' and 'The Moonlit Journey' [35]:

> The crescent road is ivory
> Between the silver water:
> But squat and black and creeping, see,
> Blank as the shadow of a tree,
> Old Robert and his daughter
> Toil on: and fearful, each descries
> Moon-gleams in others.

and of the lives of vagabonds or gipsies in 'Gipsy-Night' 'Tramp' and 'Winter' [36]:

Hunger-weak, snow-dazzled,
   Old Thomas Kelly
Thrusts his bit hands, for warmth,
   'Twixt waistcoat and belly.

The story 'Poor Man's Inn' draws upon a chance encounter with a singular showman, and was later translated into the one-act play *The Man Born to be Hanged*.

Before leaving Charterhouse, Hughes had acted as sub-editor (to G.H. Johnston, who later became Lord Derwent) on *The Carthusian*. At Oxford he resumed the partnership, and the two brought out four issues of the exotically named *The Topaz of Ethiopia*, the first appearing promptly in February 1919. As Hughes later put it, the magazine "flared and died"[37] — but not before it had featured a number of things by him. In 1921 he co-edited *Oxford Poetry* with Graves and Alan Porter. These literary activities did not always run smoothly. On May 25th 1921, he published in *The Isis*, under the pseudonym 'Elge', the following poem:

The Heathen's Song

Oh, give me gods of lively stone,
   Of limbs and painted eyes,
Or spirits on the breezes blown:
   I'll pay them sacrifice!

I'll dance the moon down, up the sun,
   In wine fuse night and day,
And let my flickering passions run
   Like fire in sparkled hay:

Or give me gods of grimmer mould,
   With hell-fire in their veins;
Whose lightnings crack the over-bold
   From crown to smoking reins.

And I'll stretch Beauty on a stone
   Naked and young and dead,
So Hecate's rusty light alone
   Dare show how Beauty bled.

For gods and devils give me these
   And each shall have his due:
But shall I tumble on my knees
   At name of bastard Jew?

> Or bow, while wrinkled maids devour
>   Like kine with harmless cud
> A God new-made of wheaten flour
>   With sweetened wine for blood?
>
> Thou Shapeless Master of the fold,
>   Eyeless and full of eyes:
> I see men wizen and grow old
>   To win Thy heavenly prize:
>
> I see men wizen and grow dry
>   Who live before Thy face —
> I'd sooner damn my soul, would I,
>   Than sell it for Thy Grace!

Oxford's Victorian authorities seemed disinclined to read this high-spirited squib as a product of Negative Capability. Lord Alfred Douglas(!) rose up in horror to condemn it and to recommend its author's removal from the University. Lord Curzon, the Chancellor, was shocked by it. Dr. Farnell, the Vice-Chancellor, and an authority on comparative religion, summoned Hughes before him for a lecture on the subject of blasphemy. One wonders if Hughes stopped short of declaring to Farnell what he wrote about this time in an unpublished Preface to his poems: "I must confess to being a polytheist both in religion and art."[38] An apology subsequently appeared in *Isis*, to be followed by an editorial in *Cherwell* which contrived both to disparage the poem ("artistically without merit or originality . . . in the very worst of taste, thoroughly offensive . . . and legally indefensible")[39] and the tender susceptibilities of the authorities.

But if Hughes was active *within* University circles, he was positively *busy* outside them. His poems and stories began to appear in a variety of newspapers and magazines, and in 1920 he became a regular poetry reviewer for the *Saturday Westminster Gazette* reviewing books by, among others, D.H.Lawrence, Edward Thomas, W.H. Davies, Graves, Blunden, Elroy Flecker and W.E. Henley. He was enjoying the hectic life of a literary man whilst still a student.

A developing interest in drama led him to join a play-reading group which called itself The New Elizabethans. The group held its meetings at an inn called The Paviours Arms in that part of Oxford called Paradise. Yeats sometimes came to the readings, and A.E. Coppard also joined in. But the meetings took place during prohibited hours, and one night the Proctor burst in upon them, fully gowned and mortar-boarded. He demanded the names and colleges of the students present — who could now look forward to the prospect of being heavily fined and gated for the rest of the term. But Hughes reported the disaster to Yeats, who wrote a supportive letter to the Proctors which resulted in The New Elizabethans getting off with a fine of half a crown each. Forced to abandon The Paviours Arms, the group moved to an attic at the top of a varsity club called the Hypocrites which Hughes, a member of that club also, found for them. A few hours sufficed to apprise them of the attic's chief drawback: it was infested by fleas. This was adding injury to insult. The New Elizabethans, bitten by insects as well as Proctors, abandoned their enterprise in despair.

In his second year at University, Hughes wrote his first play *The Sisters' Tragedy* : and this in a single twelve-hour sitting, without revision. When he showed it to John Masefield, Masefield invited him to mount a production in his house. This took place on January 24th 1922, with Hughes himself playing John. Unfortunately he never recorded the name of individual members of what he teasingly described as the play's "distinguished audience" — nor their reactions to it. Masefield sent the play to London, where it was quickly accepted for the Grand Guignol series at the Little Theatre. No sooner was it in rehearsal, however, than news reached Hughes that the censor had banned it — not on grounds of sexual or religious offensiveness, but "apparently . . . only . . . for the ferocity of its tragedy".[40] Fortunately the censor relented under persuasion, and the play had its first night at the Little Theatre on May 31st. On the same bill was a one-act play by Noel Coward, almost as obscure a writer as Hughes in those days. The drama critics of *The Times* and *The Observer* both thought *The Sisters' Tragedy* the best item on the bill. In the latter St. John Ervine wrote:

> Mr. Hughes has a poet's sensitiveness to the presence of human beings, but he has not yet learnt the dramatist's craft. He tells this story at too great length and repeats situations . . . but by a singularly beautiful ending averted the danger of destruction which might have overwhelmed any other dramatist . . . When all his faults are enumerated, there remains this happy conclusion, that Mr. Hughes has brought a sense of poetry and humanity to his work which disables criticism and leaves us hopeful of his future.

This verdict did not displease Hughes, who had written the previous October, in a never-sent letter to Amabel Williams-Ellis: "I still think my idea was good, but the actual writing is inconceivably crude." In the event the play's success served even further to reduce the rump of commitment that he felt towards his degree-studies. When he got his second Fourth, the provost considered sending him down. Hearing of this, Hugh Lyon, a senior student, hastily got in touch with the Provost and asked him to remember Shelley — "the only poet that Oxford ever turned out, in both senses".[41] In later life Hughes would boast of this double Fourth, though in fact he left Oxford with a Third. But at the time he was ashamed of having let down P.C. Lyon, the Bursar of Oriel. And yet, even as he apologised to Lyon, he was moved to express his disgruntlement with what he saw as the critical conservatism of the tutor who conducted his viva.

Gipsy-Night and Other Poems appeared a few months before he left Oxford. It was produced by The Golden Cockerel Press in an edition of 750 copies. Poems of the walking-road dominate the book — of tramping, vagrancy, gipsy-life. There are poems of summer heat and wintry cold, of rain and storm. Others make use of specifically Welsh material — the legend of a murdered Saint, the poet's experience of a *hwyl*-rich sermon. It is plain that, if Hughes remained an outsider to the lives of the North Welsh, the landscape and climate of Snowdonia had entered his imagination:

> The clouds sail past in argosies
> And cold drips the rain:
> The whole world is far and high
> Above the tilted plain.
> The silent mists float eerily,
> And I am here alone.

('The Rolling Saint')[43]

Some time in 1921, Colonel Kirkby, the owner of Maes-y-Neuadd, returned to re-possess his property. Scandalized at finding a scruffy student occupying a half-ruined cottage in his grounds, he lost no time in giving the young man his marching-orders. So it came about that Hughes printed, opposite 'Old Cat Care' (his celebration of Ysgol Fach), 'Cottager is Given the Bird'.[43] Despite its stylistic awkwardness — the product of a desire for compression — this poem articulates a genuine sense of loss. It ends:

> Door, Window, Rafter, Chimney,
>   Grow silent, die:
> All are dead: all moulder:
>   Sole banished mourner I.
>
> See how the Past rustles
>   Stirring to life again . . .
> Three whole years left I lockt
>   Behind that window-pane.

A number of the poems in *Gipsy Night* employ either this terse ballad-like stanza or a shortened line which can be made to serve both lyric and narrative purposes. The influence of John Skelton's verse is plain. It was probably Robert Graves who recommended Skelton to Hughes, for Skelton is a palpable presence in Graves's early work. Elsewhere Hughes's poetic line expands with an air of freedom, and rhymes come as they will:

> Gone are the coloured princes, gone echo, gone laughter:
> Drips the blank roof: and the moss creeps after.
> . . .
> Only from roofs and chimneys pleasantly sliding
> Tumbles the rain in the early hours:
> Patters its thousand feet on the flowers,
> Cools its small grey feet in the grasses.

('The Ruin')[44]

Only once does Hughes write in a style reminiscent of the *fin de siècle*:

> Dim the light in your faces: be passionless in the room.
> Snuffed are the tapers, and bitterly hang on the flowerless air:
> See: and this is the Image of her they will lay in the tomb,
> Clear, and waxen, and cooled in the mass of her hair.

('The Image')[45]

This is superficially impressive, yet has more than a flavour of pastiche about it. Hughes is a poet whose romanticism likes to mask itself in anti-romanticism, but here he gives it uninhibited value: so much so, perhaps, that he did not reprint this piece in his Collected Poems. However, further discussion of these poems must wait for a later chapter.

While still at Oxford, Hughes had undertaken his first significant act of travel, voyaging steerage to America on a boat carrying emigrants. This "at the height of the post-War rush, when Ellis Island was at its prime".[46] On the boat he became friendly with a number of young Central Europeans, refugees of the Peace — Hungarians and a Yugoslav — as well as encountering Germans, Greeks, Danes, Finns, Rumanians and more besides. He noted the racial feeling amongst the travellers: for example, the fuss made by the British if they were placed at the same table as "dagoes". But it was towards the latter that he gravitated, and he took a variety of language-lessons from them. When a group of second-class passengers came to the steerage to see how the lower orders lived, holding handkerchiefs to their noses and commenting upon what they saw without lowering their voices, Hughes hated them:

I did not see one of them who had the delicacy of voice or expression of even the dirtiest peasant on our deck. They were ugly to a fault, vulgar, and bored — bored.[47]

The reversal of expectation is typical of Hughes. And when a fat American saloon-keeper lingered to roll his eyes at a young Hungarian girl, Hughes and another Englishman faked a quarrel over her, pulling out knives and pretending to fight: a ruse which promptly scared him off. At Ellis Island the emigrants were treated like criminal cattle by immigration officials who themselves were scarcely able to make themselves understood in English. But at last Hughes made landfall in America proper. He stayed for three weeks in New Jersey with the Biancos, a family he had known in North Wales. (It was probably then that Pamela Bianco did the drawing of him which appears as a frontispiece to *Gipsy-Night*.) One night, during a storm, he wrote the story 'The Stranger' which he later expanded into *A Comedy of Good and Evil*. He visited New York, but the city aroused in him a response of hatred mixed with fear. He sold some work and returned to England, where his account of his experiences on the voyage out, 'The Diary of a Steerage Passenger', was published.

Chapter Two: Playwright and Novelist

Hughes's Central European travelling-companions had projected a visit for him to the Balkans, and within a week of leaving Oxford he was in Vienna with four friends, buying a dinghy to paddle down the Danube. His day-by-day record of his experiences was serialized in seven parts as 'A Diary in Eastern Europe' in *The Weekly Westminster Gazette* between September 9th and November 4th 1922. He discovered two Viennas: the outward city and its people, which he described as "notoriously beautiful", and the dilapidation and poverty of the backstreet warrens. Rainwater dripped green from the ceiling of the room he slept in, a steady stream of curses came through the walls, and vermin romped across the floor. The party took to the river, which immediately activated Hughes's descriptive powers:

> As we put out, the sun rose ahead of us, golden in a host of small clouds, like little green fish-scales: every swirl and eddy of the river was caught with colour and light. Sometimes an eddy would seize the boat, swinging it right out of its course, or, as the river poured over some big rock deep in its bed, would slide suddenly down hill, then wriggle through the choppy water beyond.

Approaching Pressburg, he found that

> the river was like a series of lakes or lagoons, although the current was still as swift as ever. It is an odd thing about the Danube in these reaches: but it *sings*: there is a perpetual humming, as if a myriad bubbles were bursting, several fathoms deep; and where there is an eddy or a lasher, you can hear it many miles off.

The idyll was soon punctured by the appearance of officialdom. A motor-launch pursued them after they put in for a meal at Pressburg, on the Czechoslovak bank of the river. Having inspected the party's passports, however, the official handed them back with a smile, and the dinghy could continue. This incident indicated the shape of things to come: the party was to be 'arrested' a further six times on its journey south. Meanwhile, Hughes found the designation of the Danube as frontier between Hungary and Czechoslovakia an artificial thing:

> in all our landings on the left bank, we did not find a single Czech among the civilian population; it is as purely Magyar as the right, and intensely and passionately anxious to be joined to its proper nation.

A series of picturesque towns and villages provided agreeable stopping points until the party reached Budapest on September 4th. There, hotels were expensive but food cheap, and cigars and liqueurs unlimited. Here Hughes spent much of his time talking politics. At the root of current Hungarian resentments lay the Treaty of Trianon of June 4th 1920. By this the Allied and Associated Powers had liquidated the ancient multinational state of Hungary, reducing its size and population by two thirds, assigning three million Magyars to other states and two and a half million Croatian-Slavonians to Yugoslavia, and requiring Hungary to pay reparations of an unspecified amount. This dismemberment spelt economic disaster for Hungary: Budapest itself had, in recent years, experienced two royalist uprisings, a Bolshevik revolution, and a destructive occupation by the Rumanian army. Yet to the sympathetic Hughes it seemed that the Hungarians in the capital, despite their talk of invasions and insurrections, preferred a "slow death to a desperate remedy". They were waiting for others to take a revolutionary lead — the Magyars in Rumania, the Croats in Yugoslavia. When it was hinted to the Englishmen that things might be about to happen in Zagreb, they sold their boat and boarded a slow train to the Balkans.

In Zagreb, a city swarming with armed soldiers and policemen, they found they hadn't the price of a bed between them. Wandering about the moonlit countryside on the edge of the city, they were stalked by nervous vigilantes who whistled and occasionally fired their guns in the dark. Hughes, dozing in a field, was brought to consciousness by the proddings of a gun-muzzle. Armed farmers directed them back to the city where they were arrested by police in a public garden and given quarters in the University. One of the group, James Bennett, had a letter of introduction to a citizen, and the citizen in turn introduced Bennett and Hughes to Stiepan Radić. During the war years Radić had passed through phases as an Austro-Hungarian legitimist and a Yugoslav enthusiast before emerging as a Croatian particularist. His Croat Peasant party emphasized the importance of traditional ways of life and opposed the centralizing tendencies of the government in Belgrade. Hughes and his friends arrived at a time when Radić's party was pursuing a policy of parliamentary abstention. Radić swept Hughes and Bennett off on a speechmaking tour which ended at a concert given by peasant children in national dress. A week of heady political involvement followed. But a tactical withdrawal became advisable when, after noticing that his room had been searched, Hughes heard that the Secret Police were taking an interest in the Englishmen. Early one morning a car spirited them away from Zagreb, after which they travelled in a series of peasant carts to within a few miles of the frontier. A goose-girl carrying a basket of plums on her head offered to take them across by an obscure mountain-path. A patrol happened upon them, however, and they were marched to a frontier-post. There, overcoming thumping hearts, they enterprisingly dropped on the ground the only important papers they were carrying (Bennett had a letter from Radić to the Soviet Foreign Minister). When they were released, they simply pocketed them again. At Trieste, compelled by lack of funds to put up at a doss house, Hughes met a Montenegrin who possessed a fund of good stories — stories chiefly concerned with the smuggling trade. Later, Hughes would write up one of his tales under the title 'Lochinvárovič. He and his remaining companions (two by this time) eked out a precarious existence until money arrived, and then set off home.

In retrospect the Balkan interlude had about it an air of romantic escapade. While Hughes might be so fired by Radić's brand of nationalism that he made speeches to the native peasantry (in English of course — they had to be translated by an interpreter), he could never be more than an outsider dabbling in affairs that couldn't claim more than a momentary act of attention in his life. He, the artist-traveller, was no T.E. Lawrence: the romantic Lawrence actually succeeded in translating his favourite reading, the chivalric tales of Sir Thomas Malory, into lived experience. Hughes, by contrast, was a game-playing naif. And yet, there were implications of an unromantic sort to be drawn from his Balkan adventure and its aftermath. One turned upon the gulf that yawned between the artist and the politician: the first must practise detachment, the second involvement; the first must work in isolation, in a lonely functional room, the second impose his will upon others while moving on a public stage. Back in London, Hughes found that

> my finer perceptions, both in intellectual and in human relationships, were badly damaged. It was many months before I returned to normal, and before I was able to write anything except a florid and worthless kind of journalism.[1]

Then, Hughes could muse upon the real constraints which operated against the realization of political ideals. Lawrence's Arabian experience exemplified the forces of compromise which global *realpolitik* exerted upon local romantic aims: for even as Lawrence preached a fierce Arab nationalism, inspiring the desert clans to drive out their Turkish oppressors, he knew that it was unlikely, given the political ambitions of Great Britain and France, that he could deliver self-government to those he sought to galvanize into motion; and so it proved. As for Radić, he supplied a magnifying lens through which Hughes might ponder the precarious nature of the political life. In 1923 Radić embarked upon a tour which took him to Britain and North Wales — where he stayed for a while with Hughes at Garreg Fawr — and to Moscow, an experience which caused him to formulate new ideas about the partnership between peasants and workers as the basis of a future society. Back in his own country he was imprisoned, "given the choice of being shot or becoming a Cabinet Minister, and chose the latter",[2] as Hughes (who sought to draw the British government's attention to his plight) laconically puts it. For a time Radić supported King Alexander. But, having gone back into opposition, he was shot in the stomach by a Montenegrin deputy (who went unpunished) in the Belgrade *skupština* on June 20th 1928, and died seven weeks later. Whilst Hughes was not finished with romantic adventuring, it would never again assume political features.

Back in North Wales, he eventually settled down to work upon his only full-length play *A Comedy of Good and Evil.* He was now living at Garreg Fawr, a cottage near Croesor which his mother had bought by 1921, and which they shared. Mrs. Hughes was a formidable woman and, as she grew older, an eccentric one. She continued to write for little magazines, dabbled in theosophy, and had met Edith Sitwell, who corresponded with her and sent her an inscribed copy of *Façade.* As an old lady she remained fit and energetic, and surprised her grandchildren with her ability to scramble up rocks. She enjoyed gardening, believing it to be an excellent occupation for bossy people. She would say, as she busied herself with hoe and trowel, "You're a weed, out with you; you're a flower, in with you". Her *ménage* with her son, however, seems to have fostered tensions in him which, a few years later, would actually result in nervous illness.

Hughes wrote at the comparatively sedate rate of approximately two minutes of acting-time per day, and the play took precisely six months to complete. While writing it he grew a neat Van Dyke — the earliest version of his famous beard. He then had a disguise of sorts when, half way through, he broke off for a holiday which took him first to Sicily with Peter Quennell, and then back to Croatia where he stayed a few nights with Radić. The first performance of the *Comedy* was given before the Three Hundred Club at the

Court Theatre in London on July 6th 1924. J.B. Fagan then took it up, producing it first at the Playhouse, Oxford, and later at the Ambassador's Theatre in London, where its first public performance occurred on March 20th 1925. The London run was brief: the dramatic critics were divided, and even a positive review by Shaw, making one of his few appearances in a theatre audience ("anyone who can't enjoy all this must be an idiot"!), failed to save it. James Agate found it "baffling, provocative . . . even irritating", and declared that the promise of the first two Acts was not fulfilled. Lennox Robinson, who had seen the play in Oxford, gave it as his opinion that Hughes was "likely to prove one of the most important figures in our theatre".

He was wrong, for by the time the *Comedy* opened in London Hughes was finished with the theatre. He did not even see the London production. *The Sisters' Tragedy and other plays* (1924) was to be definitive — though he would later write for both radio and the cinema. The period extending from the beginning of the writing of the *Comedy* to the play's London run encompassed all of Hughes's theatrical activity after *The Sisters' Tragedy*. I say "theatrical activity" because by then he had worn the garb of an actor-manager as well as a playwright.

Early in 1923, he co-founded the Portmadoc Players with A.O. Roberts. The group was quick to publicize itself. *The Manchester Guardian* of February 27th carried the following summary of its aims:

1) To read and produce as artistically as we can plays by the best authors, especially those of young Welshmen, whether writing in Welsh or in English.
2) To encourage the serious study of the technique of playwriting, acting, and play production, and of all those crafts which help towards artistic stage production.
3) To support enthusiastically all those who are striving towards the common ideal of a Welsh national theatre which shall be worthy of the race and country to which we belong.[3]

The company's aims were more impressive than its funds, which initially consisted of 5 which Hughes himself put up. It was composed entirely of local people, some of whom Hughes would ferry to rehearsals on the pillion of his motor-cycle. The Players' first bill comprised three one-act plays: *Cloudbreak* by Roberts, *The Poacher* by J.O. Francis, and Hughes's own *The Man Born to be Hanged*. Hughes took the part of Davey in his own play. The company moved to the Portmadoc Town Hall after a single night at a converted brew-house, and the first public performance took place on March 4th. The plays were controversial: some of the populace were shocked by what they saw; one lady in a letter to *The Cambrian News* declared: "I have yet to learn that suicide is a fit subject for drama!" (Her call for the Players to act Shakespeare suggested that she was not exactly *au fait* with the works of the bard.) Local opposition to the plays arose, as Hughes saw it, not only from the 'tyranny' of the chapel in a 'Religious State', it arose also from the lack of a deep-rooted dramatic tradition in Wales, the absence of an unbroken line of significant dramatic writing. Wales possessed a rich vernacular culture which he saw as being dispersed and centrifugal as against that of England, which was metropolitan and centripetal. Whilst there was much vital local activity in communities such as that of the Glaslyn area (Portmadoc itself, a town of three thousand inhabitants, boasted three dramatic companies and an opera company), there was no process by means of which the best might be distilled from the good. Hughes and his *confrères* wished to see a national company emerge from the many local ones, the most talented actors performing the best plays. The chief misunderstanding that would arise in connection with the Players would be that this was that national company — whereas in fact the Players was only a scratch group from the Glaslyn area. Present at the first night was John Strachey, editor of *The Spectator*, who praised highly what he saw, finding in *The Man Born to be Hanged* "a note . . . which recalled some of the most poignant and menacing of Goya's 'Caprichios'", and in *Cloudbreak* the working of a dramatic mind akin to Renan. Also in the audience was Nigel Playfair, who lost no time in inviting the company to perform at the Lyric Theatre, Hammersmith. Hughes went down to London to raise money and organize matters, and the performance took place on February 26th 1924. The invitation was premature, and, despite the arguments in favour of acceptance, Hughes felt in retrospect that the Players ought to have refused it. For, although in press interviews and programme notes the company took care to explain precisely its nature and provenance, it was treated by the London critics as a National Welsh Company and, inevitably, compared to its detriment to the Irish Players of the Abbey Theatre. In spite of this adverse comparison, however, the critics were in general not discouraging, and the Players returned to North Wales with more laurels than brickbats.

Hughes now resigned as actor-manager. He felt himself "no longer necessary" to the Players, and wanted to get back to writing. But he was wrong in believing his scheme to be "well-launched", that he had "only . . .to sit back and watch the other district companies . . .spring up, and the whole movement for a Welsh National Theatre gather momentum".[4] A.O. Roberts entered the Civil Service, and the Players did not long survive.

Hughes's association with Nigel Playfair was productive in another way.

While they were dining together on Friday January 11th, Playfair happened to mention that the BBC had invited him to produce a programme of a semi-dramatic kind. He had decided on three items — "some of Vachel Lindsay's chanted poetry; one of A.P. Herbert's humorous dialogues, read in parts; the proposal scene from *Pride and Prejudice*, also read in parts"[5] — but wanted a fourth. Radio was at this time in its infancy; the first scheduled programmes had been put out early in 1922 at the rate of half an hour a week. Concerts, and even opera, had been broadcast by the end of 1923, but no drama. Playfair told Hughes that what Radio really wanted was something especially written for it. What a pity it was that he had to cast his programme on the following morning — he might otherwise have asked Hughes to write something for him! Undaunted, Hughes replied that he was confident he could produce something in the time available.

> Sir Nigel's eye went small and bland, like the eye of a calculating fish. "Ten guineas," he said, "for all rights."
> "You mayn't like my play when you read it. Let's leave terms till the morning," I countered.[6]

And so it was that Hughes came to write the first listening-play, the first dramatic piece conceived specifically for the medium — *Danger*. The chief problem facing him he took to be overcoming the difficulties of an audience used to *seeing* a dramatic situation, and now, all of a sudden, struck blind. But then, if the story happened *in the dark*, with the characters themselves unable to see . . . Playfair suggested an opening line as he showed Hughes to the door: "The lights have gone out!"

Back in his attic flat in New Oxford Street, Hughes considered various scenarios. A bedroom scene? No: "I did not know much about bedrooms, even at twenty-three."[7] An accident in a coal mine seemed to offer possibilities: "sudden total darkness, the dramatic sounds of explosions and running water, the picks of a rescue team."[8] He decided to lose a group of visitors underground — say, a young man, an old man, a girl — in order that he might make use of a greater variety of voices than a cast of miners would offer.

He delivered his play to Playfair at breakfast-time next day. The real problems arose in rehearsal. In a studio which hadn't been designed with listening plays in mind, and with transmission a primitive business, every sound effect which the script called for proved an obstacle to be overcome. It was even a task to make the speakers sound as though they were cramped in a flooded tunnel. Unable to produce an artifical echo by technological means, Playfair "decreed that his whole cast must orate with their handsome heads in buckets".[9] And, conscious that he couldn't broadcast more than a modest explosion (since anything stronger would have blown every fuse in the building), Playfair decided that the press at least shouldn't be disappointed: and secretly arranged that an ear-shattering bang should occur in the room next to the one in which it gathered to hear the programme — synchronized with the latter, of course. It worked!

Danger signalled the beginning of a long association. Hughes contributed stories, plays and talks to the BBC over a lifetime — thus earning himself a significant place in the history of radio.

But he had finished with the theatre. His reasons for ceasing to write stage-plays are not far to seek. In later years he would, when sounded on this issue, quip: "You can make a fortune as a playwright, but you can't make a living." A more serious though less witty reason was that he "resented the necessity of actors operating as a screen between the writer and his audience".[10] The poet or prose-writer works directly upon a reader and, if he cannot make himself understood, has only himself to blame; but the playwright is subject to annoyances he may be able to do little or nothing about. "No dramatist is ever content with anything but the finest possible production",[11] and with *A Comedy of Good and Evil* Hughes had found the reality far from his ideal. Whether the play was performed in Oxford, London or (in later years) Birmingham or Dublin, its Welshness

> proved a severe handicap to it. Few actors could be found who had any knowledge of the Welsh accent, or any understanding and sympathy for the Welsh character. As a result, a play which I feel sure would have appeared simple enough and clear enough if it had been performed by Welshmen for Welshmen, seemed wild and incomprehensible when performed by Englishmen for Englishmen; and on this account came in for exaggerated blame, and, paradoxically enough, for exaggerated praise too.[12]

A third reason given by Hughes was "shyness: I was scared stiff by the extrovert manners of stage people".[13]

As I have said, he never saw the London production of his *Comedy*. He had gone off to America two weeks before it was due to open. This was his second transatlantic trip, and a substantial one, for he stayed six months. Now he found himself falling under the spell of rural America, and even beginning to like New York. He revelled in the anonymity that the country conferred on him:

> I was not so fatuous as to suppose that all London was ringing with my name; on the other hand, there was at least the liability that anyone I met there might already have heard of me, to which I was abnormally

sensitive at that time, and for which I had a ridiculous and unnatural dislike . . .[14]

This sensitivity was to remain with him at least until he was thirty. The advantage of being unknown and disregarded is that one can please oneself. Again Hughes indulged his penchant for dwelling in insalubrious places: it was in an Eighth Street garret — "sitting on a table to escape the vermin" — that he filled out his first questionnaire for *Who's Who*. Then, without the least preparation, in town clothes, he drove to Canada with a friend and crossed two ranges of the Laurentians in a Chrysler. Travelling by bridle-paths, they got to Lake St. John: and so could boast that theirs was the first automobile to get there overland — the hard way. Abandoning the car, they set out with a party of Red Indians migrating towards Hudson Bay for the winter's trapping. It seemed to Hughes that the Indians poled their canoes up rapids which were virtually waterfalls, skilfully and dangerously. He tried it himself, standing on the thwart. They thus came down in an hour what it had taken them three days to work their way up.

Back in England, Hughes took stock. He felt he was slowing down, no longer subject to the rapid mental change which characterizes youth. He had been accustomed to tell himself that one should wait until one was twenty-seven before embarking on a novel. Now, however, he felt ready to ignore that prescription. For a subject had fallen upon him out of the blue.

A family friend turned up one day with a strange manuscript. Written by an old lady called Miss Jeanette Calder whom the friend had known in her childhood, it was a record of a personal experience Miss Calder had been in the habit of recounting. Her story concerned a brig, *Zephyr*, which set sail for England from Kingston, Jamaica, in April 1822, carrying a family of children. Pirates waylaid the vessel off the Cuban coast and, convinced that the Captain was carrying a large sum of money, shut the children in a deckhouse and threatened to kill them if they didn't get the money. Even when they fired a volley into the deckhouse above the children's heads, Captain Lumsden refused to talk.

> Now this was where the story took a strange turn. The pirates were not so blood-thirsty as they pretended. They let the frightened children out, and petted them, and comforted them, and took them on board their schooner and fed them on crystallised fruit; and the old lady was positive that except for the little matter of that harmless musket-volley, the pirates did nothing to harm, or frighten, or offend them in any way.[15]

No doubt the pirates wanted the children out of the way, for they proved to be less accommodating to the Captain. Tieing him to a pump, they sprinkled gunpowder under his toes. The sight of flaring matches was too much for Lumsden, and he surrendered the whereabouts of the money. The pirates seized it, returned the children to the brig, and sailed away with *Zephyr*'s new mate Aaron Smith, leaving in their wake the suspicion that Smith was in league with them.

Hughes's imagination went immediately to work:

> suppose through some accident the children had *not* been returned to the brig and the loving care of Captain Lumsden at all? Suppose these all-too-human pirates had found themselves saddled indefinitely with the whole lethal nursery-load of them . . .[16]

An odd coincidence contributed to the growth of his idea. Glancing through the endpapers of an old book, he saw announced for publication in 1824 a volume entitled *The Atrocities of the Pirates* by one Aaron Smith. Hughes located a copy of Smith's book in the British Museum: the Mate, having escaped from the pirates, had been tried and acquitted of complicity in the piracy. His story tallied in the main with Miss Calder's. Hughes then turned up old copies of *The Times* which contained Captain Lumsden's account of events.

> Naturally the Captain's own account of his conduct showed his valour in a somewhat different light from that which the others had seen it in. But, even expecting that, I was surprised to find that he never mentioned the presence of the children on his ship at all — though Aaron Smith referred to it again and again. That seemed carrying forgetfulness rather far, I thought.[17]

Just so. It was natural that Hughes's own Captain Marpole would become an object for satire; and, indeed, be made to condemn himself out of his own mouth by means of his letter to Mr. and Mrs. Bas-Thornton. But Hughes's researches didn't stop with Lumsden. He proceeded to read everything he could lay his hands on that pertained to "what might be called the decadent period of the Caribbean pirates",[18] and this general reading contributed significantly to his novel. He came across one report in which, in order to persuade captive crew members to tell them where their bullion was hidden, pirates imprisoned them below; then, bringing them up on deck one at a time, hammered on the ship's rail while one of their number screamed to simulate a flogging; then fired off a pistol, contrived a splash, and locked the sailor up elsewhere. But the crew were not fooled, and laughed in their captors' faces. Here again, what intrigued Hughes was the squeamishness of the pirates in question: "a humanitarian rot did seem to have set in. Again and again they avoided bloodshed where they could."[19]

The truly savage buccaneer appeared to be, by 1820, an extinct species.

The children, thought Hughes, would be the dangerous ones. Although, unmarried, he had at the time no children of his own, he had plenty of opportunity to observe them. He would 'borrow' the children of friends — of Amabel and Clough Williams-Ellis as well as others. He had contrived an introduction to Amabel as early as 1921 by falling off Lord Douglas, his motor-cycle, more or less at her feet, and gashing his leg: so that she found herself following up her first service to him — that of printing some of his undergraduate poems in *The Spectator*, of which she was literary editor — by acting as nurse and binding up his wound. Amabel denied that any of the *High Wind* children were based specifically on her own, but she admitted that he got a lot of copy out of Charlotte — the only one who responded noticeably to him. In Diccon's company children did things that their Mamas thought dangerous, like going out in boats or climbing mountains or waterfalls; but his size and strength were sufficient to reassure these same Mamas. At the age of eleven or twelve, Charlotte had gone through a difficult phase, suffering nightmares; Diccon would take her out walking, and was clearly good for her. But she testifies that he could be pretty alarming, and would not call a halt when something got out of hand. "There was a game he used to get us to play called Muffled Silence when you moved about in the dark and pinched people you met and they mustn"t shout. It was terrifying."[20] When she began to grow up, she felt that Diccon was disappointed: it was rather letting the side down. Amabel felt there was more than a smattering of Peter Pan in him. His eldest daughter Penny says that in his thirties her father "had a way of being able to live almost totally in the present — like an animal",[21] and that he often seemed more at home in the company of children than of adults. His capacity, when grown-up, to revert to living the timeless and unconditional life of the child, cannot be doubted: but it would be foolish to identify this child-persona as his ultimate innermost self. Such a capacity is intimately related to the negative capability of the artist, to that ability which enables a writer to 'become' what he contemplates, whether it be a cloud, a minnow, or the body of a pubescent girl. Amabel believed that Hughes had, as a child, "encapsulated" his mother's eleven-year-old Jamaican self. If this is so, and it is an attractive theory, then Emily Bas-Thornton was already potential in Hughes's unconscious, and waiting merely for the creative stimulus which would cause her to emerge. Miss Calder's story provided that stimulus.

Hughes did not visit Jamaica until long after writing *A High Wind*. But he always held his lack of first-hand knowledge of the island to be advantageous: "I seem to find it easier to write about places that I haven"t been to than places to which I have been."[22] Thus he would maintain, with that challenging logic so characteristic of him, that it is far more natural for a writer to write about what's under his *skin* than about what's under his *nose*. His own fiction, and particularly the pre-war novels, seem to argue in favour of this maxim. It is not, however, quite so simple as that. For one thing, just as he read up on pirates, he acquainted himself with Jamaica by reading travel-books about it — thus adding to that child's eye view which in his own childhood his mother had given him. For another he drew, as do all writers, on a range of material culled from personal experience — half-conscious, half-submerged — in creating his vivid and sometimes bizarre island. Thus, wild North Wales could, by a process of creative translation, become wild Jamaica. In her fascinating Memoir of her father, Penny Hughes recounts the story of an eccentric party he once attended in the backwoods of Merioneth, an experience which seems to have supplied him with the dilapidated gateway and blind donkey which crop up in the novel's opening chapter.[23]

In these last paragraphs I have written as if the writing of *A High Wind in Jamaica* went ahead without impediment. In point of fact, it was delayed:

> Just as I was about to begin, I suffered a sudden and severe illness which made all work quite impossible for a long while. In fact, it ended my career as a writer altogether for the time being; so that when it finally appeared, *A High Wind in Jamaica* was almost more like the beginning of a new career than the continuation of an old one.[24]

This "sudden and severe illness" seems to have amounted to a nervous breakdown. Hughes himself never spoke of it later, but it appears to have been brought on in part by living with his mother, in part by the demands of writing. He did, however, joke about suffering from "an anti-mother complex", a condition which doubtless contributed to his frequent flights from North Wales as well as his cultivation of the company of children. The breakdown of 1925 was only the most prolonged manifestation of a psychic complaint which troubled him on and off during his twenties. He was fond of remarking that illness acted on him like a stimulant, claiming that *The Sisters' Tragedy* was written during an attack of appendicitis — a condition which he only became conscious of when the play was finished. The illness of 1925 was not to be trifled with, however.

At this point, let us step back and consider the nature of Hughes's predilection for romantic adventuring. He himself, when he wrote of it, called it as an "anodyne", a kind of antidote to the stresses involved in writing:

> There is no excitement that I have experienced which equals the excitement of creative writing; especially of writing poetry. It lifts one

into a state of consciousness otherwise unattainable. At the same time there is nothing so fatiguing, no strain so great. If you have flown, you will be familiar with that sudden strain on the body, that uncanny increase in its weight, which comes at the moment of starting a loop. As the plane swoops suddenly upwards one is pressed into one's seat by one's burden of five hundred pounds or more of flesh. In writing, one's mind suffers the same uncanny increase of stress.[25]

Writing for him, as for all authentic writers, was inescapable. Yet, even as he bowed to the compulsion of the word, he suffered for it. Along with the need to write there grew up in him "an unconscious fear of it — a wish to escape the inhuman strain".[26] "Inhuman" is an extreme word, undoubtedly. Most writers, he felt, must experience a complex of feelings similar to his own: *their* anodynes might range from alcohol, drugs, sex, society, to writing for pulp magazines; *his* took the unusual form of a life of action. The life of action, of course, is conventionally the life that writers are supposed impotently to hanker after, believing it to be more satisfying than their own sedentary business. In a pencilled addition to a fragment entitled 'The Wall', Hughes writes: "Like all cowards I have a secret appetite for physical danger; like all introverts, a sneaking respect for action." Unorthodoxly, Hughes embraced action whilst feeling its excitements to be less intense than those he experienced when writing. This inversion is typical, and I see no reason to doubt its truthfulness. Certainly Hughes *enjoyed* danger. He was not the sort of novelist who was content to experience danger vicariously in the persons of his characters, and leave it at that: he cultivated situations in which real danger was liable to arise. When this is said, however, I do not feel it to be a complete answer. His flights from his desk in North Wales were also flights from the domestic tensions which sharing a house with his mother created in him. When life at Garreg Fawr became intolerable, he simply upped and disappeared. Later, when he was famous, his flights also were flights from people in general, flights towards anonymity. Finally, I would suggest that his deliberate cultivation of danger has about it something of the compensatory. Not only might dangerous situations supply a kind of substitute for what Hughes had missed in missing the war, they might also enable him to assuage his guilt at not being called upon to risk his life in battle. It is interesting to note Augustine's considered response to dodging the bullets of the coastguards in *The Wooden Shepherdess*:

the fact was that though he hadn't one bit enjoyed being shot at, now it had happened he wouldn't have had it unhappen again for all the gold in the world. That unbridgeable chasm at Oxford between the men who had fought in the War and the boys too young for it . . . . Now he too had been shot at and might have been killed; and for-crying-out-loud, what a load of guilt that took off one's shoulders — even admitting one's 'War' had lasted for only six seconds (or seven at most)! (pp.36-7).

Just such thoughts, I would suggest, passed through Hughes's own mind in the wake of being shot at on the outskirts of Zagreb in 1921; and perhaps at other times during his youthful adventures.

He denied "most emphatically" that his "dabblings in a life of romantic action . . . were . . . undertaken in search of copy".[27] That they were undertaken for themselves, out of a desire for experience, it is natural to allow — but I am powerfully tempted to qualify this formulation by the phrase "in the first place". For it is a fact that Hughes 'wrote up' both his steerage trip to America and his Danubian idyll and Balkan interlude as diaries for which he sought and found publication. These accounts were thrown off, no doubt, and in them his creative mind is not profoundly engaged. Some of his later adventures did, however, supply material that found its way into *The Human Predicament*, and it is plain that his broad and various experiences of peoples and places was critical in feeding and shaping his imagination. His first-hand experience of danger enabled him to treat of it with psychological verisimilitude. His travels, in showing him new ways of looking and seeing, caused him to recognize the local nature of moral conduct, the relativity of human values, and developed his pre-existing sense of irony and absurdity.

By way of clearing the decks before embarking upon his first novel, Hughes in 1926 added collected editions of his poems and stories to that of his plays. The most substantial piece in the volume of stories, *A Moment of Time*, was 'Lochinvárovič', the piece inspired by the tales of the Montenegrin he'd met in the Trieste doss-house. The collection included 'The Stranger' and 'Poor Man's Inn', out of which the plays *A Comedy of Good and Evil* and *The Man Born to be Hanged* had developed, and 'The Diary of a Steerage Passenger'. A further eighteen tales made up the book — some of them squibs of three or four pages. They ranged from the Wellsian fanatasy 'A Moment of Time' through ghost stories to 'Llwyd', a story set in Snowdonia. To publish one's Collected Poems at the age of 26 may seem, unless one is Keats or Rimbaud, a curious thing to do. Yet in fact Hughes wrote few poems subsequently. He was fond of saying that lyric poets die young — even those who live to enjoy a ripe old age; and though this dictum is more showy than truthful it is demonstrably true in his case. *Confessio Juvenis* reprints most of the contents of *Gipsy-Night* (with revisions here and there). Of its five sections, only the first (substantially) and the last (entirely) are made up of poems that did not appear in the earlier volume. The first section, 'Numeri Balbutientes', contains five poems written in early and later childhood, and I have already quoted from most of them. The final section contains verse written after Hughes left Oxford — the longest and most ambitious, if not always the most successful, of his poems. The anonymous reviewer of *The Times Literary Supplement* wrote: "Mr. Hughes's impulse is always creative, but the degree of his perception is not yet fully adequate to enrich and unify his impulse." Commenting that he "is in no danger of losing himself in abstractions when he turns 'to muse on shapeless mysteries'", the reviewer concluded prophetically in saying: "And if he can but give shape to those mysteries, he will fully realize the genius of which this book affords far more than a promise."

It was a condition of Hughes's convalescence following his breakdown that he should write for no more than half an hour a day. Half an hour is a modest allowance when what you want to write is a novel. And the novel did not go well at first. Hughes struggled at Garreg Fawr with the opening chapter, producing draft after draft of it. It wasn't until he got away to Capodistria, an island-town off the Adriatic coast, that he began to feel he was getting somewhere with it. There, because of the favourable rate of exchange, it cost him little to live. Better still, he enjoyed a condition of insulation that was conducive to writing, for Italian was the only language spoken on Capodistria and, initially at least, he understood it not at all:

> so that I could work all day in the Café della Loggia undisturbed by the chatter: to me it was just meaningless sound, no more interruptious than wind or rain.[28]

He spent six months there. In an Introduction written in 1963 for an American edition of *A High Wind*, he seems to say that he only had the first chapter to show for his time on the island. But in an interview published over thirty years earlier (in *Everyman*, April 9th 1931), Louise Morgan reports him as saying that he was a year doing the first chapter, and then wrote two more on Capodistria. Back in London, he offered the first chapter to Henry Goddard Leach in New York. Leach wrote that he liked "your high wind in Jamaica" and printed the chapter in *Forum*. Hughes in turn was taken by Leach's phrase, and adopted it as a title for his continuing opus.

Towards the end of 1926, Hughes's wanderlust overcame him again. On a raw and sleeting December day he and a painter friend, Jim Wyllie, boarded a Dutch steamer bound for North Africa. Lascar stewards padded about in bare feet, their heads wound in batik handkerchiefs. In his travel-diary Hughes described them as "Pathetic little creatures, with voices like windy mice and bodies like monkeys, who understood no request in any language" — similes entirely in keeping with the world of his part-written book. The sea had calmed by the time they landed in Tangier, and the Moroccan evening was reminiscent of a somewhat troubled English July. Next day they drove north to Rabat, where they explored old Moorish dungeons, then on, over a period of days, by way of Salé, Casablanca, Mazagan and Safi to Marrakesh. At Marrakesh they decided to mount an expedition into the foothills of the Atlas mountains. Here in Richard Hughes's life fact masquerades as fiction, for Hughes made his subsequent adventures over, lock, stock and barrel, to Augustine Penry-Herbert in Book Three of *The Wooden Shepherdess*. Just how true to Hughes's own experiences Augustine's are can be seen by a comparison of the early autobiographical piece 'In the Lap of Atlas' (never published in Hughes's lifetime, but included in the posthumous collection of stories of the same title) with the relevant chapters of the novel: chapters which, incidentally, are the only ones of *The Human Predicament* that Hughes would admit to drawing directly from his own life. Certainly he was aware of the dangers of a journey into a region forbidden still to Christians: of being abducted and held to ransom, or of being murdered for the petty cash in his purse after being subjected to the gross physical indignity which had befallen Lawrence. But curiosity outweighed self-preservatory considerations. In spite of his early and profound experience of the deaths of persons near to him, he was, it seems, still young enough not to be able convincingly to imagine himself dead. So it was that he and Jim Wyllie bluffed their way from one imposing castle to the next, enjoying the hospitality of unseen hosts: until, tipped off that their presence was unwelcome to the latest potentate, and that they were to be hunted down like wild dogs, they high-tailed it back to Marrakesh on their mules, avoiding disaster only by a hair's breadth.

Hughes returned to England and his incomplete novel. Probably he spent some time upon it in North Wales, for he showed what must have been a well-advanced draft to Amabel Williams-Ellis. She criticized the lack of sex in the book, remarking that it was inconceivable that Margaret Fernandez would not have entered into some sort of relationship with the pirates. Hughes took the point and rewrote accordingly. Then America beckoned, and in the following year he again crossed the Atlantic. This third stay was to last eighteen months. Taking up residence at a remote farmhouse near New Milford in Connecticut, he lived on ten dollars a week (which enabled him to keep a pony and a Model T Ford). There, he relished a solitude punctuated by the occasional visits of friends. It can hardly be a coincidence that Hughes opens Book One of *The Wooden Shepherdess* with his naive hero, Augustine, living in a house in the Connecticut woods. But whilst it is fascinating to speculate on the amount of autobiography contained in the novel — especially in so far as Augustine's sexual education is concerned — speculation is all that it can be. Hughes did, however, tell Louise Morgan how *A High Wind* came to be finished:

> Towards the end I finally stuck for three weeks. I could not finish. Then a girl baked me a cake and I started off for an all-day ride with the cake in my knapsack. The horse went head over heels at one point of the journey, and I landed flat on my back on top of the cake. The cake was absolutely intact. And so was I — more than intact — for I rode back and straightway finished the story. All I required was a good shaking up. Which would go to prove that all books come from the liver.[29]

For a biographer, the cake-baking girl is of greater potential interest than. the cake: but there she must remain in all her American elusiveness. As for Hughes's horse: on the morning after finishing his novel he leapt on its back, his face to its tail, and slapped its rump like a madman playing the drums.

But it was cold in Connecticut. He would crack eggs to fry, and find they had gone solid in the shell. He spent Christmas 1928 at the house of a neighbouring farmer, riding there

> through starlit air held motionless in the grip of thirty degrees of frost. We supped solidly in the roaring furnace that was his kitchen. After that I was lulled to sleep . . . . by the midnight cooing of children . . . . By three in the morning we were up, had breakfasted on cold fried steak, and started forth with a willing hound bitch to a serious day in the woods *shooting foxes!*[30]

When it got so cold that he couldn't boil water on his oil stove, he went south to Virginia. Summer 1929 saw him cruising on the New England coast with Hal Smith. Fog-bound for a while in Nantucket, he swapped books with Smith, receiving Faulkner's *Mosquitoes* and *Soldiers' Pay* in exchange for Waugh's *Decline and Fall.*

By this time he was a celebrity. *A High Wind in Jamaica* was published in the U.S.A. in 1928 under the title *The Innocent Voyage*, and was an immediate success. Hughes didn't actively seek publicity, yet he seemed to attract it, to attract it indeed by "silence and reserve" rather than any extrovert display of personality. At least one gossip columnist, Herbert Corey in the *Brooklyn Times*, began to feel that Hughes's "modesty" was suspect, his "apparent diffidence . . . . merely rheumatism". Had he "played a reverse English" on the Americans, outsmarting them by a calculated inversion of behaviour? Before boarding a liner for home on September 26th 1929, Hughes delivered a farewell message to the press that might have been prepared, so quotable was it. Declaring that he had failed in an attempt to learn the American language, and that it would take an Englishman twenty years to pick it up, he went on:

> Get a load of this — in literature, England has more to learn from America than America has from England. Present day American authors are the goods. I give every new one the twice over. It wouldn't burn me up if one of them kicked in as the biggest noise since Shakespeare.[31]

Hughes arrived back in England to find *A High Wind in Jamaica* — published there in 1929 — a subject both for accolade and denunciation, the former predominating. Reviewers were agreed on the brilliance of his descriptive powers, and uniformly praised his hurricane chapter. On the other hand, objections of various sorts were raised to the novel. The critic of the *English Review* found what he or she called the book's "naturalism" not entirely to his or her taste: "Some, at least, of the horrible and cruel and disgusting things described add nothing that we can see to the book"; and cited the cutting off of the monkey's cancerous tail and the belching sailors. Gerald Gould, in the *Daily News*, deplored Hughes's illegitimate tearing of the novel's imaginative fabric with his late declaration that he can "no longer read Emily's deeper thoughts, or handle their cords"; St. John Ervine accused Hughes of whimsicality and declared: "The trouble with Mr. Hughes is that he cannot make up his mind whether he is writing literature or performing in a circus", and dismissed *A High Wind* as "an amusing stunt". But the issue which provoked the liveliest disagreement was Hughes's grasp of child-psychology — or lack of it. Clemence Dane, Arnold Bennett, Leonard James, Hugh Walpole and Cyril Connolly all found the children's behaviour authentic; Humbert Wolfe, however, concluded that they were "brilliant robots", while J.E.S. Arrowsmith in *The London Mercury* found them "not as other children are", and remained unconvinced by Emily's behaviour at the trial. Controversy raged in the letter-pages of a number of papers and journals, most interestingly and protractedly in *Time and Tide* whose critic applauded Hughes's portrayal of his children as "the cruel, inconsequent, unpredictable little mechanisms they are". Miss Steel, Headmistress of the Royal School, Bath, objected to this verdict on the basis of thirty years in education: finding "unthinkable" the children's silent acceptance of John's sudden disappearance and Emily's killing of the Dutch Captain, she wrote:

It is this distortion combined with an unnecessary coarseness of expression and incident that makes so much of the book a disgusting travesty of child life.[32]

Another correspondent, Philip Jordan, countered with an assertion that children "in the first months of freedom from irksome and well-meaning discipline" were capable of all sorts of anti-social acts; he instanced the case of two children removed from a typical school to a laissez-faire one:

> Their first reaction to freedom was to buy a hatchet apiece and to slaughter in the most brutal way every chicken and duck they could lay their hands on.[33]

Now that these children had grown up, they were pillars of the community. At this point Dame Ethel Smyth wrote to defend Miss Steel and denounce Mr Jordan:

> My own feeling is that if normal children are like Emily, then (if one may say so without irreverence) Christ must evidently have been pulling one's leg when He bid us take them as our example![34]

And so it went on for another couple of letters.

Chapter Three: *In Hazard* and the War

From the fame — or notoriety — that *A High Wind* earned him, Hughes retreated to Morocco. For two months he camped in the cork woods of the North in a glade brilliant with marigolds, asphodel and wild gladioli. His tents had belonged to Kaid Sir Harry MacLean, and were sumptuous brocade-lined affairs. He took to wearing Arab clothing.

> I ate my food propped on embroidered cushions, and took my snuff from a silver snuff-box. Woolly-looking gentlemen who lived in straw huts used to bring me eggs and butter, and cheeses, and lashings of truffles. Wandering scribes, and story-tellers, and other travellers, would blow in for a night or two: would help with the work of the camp by day, and in the evening would come to my tent and sing, or dance, or tell long, pleasant stories that either came or ought to have come out of the Arabian Nights.[1]

His only human companions were Arabs. At night the singing of innumerable nightingales, the growling of a wild boar, or the high-pitched howling of a jackal would detain him on this side of sleep. He then moved to a pig-sticking camp, where at first he refused to carry a spear. But one day a pig — driven by beaters, as was the custom, towards the hunters — turned on a horse which reared, unseating its lady rider; whereupon Hughes grabbed a spear and chased the pig away. After this he further captivated the young English women in the camp by his ability to remove a match from a matchbox and light a cigarette with his toes. Soon, however, he was off travelling again — to the South, this time, in the company of a Moorish-Jewish friend (the original of Ludovic Corcos in *The Wooden Shepherdess*?) and his friend's father's personal assassin. In Agadir they took a dish of tea with the town poisoner, who seemed bent on poisoning them:

> and he knew that we knew, and we knew that he knew that we knew, and both sides kept their eyes skinned and chaffed each other bitterly and timorously.[2]

Passing themselves off as slave-smugglers, they almost made the mistake of purchasing a cargo of little black boys, at £1 a head. Still further south Hughes encountered an old snake-charmer who, "after saying over a spell to make me immune as himself from snakebite", held up "two cobras to kiss my hands and forehead with their flickering, tickly tongues . . .'[3] And these were only a few amongst many strange experiences.

It was during this visit that Hughes bought his house in the citadel — the Kasbah — of Old Tangier: price — two donkey-loads of silver. He thus became the first Christian to own property there since the reign of Charles II, when the British held the town. One of the house's attractions was its garden — the only one, apart from that in the Old Palace, in the entire citadel. The last-remaining portion of the gardens of the seventeenth-century British governor of the city, it was called, for that reason, and still, 'The Captain's Garden'. But the house was so deeply embedded in the native quarter, tucked in amongst a labyrinth of streets, that Hughes found it very hard to locate once he'd left it. This tickled the Arabs, who would say: "Here's a man who owns a house but doesn't know how to find it!" It seems likely that it was on this visit that Hughes began to collect Berber folk-tales with a view to recomposing them for an English-speaking readership. The first to be published (in *The Listener* for December 1931, following the story's broadcast) was 'The Fool and the Fifteen Thieves'. This tale is given as having been told to Hughes during his cork-wood period by Hamed, his man-servant.[4] Hughes's 'Arabian Nights' tales were collected after his death in the book *In the Lap of Atlas*.

The 1930s were busy years for Hughes — and yet he published only one novel during the decade. Two major projects remained uncompleted: one, indeed, was virtually stillborn. He had begun a new novel by April 1931, but it ground to a standstill. He reported much later (in *Time and Tide* for July 6th 1940) that the idea for it came to him in 1925:

> The central characters were a family of Italians, destitute to the point of starvation, completely incapable of work, by no means picturesque, and always merry. The theme of the novel was the contrast of their insecurity against the security of the background upon which they were set. For its effect, of course, it depended on a feeling of complete security on the part of the reader. But I had barely worked on this book for a couple of years when I found it impossible to go on with it. *Security had gone out of our background.* The post-war period was over (this was about 1932): a new pre-war period had begun.

(This retrospective account, no doubt, was coloured by the novel which he *did* complete — one entirely in keeping with the pulse of the times.) The other project which never came to anything was a biography of Walter

Harris, *Times* correspondent in Tangier from 1887 to his death in 1933. Hughes knew Harris during the last years of his life, and after his death his family asked Hughes to write his biography. Harris was a nonchalant, witty and resourceful man, and his many extraordinary experiences in Morocco (including his abduction by the bandit chieftain Moulay Ahmed er-Raisuli in 1903) would have composed a tapestry eminently suitable to Hughes's ironic pen. Hughes accumulated a quantity of papers relating to this project from 1933 onwards — including letters and personal recollections of Harris. But he never got further than drafting an opening chapter: *In Hazard* had by that time taken possession of his imagination, and soon after this novel was finished, the war began. Quite simply, he never got back into touch with the Harris material. His knowledge of Harris wasn't wasted, however: Harris makes a supporting appearance in the Moroccan chapters of *The Wooden Shepherdess*. His adventures also left a significant mark on Hughes's long short story 'A Woman to Talk to' — another piece of writing that he never brought to a conclusion satisfactory to himself. He mentions "working on a short story that's gradually developing into a longer one" early in 1931, and there seems to be no candidate for identification as this piece other than 'A Woman to Talk to'. This story is included in *In the Lap of Atlas*.

In February 1932 Hughes married, and the texture of his life inevitably altered. His bride was Frances Bazley, daughter of Sir Thomas Bazley of Hatherop Castle, Gloucestershire. She was a painter. They met on the platform of Dolgellau Station in North Wales, whither Hughes had been despatched by Amabel Williams-Ellis to collect this particular guest. The courtship was a rapid affair. When one day Diccon and Frances announced that they were getting married on the following Wednesday, their families naturally objected to the suddenness of the decision; in deference to which, the couple put off the wedding till Thursday. There was no time for proper invitations to be dispatched; a Duchess — 'the Flying Duchess' — came by plane, landing in the castle grounds. But a host of little girls attended, for Frances was the leader of the local Brownie troop.

Hughes had made two further trips to Morocco in 1931, spending time on directing repairs to his house; so that it was natural for Frances and himself to go out there a month or so after their wedding. Indeed they considered making Tangier their permanent home, but decided against it on the grounds that it was an unsuitable place for their first child to be brought up. (A secondary consideration might have been Tangier's decidedly rudimentary medical facilities; within a week of arriving, Frances had an appendectomy under a local anaesthetic, an operation performed by a trio of doctors who seemed to find the offending organ hard to locate; she left hospital having contracted gangrene in a toe — which Diccon somehow cured.) Returning to England, they took up residence in Stiffkey Hall, Norfolk, a partially-ruined Elizabethen house built by Sir Nicholas Bacon, father of Francis Bacon. The choice of domicile was typical of Hughes, whose passion for living in dilapidated castles testified to his submerged romanticism. Stiffkey's other attraction was its Rector, the Reverend Harold Davidson. Davidson had begun as an actor, experienced the Call, and got himself ordained. Much of his time was spent in London, trying to save the souls of the ladies of Leicester Square. After being defrocked, he appeared in a variety of eccentric shows until a lion with whom he was encaged killed and started eating him.

Despite its diminished state, Stiffkey Hall was so large as to be impossible to heat, and so cold that Frances remembered breakfasting in the courtyard one February morning. There the Hugheses lived with their first child, Robert Elistan Glodrydd, Hamed their Moroccan manservant, and the 113th Bentley to have been made, until their move in 1934 to Laugharne Castle — a pink Georgian house again in close touch with ruins. Their second child, Penelope, was born three months before the move; their third, fourth and fifth arrived in Laugharne — Lleky Susannah in 1936, Catherine Phyllida in 1940, and Owain Gardner Collingwood in 1943.

The move brought Hughes back to Wales, and to the sea. There he could develop his love of sailing. In the early twenties he had helped to rig an ocean-going schooner in Portmadoc harbour. Later he worked his passage on a brig carrying slates to Belfast; it was designed to be manned by a skipper, a mate and a crew of six, but Hughes was sole crewman. Now he initiated a sailing-race from Tenby to Laugharne. On a grander scale, he and his crewman, Jack Rowlands, won the Bristol Channel Pilot's Race in 1937 in *Tern*, his pilot cutter. Of this his daughter Penny writes:

> It was blowing so hard that two yachts were dismasted before they crossed the starting line. The race lasted three days and nights, and our father and Jack never once went to bed. Diccon said he was so absorbed he felt no need of sleep.[5]

At Laugharne the Hugheses did a good deal of entertaining. Augustus John was a frequent guest: his father lived at Tenby, and he would often use Hughes's house as a base-camp for the final ascent to the parental home. Hughes was a little afraid of John, who "loathed fools and bores: and who in his company felt wholly guiltless on either charge?"[6] John would telephone unexpectedly, then appear: to stay for a few hours or a few weeks.

He never spoke unless he had something to say, and with a simple explosiveness and a flash in his words — the intensity he gave to his painting, though briefer. He was then the best possible company. But if ever his whole mood was silent, thunderous, the warning sheet-lightning flitting across his face, then the prudent also were silent. Only children sometimes could safely break it.

In July 1936 John brought Caitlin Macnamara, who modelled for him, to Laugharne for a few days. Possibly at Caitlin's prompting, John suggested that Hughes ask Dylan Thomas, who just happened to be in the vicinity, over for lunch. Dylan and Caitlin had already had a love affair. It was thus that Hughes and Thomas's friendship began. It was Hughes who found the poet his fisherman's cottage in Gosport Street; he occasionally gave him small sums of money, and was godfather to his son Llewellyn.

Hughes was proud to be made Petty Constable of Laugharne, even though the duties were chiefly honorary, and his mace of office an old chair-leg with a piece of string attached. During his time at Laugharne he did not, however, neglect North Wales. In his last years as a bachelor he had borrowed, from Clough Williams-Ellis, a house near Croesor, Parc, that had last been 'modernised' in the reign of Charles II.

> . . .here I could snap my fingers at power-cuts, and the water-pipes could not freeze since there were no pipes. A modern tiled bathroom is about as cosy as a fishmonger's shop; but *I* could take my bath in real comfort in front of the open kitchen fire — and there is no luxury greater than sitting in a hot bath in front of a roaring fire. . ., frying the bacon with one hand while you sponge yourself with the other. Breakfast finished, too, I had only to spill the soapy water over the stone floor and chase the suds out-of-doors with a stable broom (saving one bucketful to pour down the stairs of course), and my house was clean in a time no vacuum-cleaner could rival.[7]

Such a house was ideal for a bachelor-writer, since it required no following. He even found its two ghosts congenial company. Now, in 1934, he leased it. Parc proved a perfect place for the growing Hughes family to take its summer holidays.

Between 1933 and 1938, Hughes worked on his second novel *In Hazard*. Much of it was written in a little eighteenth-century summer-house perched on top of the watch-tower of Laugharne Castle. Few people bothered him there, as the approach to this retreat lay through a shrubbery reputed to be haunted. That he came to write the book is due, in part, to the Williams-Ellises. Early in 1933, Lawrence Holt, the director of the Blue Funnel Line, dined with them and told them of a ferocious hurricane which one of his steamships, *S. S. Phemius*, had experienced between the 5th and 12th November in the previous year. Crossing the Caribbean Sea from

Florida to Panama, *Phemius* had encountered winds up to 200 m.p.h. —
winds beyond any velocity measurable by the Beaufort Scale and strong
enough to break the guys restraining her funnel, which was then plucked
out of the ship like a cork from a bottle, and to blow away her hatch-covers:
thus placing her in extreme jeopardy. So remarkable was this occurrence
that Holt said it ought not to go unrecorded. But who could do it justice?
Amabel suggested Richard Hughes, and wrote to him to sound him out. If
Hughes was intrigued by her verbal report, he was hooked when he saw
Phemius herself:

> while a crusted water-line (from the 1,000 tons of sea she had shipped),
> slanting diagonally up the bulkheads dividing her holds, was still there
> to prove the incredible angle of the list she had taken and how near she
> had been to filling; while one could still see and handle cold steel torn
> and twisted like paper, tangled like string.[8]

He began to research the task, for it was plain that a real theme for a novel
had fallen into his lap. He interviewed *Phemius*'s ex-master, Captain Evans,
the Chief Engineer (R.J. Wolfe), the First Mate (Mr. Kavanagh), and as
many of her crew as he could find. To their first-hand reports he added
Captain Evans's Offical Report and the Report prepared by Roscoe and
Little, Consulting Engineers, Naval Architects and Arbitrators, on the
incident. He studied *Phemius*'s charts and logs, including those of wireless/
telegraph messages. He undertook a voyage, in another ship, under
Captain Evans. When he had completed these preliminaries, he felt that he
knew, "in the material sense", everything that had befallen the ship — more
in sum than any of her crewmen could know individually.

In giving the following brief account of what happened to *S.S. Phemius*, I
am drawing upon Captain Evans's Report to his Owners.

Having passed between the islands of Jamaica and Haiti on the morning
of November 4th, 1932, *Phemius* at noon received reports of a hurricane of
small intensity, sixty miles in width. Captain Evans altered course in order
to avoid it. After rising steadily all night, his barometer began to drop from 6
a.m. on November 5th, puzzling him. At 9 a.m., barometer 29.55, he hove
to with the intention of riding out the storm. By 2 p.m. the wind was "of
hurricane force with terrific squalls"; shortly after, it "reached
indescribable violence"; by 3 p.m. it was of such "terrific force as to be
beyond human conception". It was no longer possible for the ship to heave
to. All the covers of No. 2 hatch, and some of No. 6 hatch, were blown
overboard; pumps were put on these hatches. Towards 8 p.m. he discovered
that the funnel had gone. He put his hand out into the wind in an attempt to
gauge its speed: "the force of the spray striking the hand was agony, and for

some minutes after numbed as if after a severe electric shock". The wind could not, he thought, be less than 200 m.p.h. At 9 p.m. steam failed, leaving the ship powerless in darkness. He estimated that ten tons of water an hour went down No. 2 hatch, and five tons down No. 1 and No. 6 hatches. The crew was without fresh water and denied access to stores. *Phemius* was being carried along by the hurricane. Throughout November 6th engineers attempted to raise steam by means of a donkey boiler and an emergency engine — but without success. By noon the Captain saw that their situation, with the pumps unusable and the ship taking a heavy starboard list, was very serious. Brief lulls enabled the hatches to be secured with awnings. Violent winds on the morning of the 7th again stripped the hatches; a lull allowed them to be secured once more. *Phemius* was rolling dangerously; the wireless was out of commission. At 1 p.m. Captain Evans observed the ship to be passing over a reef. The seas were terrific. He ordered oil to be poured down the latrines continuously; only this in his opinion saved the ship from foundering. A lull at 5 p.m. again allowed No. 2 hatch to be secured. Oil continued to be poured through midnight into November 8th. At 2 p.m. the wind lulled as *Phemius* entered the centre of the disturbance. Immediately it was overwhelmed with birds and insects — in particular large birds of the heron species — to such an extent that the Captain thought they added to the danger. It was impossible for the sailors to walk deck and bridge without crunching them underfoot. Evans was glad when the blast came, carrying to destruction their strange freight. Late in the evening a little water was obtained from a tank; and early next morning some fruit, vegetables and cheese from a cooling chamber. By 2.30 a.m. on November 9th the wind was moderating, the barometer rising. The wireless was dried out and an emergency aerial rigged. *S.S. Killerig* was contacted. Now, however, *Phemius* was bombarded with offers of assistance and, to conserve his emergency set, the Captain had to send out: "Do not require immediate assistance". By noon the wind was a fresh breeze, but the ship's lurches to lee gave Evans more concern than they had when she was in the storm, due to the amount of water the starboard cargo must have absorbed. He estimated that *Phemius* had been carried 209 miles by the hurricanee. Another attempt to get the emergency engine going failed. At 10.45 a.m. on November 10th *S.S. Killerig* arrived. But when Captain Evans counted fifteen men leaving her in a boat, he gave orders that no one but Captain Tooker should be allowed on board. The two Captains agreed salvage terms according to "Lloyd's Contract", but Evans would only allow *Killerig's* men onto his ship on the understanding that their presence would have no influence on the terms of towage. Towing commenced. Evans ordered a temporary funnel to be rigged and finally, by 10.30 a.m. on

November 11th the ship's engineers succeeded in raising steam on the donkey boiler with wood fuel. *Phemius* was steering again. At 4 p.m. on November 12th, she anchored in Kingston harbour, Jamaica.

If this account is compared to that of *In Hazard*, it will be seen that what Hughes called "the inanimate side" of the novel is factual. What then of the *animate* side? Hughes in his 1966 Introduction to the book says:

> For purposes of my novel I signed on a new and wholly imaginary crew. There are no *human* portraits there, for this would neither have been decent behaviour to the men themselves nor would it have served my purposes as a novelist.[9]

This statement is to a degree ingenuous. For while the names and life-histories of the officers and crew of Hughes's *S.S. Archimedes* came out of his imagination, his characters must, of necessity, *behave* exactly as did their counterparts on *S.S. Phemius*. In imagining the emotional and psychic lives of his sailors during the storm, Hughes is not free: he must imagine within the constraints which historical events impose on him. The kind of constraints I am thinking of may be indicated by taking the case of *Archimedes*'s Second Mate, who, like the Supernumerary on *Phemius*, suffers a breakdown under the stress of the hurricane. Captain Evans told Hughes that his Second Mate, having broken down in the wheel-house, refused to leave the bridge until Evans, simulating fear, exclaimed: "My God! The next wave that comes will carry away the bridge and everyone on it." Only then did the Second Mate leave. Ordered subsequently to superintend oil-pouring operations, he collapsed completely, and went and hid in the Chinese quarters. So badly did he behave that Evans said that the First Mate would have shot him if he'd had a revolver. Yet under normal circumstances the man had been a good officer, pleasant-spoken and liked. Plainly, Hughes's Mr. Rabb acts precisely in the way *Phemius*'s Second Mate did: so that any portrayal of his inner life which Hughes attempts must harmonize with his behaviour.

Yet if Hughes is, in both general and particular matters, constrained, it is also the case that many of the incidents that occurred on this epic voyage must have struck him not so much as givens but *gifts*, so fresh and demanding of incorporation into a novelistic narrative are they. Among the jewels Hughes gleaned from his human sources were the following, which I quote verbatim from Hughes's typescript of his conversations with Captain Evans:

> Almost the last day steward came to Captain with an apple and an orange. Captain started to eat half the orange, meaning to keep the other half for the Mate, and then found he could not stop, and ate it all.

He gave the apple to the mate and said to him "Mr. Kavanagh, I've played you a dirty trick. There was an orange too, and I ate it all."

Chinese quartermaster at the wheel flung from the wheel and slid along the bridge on a mat, (bridge tilted at about 35 degrees). He struck the edge of the bridge and carried away the navigating light, but this just saved him from going overboard. Captain managed to grab him and hold on, but did not know if he was dead or alive. If dead, of course, would have let go. Then he saw his lips moving and knew he was alive, and managed to drag him back.

Hughes incorporated both these incidents into his text. The first he left almost as he annotated it; the second he developed with all his cunning in a manner characteristically Hughesian (see Chapter 9 section iv and Chapter 3 section ii respectively). As a final example of the way *In Hazard* relates to its sources, I will quote from Captain Evans's Official Report his account of his meeting with Captain Tooker of *S.S. Killerig* — the originals of Captain Abraham and *S.S. Patricia*.

> 11.15 a.m. Capt. Tooker Salvage Officer boarded. I received him on the lower bridge. His first words were:- "Captain I congratulate you"! I then invited him into my room having previously instructed the chief officer to be present. I asked him what the good old ship looked like. His reply was — "You look pitiful"! Then to business — He asked me what I required. I replied "Lloyds Contract", to which he agreed. This was then duly signed by the two of us — destination Kingston. He now wanted to know the reason why I would not allow his men on board. I replied that no man boarded my ship without my permission. He then wanted to know whether there was any illness on board to justify me in my action. The reply was no. He then said that he insisted on having his men on board. I still stood my ground. He then threatened to tear up the contract. I replied that he could do as he pleased but I pointed out that my copy would not be torn up. I then asked him what bearing these men boarding would have on the towage question. He replied "none whatever, that it was the usual procedure". I was still adamant and pointed out that my men could still do all the work necessary. He then gave his solemn assurance that his men boarding would have no bearing on the matter at all. I was then satisfied and now instructed the chief officer to allow all the 'Killerig's' men to come on board.

Hughes turns this encounter back into dialogue in Chapter 13 section ii of *In Hazard*. A reader who compares the two accounts might well point out that Captain Abraham falls on his knees to swear that his fifteen men will not "affect the salvage question". A fanciful invention, then? No: in fact, the simple truth. Captain Evans told Hughes that this was what Captain

Tooker did: it was a detail that he probably felt unsuitable for a sober Report to his Owners.

In two highly significant instances (I mean *novelistically* significant), Hughes felt free to add to what actuality delivered into his hands. He was able to do this, I think, because neither instance belonged strictly to the 'inanimate side' of the novel. The first is the 'mutiny' of the Chinese crew, which Dick Watchett is instrumental in putting down when in Chapter 11 he arrests Ao Ling on Captain Edwardes's orders. Nothing of this order of significance is logged in Hughes's sources. R.J. Wolfe, *Phemius*'s Chief Engineer, told him, somewhat disconnectedly, that while his own engine room Chinese behaved well, the deck hands became unruly. For six nights he did not sleep because of them. Hughes seems to have gathered the impression that strict discipline over the Chinese had to be relaxed during the hurricane. This so demoralized them that it proved impossible to re-introduce afterwards, and the lot had to be sacked. These hints sufficed to provoke Hughes's imagination. With the Chinese a whole region of potential interest lay awaiting development: what might he do with them? His second addition is the death of Ramsay MacDonald, his Chief Engineer. In actuality no member of *Phemius*'s crew — an astonishing thing — received any physical hurt beyond cuts and bruises. Yet, in having MacDonald fall overboard, Hughes is still relying upon source-material: for he had read, in a newspaper account, how, on January 29th 1933, one Midshipman Miller, of the merchant vessel *Dolius*, came to fall overboard in precisely the same way as Mr. MacDonald. Miller was picked up by another ship; MacDonald is not so fortunate. It is a curious coincidence that the Prime Minister of England whose name Hughes's Chief Engineer bears did in point of fact die at sea — of heart failure on a voyage to South America on November 9th 1937. Hughes's engineer meets his end just one day short of five years earlier — on November 10th 1932.

Sheila Rowlands, at one time Hughes's secretary, reports that after finishing *In Hazard* Hughes emerged from his summerhouse

> with this enormous look of relief on his face, and said :'Oh, thank God for that.' And then he looked up and said: 'Look, even the heavens are rejoicing.' That night, there was the one and only display of the Aurora Borealis that I've ever seen![10]

To read the British reviews of *In Hazard* is an amusing and instructive exercise, for the reviewers' responses to the book were various to say the least: on every significant issue there were violent disagreements of opinion. Much was made of the amount of 'science' in the novel: on one side were V.S. Pritchett and Richard Church, on the other John Brophy and David

Garnett. Pritchett declared that Hughes had "revived our lost sense of wonder by turning to the scientific though none the less imaginative view", Church that *In Hazard* was "more imaginative than anything he has written"; he commended its "fairylike, gay wilfulness". Brophy, however, was irritated by what he interpreted as "lectures . . . about engine-rooms and meteorology, and so on", and Garnett wrote that Hughes's approach involved the sacrifice of imagination: "The book is just a piece of flat objective reporting". The balance of the novel also occasioned differences of opinion. James Hanley felt that "the human element" was "entirely subservient to natural ones"; *The Irish Independent*'s reviewer, however, declared: "it is men and how they react individually to their awful experience who interest [Hughes] more than the hurricane and sea". Frank Swinnerton, Graham Greene and Glyn Jones all criticized the extended biography of Ao Ling; but A.M.A. in the *Liverpool Daily Post* wrote: "it is, I think, a sign of inspired story-telling to introduce two unexpected digressions into the narrative". Several writers voiced doubts about Hughes's taste for the bizarre, his penchant for surprising the reader. Marie Scott-James said that *In Hazard* revealed "perhaps an excess of artifice": "He can excite, amuse and stimulate, but is too self-conscious to be moving." Graham Greene, however, exclaimed delightedly at "the old simplicity, surprise, outrageous humour". A number of critics felt that the novel "petered out" at the end: Desmond MacCarthy, for instance, found nothing in the book to match the conclusiveness of the trial scene in *A High Wind in Jamaica*; why had Hughes left us in doubt as to Captain Edwardes's treatment at the hands of his owners? Conrad's *Typhoon* was liberally invoked by way of comparison. *In Hazard* came out of L.P. Hartley's and Desmond MacCarthy's accounts decidedly favourably; but James Hanley felt the comparison to be "ridiculous and hardly fair" to Hughes. In conclusion, Gerald Bullett greeted the novel as "a little masterpiece", Edwin Muir described it as "outstanding" and Richard Church as "memorable"; Frank Swinnerton found it, ultimately, "creatively, a failure".

A High Wind began in Jamaica; *In Hazard* ended there. In February 1939 Hughes visited the island for the first time. Entering Montego Bay, he imagined it to have changed little from the time when his children set sail for England in "the unlucky *Clorinda*":

> Ahead, two schooners lie at anchor: and there is just enough swell for their reflections to wriggle uneasily a little, like the tails of sleepy tadpoles.[11]

Hughes's account of the island settles, after an atmospheric opening, into a steady factuality: it is concerned with economics rather than hurricanes and earthquakes, with Trades Unionists rather than children. By the time the article appeared, the War had begun: Hughes, perhaps, was rehearsing that sobriety which his public face would wear for the next half-decade.

In the summer of 1939, when the Hugheses were at Parc, over a hundred evacuee children from Birkenhead arrived at the neighbouring village of Llanfrothen. The Hugheses took in six of them. In the evenings Hughes would tell them stories. These he came at in the manner of a cook: each child present had to suggest an ingredient which he then kneaded *extempore* into a narrative mixture. Immediately after he had invented these tales he would forget them. His audience, however, did not. The children who had heard them might retell them to him — "almost word for word in the form in which they were first told"[12] — up to six months after their original telling. It was in this way that they came to be written down: they had to pass, as it were, a memorability test. Hughes, in fact, had already published one collection of children's stories: *The Spider's Palace* in 1931. Out of his 1939 storytelling came *Don't Blame Me* — it appeared in 1940. Some of its contents were not simply entertainments, but embraced a therapeutic element. Often the Llanfrothen evacuees were bewildered and miserable at being so peremptorily uprooted from their homes. No psychiatric help was available for the worst cases and problems. Hughes's story 'The Doll and the Mermaid' was designed to combat one little girl's tendency to wet herself, and seems to have succeeded. Amabel Williams-Ellis recalled another girl who was convinced that she'd murdered her little brother by letting him topple out of his high chair onto his head. Between them, she and Diccon cured her of bad facial eczema by means of telling her stories such as 'The Happy Thief'.

In the summer of 1940 Hughes joined the Admiralty. His section was soon transferred to Bath. One of his earliest assignments was to suggest a place of retreat for the Admiralty should London by invaded. Off the top of his head he suggested the hotels around Lake Windermere — connectible, of course, by boat — and was sent north to reconnoitre. Another related to two early British successes in the war at sea. On December 13th 1939 a British cruiser squadron under Commander Henry Harwood — *Ajax*, *Exeter* and *Achilles* — engaged the pocket battleship *Admiral Graf Spee* in the South Atlantic: the Battle of the River Plate. *Exeter* was badly hit and retired, but the *Graf Spee* turned away and ran for the neutral port of Montevideo. When on December 17th it left there, it was only to scuttle itself in mid-channel. The British were surprised, to say the least. The battleship's Commander committed suicide, and its crew was interned. Then, on February 16th 1940, the armed merchantman *Altmark* was captured in Josing fiord by the British cruiser *Cossack*. Three hundred British prisoners of war — the fruit of *Altmark*'s South Atlantic campaign, were liberated. Feeling that there was considerable propaganda-value in these events, Hughes's masters sent him off to gather material about them: a series of articles, perhaps? His informants treated him to eye-witness accounts. The information he obtained about the *Graf Spee* included a detailed description of the stateroom of her late commander, Captain Hans Langsdorff — even down to the potted aspidistras it contained. Hughes did not write any of this up, but it seems to have given him the idea for a novel: one that would deal with the experiences and destiny of the *Graf Spee*. Here, then, are the first tentative shoots which grew into *The Human Predicament*.

Now he became Chief Priority Officer at the Admiralty, which "meant acting as a mediator between the rival claims of powerful departments competing for production facilities".[13] In Bath he was billeted on the elderly writer Horace Annesley Vachell, who lived in a handsome manor house whose garden boasted an Italian temple, a Greek fountain, and a Roman bath. Vachell was determined to drink his cellar dry in case the Germans arrived to do so. Thus, each evening, he and Hughes sat down in evening dress to dine, and, waited upon by Vachell's aged servants, drank their way through exquisite chateau-bottled wines and vintage ports.[14]

Hughes seems to have looked upon the job of civil servant as a role to be perfected. It demanded a particular uniform — pin-stripes, black trilby hat, briefcase and umbrella — and a particular style — that of a stickler for correctness — and Hughes assumed the two with such conviction that it was as if he had never known any other way of living. His success in playing the part seems to have been made possible because he was acting out a genuine self. The 'civil servant' (like 'the adventurer', 'the old salt', 'the visiting novelist' and, later, 'the Tolstoyan sage' and 'the church warden') represented an upwelling from within of an authentic persona. The novelist, he believed, *becomes* his characters in the act of creating them; and in actual life he appears to have had the capacity to slip from self to self; shedding one and assuming another as a chameleon changes its colour in order to blend into its environment. After the war, Lance Sieveking found his civil servant's clothing abandoned in a tiny room off Eaton Square — sloughed like a dead skin.

Whilst in Bath, Hughes acted as a fire-watcher. Positioned high on the flat roof of the Empire Hotel, he witnessed the first night of the blitz of 1942. Later, in November 1943, when he moved back to Whitehall, he gave a broadcast on the West Indies Programme in which he expressed first what had come to him "as a complete surprise":

As a spectacle, for sheer pyrotechnic grandeur, this was being one of the most beautiful sights I have ever witnessed. Far too beautiful to be frightening. You may be shocked at this: I can't help it, I am telling truly what I felt. Every fire had a colour of its own, which changed from minute to minute. Burning buildings were flung so high they almost seemed to hang in the air before they fell again. The crescendo howling of the falling bombs, the enormous thudding of the burst. And then another kind of howling, as aircraft dived, bombed, and towered again, spitting a golden rain of tracer from their tails. . . . .they were machine-gunning the streets and roofs as well as bombing. Golden showers of incendiaries. The whole town was now lit almost as by day. The attackers dived so low I could see every detail of the aircraft, lit up by the flames. I even thought I saw their faces, for some of them seemed to dive even below the level of my roof-top. Once the tall building I was on swayed like a tree: blast took me off my feet and turned me on my back. I fell into a doorway. Even that was not unpleasant: one seemed to float slowly on the air, as when you dream you are falling.

Against the strange but authentic[15] purity of this vision stands his briefer account of the aftermath of the bombing:

Morning showed the town surprisingly still standing. It showed also strange and gloomy sights. The strangest of all was the glass. Not a window was left, and all the broken glass was in the streets. It covered them, like crushed ice — for days we were still sweeping it up into huge piles. It was now that the horrid and sordid aftermath of that wild night could be seen. The broken buildings, the buried and the wounded and the dead.

Four days later they were still digging people out. In one ruined building a warden saw a kitten run into a hole in a pile of debris. He put in his hand to pull out the kitten. A small hand clutched hold of his.

Addressing a remote audience over an auditory medium, Hughes seems to be aiming, in these simple sentences, for a rhetorical effect. Nevertheless the pathos of his closing words, a tender pathos untouched by irony, represents a tone new to him. The War, and his years as a civil servant, appear to have taken toll of him. Penny Hughes in her memoir writes: "It seemed as if he could not come to terms with the destruction wrought by the War", and: "It was as if the years in the Admiralty had destroyed his sense of fantasy, had snapped a thread in his life which it would take a long time to replace."[16] At the end of the War, having rejected the Governorship of South Georgia but accepted an O.B.E., Hughes returned to his family. The years had left a kind of deposit in his psyche, and the novels that he would afterwards write would, from one point of view, constitute an attempt to understand the nature of that deposit.

Chapter Four: *The Human Predicament*

For two winters after the war the Hughes family occupied Lyulp's Tower on Ullswater. Then Frances put her foot down. It was time her husband got over his romantic affair with castles and found them a proper house to live in. The result was a move to North Wales and Môr Edrin, a large house on the Dwyryd estuary opposite Portmeirion, Clough Williams-Ellis's eccentric pseudo-Italian show-village. Môr Edrin, however — still reached by a rough track which passes through a farmyard and a couple of gates — was without mains electricity; so Hughes constructed a small windmill. This, linked to a battery, supplied the house (albeit erratically) with lighting for a decade or so.

Since Hughes's pen was rusty in these post-war years, it was necessary for him to get it working again. It is doubtful, however, whether the means he chose was the best available, given that his imagination also was rusty. He'd always contributed articles to a variety of publications — so that a resumption of literary journalism could not really be objected to. But his acceptance of an invitation to write that part of a volume of Official War History which dealt with the Administration of War Production in so far as the Admiralty had experienced it, can hardly strike the delighted reader of *A High Wind* as other than perverse. Producing page after page of bureaucratic prose can have done little to resuscitate a jaded sensibility. At times there *are* flashes of Hughes the novelist in this book: a phrase, a metaphor, a momentary irony testifies that a genuinely literary sensibility is at work here, cramped and almost smothered as it is by the generalities in which it is compelled to deal: the following, for example:

> But most of the Bath Admiralty departments remained at Bath throughout the war, and after it: indeed at the time of writing they were still at Bath, so considerably expanded after more than twelve years (like a hermit-crab in a new shell) that it would seem to an observer unlikely they could ever return to Whitehall.

J.D. Scott, who collaborated on the volume with Hughes, was maddened by the snail's pace at which the latter wrote. It needed repeated efforts to get Hughes to drive down in his jeep from North Wales to discuss the work in progress, and when Hughes *did* arrive he behaved as if an infinity of time was available to them:

> suddenly it's eight o'clock, time for a drink, and we go to the United University Club nearby, where Richard Hughes orders a Manhattan cocktail. It must be exactly right — Hughes, although indifferent to comfort, is a finicky gourmet. When ready, the Manhattan looks suitably splendid — of course. Manhattan is a good-looking cocktail. Richard Hughes has drunk it — he's not absolutely certain if the orange slice was not perhaps, after all, a shade too sweet?[1]

Rather than an exercise to get his imagination running, Hughes's contribution to the *Administration of War Production* looks like an excuse for delaying novel-writing, and it seems to have been in such a light that Frances viewed the project.

In 1948 a late invitation took him, as one of a party of British intellectuals, to Poland. He visited Wroclaw (Breslau newly renamed), and then Warsaw.

> The ruins of Wroclaw were no preparation for the ruins of Warsaw. Wroclaw is shattered, but Warsaw has been demolished. No great city in human history has been treated like this since Carthage. This was not merely the battering of artillery; it was the uniform, methodical, efficient work of Nazi demolition squads. They had orders not merely to leave Warsaw uninhabitable, but to leave it beyond the remotest hope of rebuilding. Mediaeval churches and the Singer skyscraper, shops, tenement buildings, houses, palaces, sewers, offices — all equally were just so many technical problems in destruction.

Despite the impressive energy displayed by the Poles in rebuilding their city, it was the completeness of its destruction which took hold of Hughes's imagination. And he wrote, of the power which had commanded it:

> Whatever Russia has done or does to arouse Polish hatred, it pales beside what Hitler did. Against any possible question of a revival of German power Russian domination seems the lesser evil. If there is any hundredth possibility of truth in the Russian allegation that Fascism is being reborn in America — well, even Communism would be better than that.[2]

How might one imaginatively grasp and intelligently account for the doings of such a political movement as the ruins of these Polish cities witnessed?

But the purpose of the visit was the Wroclaw Congress, which aimed to study the contribution which non-politicians might make to the furtherance of world peace. Hughes was not impressed by the level of the discussion, which struck him as failing to rise above that of a village debating society. The problem, as he saw it, was that the intellectuals present discussed world issues *politically* rather than from vantage-points afforded by their respective specialisms:

> It was like watching animals at a circus performing with painful clumsiness carefully-learned evolutions for which Nature never intended them.

Politics, he felt, was a specialized subject. Why should the political views of a Picasso or a Haldane be worthy of more respect than those of a Don Bradman or a Clark Gable? The Wroclaw intellectuals were playing at politics, and politics deserved better. After which he argued that the Congress might have been more productive if the delegates had spoken as biologists, anthropologists, historians, novelists, poets, or whatever.

> If a congress of 'intellectuals' is to be held at all, surely it is because they have some special contribution to make: because the roots of war and peace spread wide, beyond politics, and even beyond economics; because they permeate, multiform, the entire fabric of human and animal nature.[3]

This recognition of what one might call the immanence, the indwellingness, of history in human lives, is an important one, and indicates the nature of the reflection going on in Hughes's mind at this time. Like everyone else, the novelist is an atom in the historical process, embedded in it like a wasp in amber whether he or she likes it or not.

That Hughes at this time found the creative writer's relationship with the stuff of politics problematical is demonstrated by two very different articles which he published in July 1948 and November 1949 respectively. In the first of these, 'The Writer's Duty',[4] he developed his response to the Wroclaw Congress, arguing for the distinction "between pure literature and propaganda", or "the pure novelist" (himself) and the political novelist (for example Arthur Koestler, with whom Hughes had debated the matter at Môr Edrin[5]) who uses "the form of literature as his means of persuasion". What should "that curious but not wholly fabulous creature, the pure writer" do in a highly politicized age when pressure is brought to bear on him to exercise his professional skills on behalf of a particular party, policy, or cause? He should refuse, quite simply. The writer's duty "lies in the framing of new riddles", the posing of new questions — "he works in imitation of his Maker". To *answer* questions is not his business: *that* is the business of the propagandist, the politician. And yet in the later article, 'Dry Land',[6] he writes precisely as a propagandist, a passionate advocate of a particular cause. The issue that so stirred him, stirred him as a Welshman: it was a scheme, then under consideration by the Electricity Authority, to generate power hydro-electrically from a string of power-houses which were to be fed by water from a network of dammed and flooded North Welsh valleys. Hughes attacked the scheme not only on the grounds that it would have disastrous consequences for Welsh farmers, but that it would be seen in Wales — since the power so generated would go to the English industrial midlands — as a policy of "Imperialist grab". He went on:

> Remember, too, that the mountains of Snowdonia have something of the significance for Welshmen, all over the world, that Jerusalem has for the Jews, all over the world. "A land of mountains — that is the abiding fact in the history of Wales." Nations, like men, have bodies as well as spirits. The mountains are the body and the rivers are the blood of Wales. You can't hack and chisel away at a man's body and pipe off his blood without affecting his spirit. If this is done to Wales, then as a nation she will be brought very near to death, as a man would be; and I think it will evoke the same instinctive resistance.

And he concluded that it lay, conceivably, within England's power to make Nationalists "of every one of us", to sow in Wales "seeds of *hatred*, where today there is no hatred". There is, in the many articles which Hughes wrote about his adopted country, no statement expressive of his sense of Welshness of comparable force. When the situation demanded, he would forget his abstract theorizing, his self-defined status as "pure novelist", and become that from which he had only months before dissociated himself. But then — have I not suggested that Hughes had many personae?

Around 1950, when his son Robert and daughter Penny's religious sensibilities were developing, Hughes's own religious instincts seem to have redefined themselves. Robert, who had conceived the intention of taking orders, began to read morning and evening prayers; and his father adopted the same custom. But whereas Robert dropped the practice after five years or so, Diccon seems to have continued it to the end of his life. He accepted the forms and rituals of the Church in Wales, and took on responsibilities at his local church at Llanfihangel-y-traethau. When the Reverend Gomer Davies was Rector there, Hughes regularly took part in services. At Matins he would read the epistle, and at Evensong the two lessons — the first in Welsh and often from the Prophets. Gomer Davies felt that this brought out the prophet in Hughes, for his reading was wonderfully expressive. Hughes sat on committees which decided the provision of churches in areas subject to slow depopulation, and considered the question of the revision of the liturgy. His thinking on this last issue is set out in a talk he gave to a Clergy School for the Dioceses of St. Asaph and Bangor in the summer of 1962.[7] But it seems that Hughes's embracement of the Church was, like R.S. Thomas's, conventional:[8] he elected to worship as a Christian because Christianity was the traditional religion of the culture he was born into. He would say that if Mithraism had become established in Europe by the Romans as the dominant religion and had remained so — as he thought it easily might — then he would have been perfectly content to be a Mithraist, and follow a ritual elaborated by the Platonizing of an ancient Persian cult of the god of light.

In 1950 Hughes was approached by Ealing Studios. They had bought a Welsh story and wanted a Welshman to script it. When Hughes suggested Dylan Thomas, they looked cross-eyed at each other; so he took it on himself. The film was *A Run for your Money*: it portrays the adventures of two Welshmen up in London for a rugby international. Hughes wrote most of the script but balked at the love-scenes: a woman was called in to do them. But now he found his carefully-written scenes hacked about, reshuffled, and in general treated as the rawest of raw material. Speeches written for one character would find their way into the mouth of another. Nevertheless he had grown enthusiastic about the medium. He rewrote a script which had gone stale on the Studio — *The Divided Heart* — and then sold them an idea which he persuaded them to let him script entirely by himself. This was *The Herring Farm*, a satire moving between Wales and Whitehall and inspired by the same strong feelings about conservation which had prompted 'Dry Land'. In order to stop a variety of Ministries from requisitioning Snowdonia piecemeal for a variety of state purposes, Sir Peregrine Madden, a Senior Civil Servant, conceives the idea of forging a requisition for the whole region on behalf of the Ministry of Land and Water. This, cunningly backdated, takes precedence over all others. The ostensible purpose of the requisition is to create, by damming and flooding a series of valleys, an inland sea for the farming of herring: but it is, of course, to be no more than an impracticable paper scheme. When, however, Sir Peregrine's Minister, the megalomaniacal Dearborn, takes it into his head to realize the scheme, and so erect a lasting liquid memorial to his name, Sir Peregrine and the inhabitants of 'Llanmadoc', the village where he has spent his vacations for many years, resort to various comic strategies to persuade the Ministry that the scheme is going ahead, when in fact nothing is happening. At last the truth is revealed to Dearborn, he accepts resignation rather than make a national fool of himself, and Snowdonia is left alone. The film was assigned a producer, Monja Danischewsky, Alastair Sim agreed to play Sir Peregrine Madden, and Hughes got as far as completing the Third Draft Script. But *The Herring Farm* was never made. It has been suggested to me that the reason for this was the collapse, due to financial problems, of Ealing Studios. But the Studios did not in fact close until 1954. Almost thirty years later, and understandably tentatively after so much time, Monja Danischewsky proffered other reasons for the film's non-production:

> Perhaps it was a little too fanciful for the studio whose comedy films tended to be based on a documentary approach. Perhaps satire was considered a questionable style of comedy from the box office point of view. Certainly it presented considerable technical problems and it may have been made too expensive for that reason.[9]

Between 1954 and 1956, Hughes gave twenty lectures, at the rate of four per term, at Gresham College in the University of London as Professor of Rhetoric. Drawing upon the work of a number of literary theorists — notably I.A. Richards and William Empson — he investigated rhetoric as a written rather than an oral phenomenon. Defining it, in his early lectures, as the art of producing a desired impression, he saw no reason why the impression should not be produced in a reader as well as in a listener. Later, however, he came to distinguish between what a writer puts into his writing ("the cerebration resulting *in* a poem"), which he called Poetic, and the effect that writing has upon a reader ("the cerebration resulting *from* a poem"), which he called Rhetoric. He discussed both poetry and fiction, continuing to maintain, as he had done in argument with Robert Graves, that the novelist might tap the same deep streams of the unconscious as the poet. In the sense that both poets and novelists make words (quoting Richards) "'the meeting points at which regions of experience which can never combine in sensation or intuition, come together' . . . the novel is only the poem writ large".[10] But, of course, the *experiences* that a lyric poem and a long novel constitute for a reader are quite different:

> In the case of a short poem, particularly if we learn it by heart, we can perhaps say that the whole effect of the poem is present in the mind at one time. But in the case of a novel no one that I have ever met has learnt a novel by heart, or indeed has any but the haziest recollection of it when he has finished reading.[11]

He then coins the phrase "the novel behind your eyes" to suggest the element of "extended duration" in novel-reading. Not to be able to hold a whole novel in his or her mind is not a shortcoming in a reader, as certain critics think, but an essential condition of novel-reading:

it is characteristic of that experience that the reader moves through his experience of the novel behind his eyes as he moves through life — a present moment, moving always from a partially-remembered past towards a partially-foreseeable future.[12]

What a long novel offers is a polyphony of meanings, a procession of connectings as the mind moves through a series of inter-related narrative parts. This kind of experience he calls "wisdom" — similar to the "knowledge" which we gain from living our daily lives, but "wider", since direct experience is bounded by certain physical laws. "The novel, then, does not only provide an additional storehouse of knowledge, it enables the mind itself to grow."[13]

Frances Hughes has said that one of her husband's reasons for undertaking the Gresham Lectures was to "clear his ideas for starting the long novel". If Hughes was not in the immediate post-war decade actually writing a novel, he was continually thinking about the one he was going to write. At this point it is important to recognize a crucial datum — or rather, a series of related data — about his novels: that none of them is a 'pure' invention, a construction of unprompted imagination (although, no doubt, imagination must always be prompted by something); that all of them were, in greater or lesser degree, 'given' to him from without; that all are in some sense of a slippery term, 'historical novels'. *A High Wind in Jamaica* feeds off an actual event before going its own way. *In Hazard* is an historical novel in two ways: literally, and most obviously, because it reconstructs an actual happening. And — as Hughes himself came to recognise as he worked on it — *metaphorically*. For was not the *S.S. Archimedes* —

> a modern and well-found merchant-ship, caught in a hurricane which beat all records and broke all rules and belied all prognostications, which stripped her to the bone and battered her and left her in such a state that by all the rules she should have sunk, but still, because of the ceaseless professional heroism of all but one of those who manned her, *alive*[14]

(as he put it in 1940) — was not this ship an imaginative symbol? Hughes denied that *In Hazard* was a work of 'prophecy': it was "a sensitiveness to the present, not the future": to the peril imminently threatening the Ship of State. When he then came to feel that he would be false to his calling as a novelist if he did not write about his own time, take the rhythms of contemporary history as his subject, he had travelled to an entirely logical creative destination. Specifically, as he considered the undertaking, he perceived that the rise and fall of German National Socialism must generate its base-rhythm. This meant handling a time-span of twenty years and more — from the early twenties to 1945. Various questions then arose. Should he restrict his cast of characters to imaginary ones, or should he mix historical personages with invented ones? What place might specific autobiographical material have in this novel? What relationship should 'objective' historical time have to 'subjective' narrative time? Time, indeed, was of the essence: he needed time not only to consider theoretical issues such as these, but time for reading and research, time to familiarize himself with historical persons, places and events, time to attempt to chart the currents and undercurrents of history. It is easy to see Hughes, as many have seen him, simply as a procrastinator, as a man reluctant to write, to get down to doing what he did best. Certainly there were barren periods in his life, and he seems to have experienced, more than most writers, an inner resistance to writing; yet two factors should not be underestimated when a critic comes to consider, and to pronounce upon, the size of his novelistic output, and his failure to complete his major project. The first, its size and ambitiousness, is indicated well enough by its Balzacian title: *The Human Predicament*. The second is Hughes's perfectionism. It is common to hear critics speak of the ease, the effortlessness, the unstudiedness of his prose. That effortlessness, of course, is the result of immense pains, of draft upon draft, of perspiration out of all proportion to inspiration. *A High Wind* took three years to write, *In Hazard* five. How long then for a serial novel of Hughes's own times?

At this juncture it is appropriate to consider Hughes's novelistic method: or, if 'method' is a term too suggestive of the worked-out, the cut-and-dried, of his novel-writing practice. When Louise Morgan asked him in 1931 if he had 'planned out' the novel he was currently writing (his abortive Italian one), he replied:

> I can't write that way. I can't add living flesh to a skeleton, any more than a doctor can. I start the first sentence with very little idea of how I am going on, sometimes without knowing the name of a single character.

When the interviewer countered that he "must have some idea of the construction" of what he was about to write, he went on:

> The *shape*, yes. I have a very clear idea, a fully detailed and vivid idea, of the pure shape of the thing. You can get that without a single character or event. A sense of the rise and fall of intensity, a sense of the pattern worked out between the pictorial and the emotional, between Time and Event. I suppose it is that old cliché 'significant form' applied to literature, more or less.[15]

Such an approach, which concentrates on large motions and rhythms, on cadence, texture and colour, leave specifics very much to define themselves in due course. Thus Hughes would conceive of *A High Wind* or *In Hazard* as an Event (capital E) imbued with a necessary pattern; the elements in that pattern are the individual events (in lower case) which constitute it and which, day by day as the writer writes, derive from it their inevitability. Hughes's description, however, may be thought to err on the side of the ideal, given that parts of *A High Wind* derive from written sources. Later, with *In Hazard*, all the transactions between storm, ship and men are predetermined; and the Munich Putsch (*The Fox in the Attic*) and the Night of the Long Knives (*The Wooden Shepherdess*) are pieces of history. It would be true to say, then, that in all of his novels there are events which are *données*, events which do not await intuitive discovery by the creative mind. Asked by Peter Firchow some time in the early 1970s if he had the whole of *The Human Predicament* "plotted out" when he began *Fox*, Hughes replied:

> Absolutely not. I'm tied to historical events, on that side of it: but on the fictional side I never know from one chapter to the next what's going to happen. The most unexpected things can happen.[16]

These "unexpected things" are often violent in character. One relates to the nativity scene in *A High Wind in Jamaica*: having got his children to the warehouse to watch the cow being hauled up, Hughes stuck for three weeks, unable to write a word. When at last he sat down, it was to write that John falls and breaks his neck. It is no wonder that this event surprises the book's readers — Hughes himself was surprised by it. It is as if Hughes's frustration had struck a violent spark in his unconscious. A later unexpectedness is recounted by his secretary Lucy McEntee. One morning, whilst he was writing *The Wooden Shepherdess*, she entered his study to find him gazing in some perplexity at what he'd just typed. "Is something the matter?" she asked. "The most extraordinary thing," he replied: "Mary has fallen off her horse and broken her neck!" On this occasion his imagination had played a mischievous trick on him: for while Mary Wadamy's neck was irretrievably broken, she was not — like John Bas-Thornton — dead. It was most inconvenient, for Hughes could not write a word more until he had found out, from specialists, how a person manages to live with such an affliction.

His own account of how, in 1955, he came to begin *The Fox in the Attic* constitutes a fine example of his intuitive approach to novel-writing.

> I was sitting in the sunny garden of a village inn in southern Spain. There were foreign voices all round me; and four feet away a party of children hung on the railings and stared straight into my face . . . But what my mind's eye saw suddenly was a West Wales sea-marsh, a

> windless damp afternoon . . . I saw two figures approaching — I had
> not the least idea who they were, but as they loomed nearer out of the
> mist I suddenly saw with a shock what one of them had on his shoulder.
> And out of that the whole story grew, spreading and ramifying out of
> those two lonely figures and the burden one of them carried.[17]

So unpremeditated, so uncalculated an approach plainly hands the writer
over to the obscure motivations and processes of the unconscious mind: a
point that I shall return to in a later chapter.

What then of the autobiographical content of *Fox* and *Shepherdess*?
Augustine Penry-Herbert, the reluctant hero, is exactly Hughes's own age
and has, like him, had an Oxford education. Hughes's response to Peter
Firchow's rather tentative enquiry as to whether Augustine was intended as
an autobiographical character was to say: "I'm not and never have been a
hereditary landowner."[18] This pronouncement, for all its firmness, is
something of a red herring. Hughes not only makes Augustine exactly his
own age and sends him to Oxford (where, incidentally, he meets
T.E.Lawrence!), but imbues Augustine with what looks like an intensified
version of his own response to the War's unsettlingly sudden ending. Penny
Hughes[19] quotes early drafts of *Fox* which show that Hughes had to write his
way through some of his own childhood experiences in order, as it were, to
slough them before he could come at an Augustine who was not disablingly
close to himself. In the end, Hughes seems to have attained a workable
equilibrium with Augustine: intermittent irony enables him to preserve a
necessary detachment from Augustine, while at the same time he is able to
graft pieces of his own life and feelings of his own onto the character. His
self-borrowings range from the small to the large. An example of the small
are the four lines of a poem which Augustine composes in *Fox*: these come
(with slight changes) from a poem in *Confessio Juvenis*. More significantly:
in portraying Augustine's preference for the company, when staying at
Lorienburg, of the young von Kessens over their elders, he seems to be
drawing on one of his own earlier personae. Consider his comment that
Augustine "far too often . . . would lead the twins into some shocking piece
of mischief . . ." (*FA* p.328).[20] More significant still is Augustine's Morocco
jaunt in *Shepherdess*, which I have already touched upon.[21] But whilst this is
the only part of the completed *Human Predicament* which Hughes would
openly admit to being autobiographical, it seems likely that other incidents
and situations are indebted to personal experience. His sojourn in
Connecticut, shrouded in obscurity as it is, afforded at the very least the
setting for Book One of *Shepherdess*. Furthermore, Augustine's abrupt flight
from Joan Dibden in the same novel seems to echo an occurrence in
Hughes's early manhood. At Oxford he met Nancy Stallybrass. They

became engaged and their marriage was announced. Wedding presents began to arrive. Then, only days before the appointed date, the marriage was called off. Nancy Stallybrass later married Hughes's friend, Peter Quennell. Plainly there can be no simple identification of Richard Hughes the ironist and Augustine Penry-Herbert the dilettante and naif: yet there is an inward persistency in Augustine which invites one to see him as more than just another character, the invention of a disinterested novelist. Might we not see him, in his typical nature, as constituting one of Hughes's personae: not lived out in life this time, but on the pages of a never-to-be-finished *roman fleuve*? — a self at which Hughes could aim a sympathetic irony even as, heuristically in his imagination, he lived it through?

Hughes always maintained that he found it easier to write about places he hadn't visited, societies he hadn't known, than places and societies he had. So with people. Of the non-historical figures in *Fox*, only one, by Hughes's own reckoning, was drawn from life. Dr. Brinley, the old coroner, is based upon a local character whom Hughes had known in Laugharne. He presumed this man to be dead; but, revisiting the town with *Fox* on the point of publication, he was appalled to hear that Brinley's original was still going strong. Rushing down to where he lived, he was relieved to be told that he had died, aged ninety-four, two years previously.

With the historical characters and locations of his novel, Hughes took infinite pains. He would be satisfied with nothing less than total authenticity, absolute accuracy — wherever, that is, the facts could be ascertained. The relationship between Hughes's sources and the final texts of *Fox* and *Shepherdess* is a fascinating one, but cannot be dealt with in detail at this point. Some general indications of how Hughes worked on the historical portions of his long novel may, however, be given. Some of his sources were written, others were oral. His portrayal in Book Two of *Fox* of Hitler in hiding at 'Putzi' Hanfstaengl's house at Uffing in the wake of the failure of the Munich Putsch, for example, is indebted to both kinds of accounts. He drew on Hanfstaengl's memoir *Hitler: the Missing Years* and on, as the Acknowledgements to *Fox* put it, "the only living person in a position to describe to me at first-hand the whole forty-eight hour period": that is Frau Helene Hanfstaengl. Hughes always insisted that he never worked directly from his sources in the sense that he 'copied out', or 'cobbled together', details or passages from written historical accounts, his own notes of conversations with eye-witnesses, or abstracts which his secretaries prepared for him. Rather his practice was, by reading and re-reading these various materials, to soak himself in history. When he had finally charged the sponge which was imagination fed by memory, he would squeeze it so that it gave up, not a scatter of varicoloured drops, but a uniform cascade.

The Fox in the Attic took six years to write. Hughes made a number of journeys to Bavaria during this period, combining pleasure with research. He stayed with distant relations of Frances in castles which piqued his imagination. Baroness Pia von Aretin gave him access to her father's memoirs and supplied him with a first-hand account of Hitler's march down Konigstrasse in Munich on the night of the Putsch. From hours of talk with her octogenarian mother, he gradually built up a picture of the Germany of the twenties. His novel, then, would move from Wales, to England, to Bavaria, playing on the contrasts between families of very different kinds.

As I have said, one of the major questions for Hughes was the relation of historical time to fictional time. Although *Fox* and *Shepherdess* approach this problem differently (as we shall see), they are alike in treating historical events in a linear fashion. It is then intriguing to learn that Hughes did not originally conceive of the temporal dimension of the *Predicament* in this way. In 1979 Penny Hughes told Michael Bakewell:

> *The Fox* originally moved about in time, as well as moving about in geographical area. And this was very complex, and it was much more like a Proustian novel originally. And I think it must have been quite important to him, this shifting about in time.

But Hughes's publishers complained that these time-shifts made them giddy: so he settled for a chronological narrative.

In the summers of 1955 and 1958 he made two voyages in a small boat, *Crab*, with his daughter Penny. The first took them from Malta to Syracuse; the second from Piraeus up the eastern coast of Greece by way of Chalcis to the peninsula of Trikeri, across the Aegean to Lemnos, and through the Dardanelles to Istanbul. In this way, two years short of his sixtieth birthday, he combined two of his favourite anodynes and loves: sailing and foreign places.

The appearance of *The Fox in the Attic* in 1961 won high praise for Hughes from the critics. Goronwy Rees's response echoed that of Hugh Walpole to *A High Wind in Jamaica* thirty-two years previously. Walpole had written of Hughes's first novel: "It has genius because it sees something that a million people have seen before, but sees it uniquely." Now Rees wrote: "There are few living writers of whom one would say that they had genuis; but somehow it seems the most natural thing in the world to say about Richard Hughes." Kenneth Allsop called *Fox* "an extraordinary creation." The *TLS*'s reviewer described it as "magnificent" and "authoritative", and allowed it "that universal authenticity that is the hall-mark of great writing". Several reviewers were driven to invoke the name of Tolstoy.

Arthur Calder-Marshall declared: "in scope and ambition it challenges *War and Peace*". The Tolstoyan qualities of the book bothered Stephen Spender, however. Was Hughes "attempting to do something essentially Teutonic or Slavonic when really his gifts are those of a painter of landscapes and interiors"? He found the Welsh and English scenes "brilliantly, surely, eloquently described", but the German ones lacking in "air and implications of life beyond their particulars". He missed in *Fox* "the sense of history as the deluge carrying not just these characters but all their contemporaries along with them". Many reviewers remarked upon Hughes's audacity in mingling fictional and historical characters. John Fuller commented: "we do not disentangle fact from fiction because, although there is a wealth of detail and variety, there is absolutely no straining after a panoramic effect", and he thought that Hughes took Hitler "very much in [his] stride". For Julian Symons, Hitler was "fresh and brilliant", but the brief appearance of Sir John Simon was "jarringly incongruous". There were, of course, larger doubts about the novel. Frank Kermode emphasized the "systematic" analysis of human psychology that underpinned the book; convinced that *Fox* was "a magnificently good piece of a novel", he still questioned whether "the disease of the social structure is correctly diagnosed as malignant egotism". Julian Mitchell disapproved of what he thought "a heavy use of coincidence and a good deal of even heavier philosophising". A number of critics felt that *Fox* could not be properly judged until the whole of the novel was before them.

If Hughes had always been a slow writer, he now became a laborious one. *The Wooden Shepherdess* took twelve years to complete: twice as long as its predecessor. The slowness of its progress was due to some extent to difficulties which the book itself threw up. For some time Hughes remained undecided about what to do with Augustine. There had been not a few complaints from family and friends (though scarcely any from the reviewers) that Augustine was too passive, too 'wet'. This might well have given his creator pause, for Hughes was not a writer who found it natural to ignore adverse criticism — especially when that criticism originated in those who might be supposed his most sympathetic readers. Then there was a hitch in connection with the German girl, Mitzi. Peter Levi, the Jesuit poet and critic, suggested that Hughes extract the scattered parts of the text which portrayed her, and put them together in the middle of the book. Hughes embarked on a reorganisation of his novel only to decide, several wasted months later, that he must revert to his original intention.

Viewed from another angle, these difficulties appear symptomatic of a deeper problem, an intractable one. Interviewed by Jon Bradshaw for the *Sunday Telegraph* in 1971, Hughes said that he worked every day but Sunday, completing "about 330 words a day":

> but, of course, what really takes the time is never what you put into a book, but what you leave out. Last month, for example, I made considerable progress. I cut out a thousand words.

The self-directed irony of this is typically Hughesian. In "his soft, almost nonchalant voice", he asked Bradshaw — or himself: "I am 71, after all. How much time can a man hope to have?" For now, even as, after ten years, he moved closer to finishing the second volume of his project, he could see no respite for himself from his "life sentence". Simply and inevitably, the third volume had moved to the forefront of his thoughts. He remarked once that a tidy God ought to grant a man born in 1900 the round century; yet now, at his present rate of progress, a hundred years would hardly be enough. In 1968 he estimated that the *Predicament* wouldn't be completed before his one hundred and twentieth birthday. "It's a race between me and the undertaker", he told Bradshaw. By 1971 it was plain that it was a race he couldn't win.

The claim that he turned out three hundred and thirty words a day is one that cannot literally be upheld. Reasons either suggested themselves — or were found — for procrastination. For example, Hughes had determined upon writing a scene in which two young Nazis stand guard outside the Hotel Dreesen in Bad Godesberg during the afternoon and evening of 29th June 1934 — the eve of the Night of the Long Knives. He now decided that he needed to know in detail about the trees standing in the hotel grounds. Instructing his secretary to write to Germany to find out, he refused to write another word until an answer came. In the event, no details about the trees appear in the Bad Godesberg chapter. On other occasions Hughes would say: "I don't think I can do much at the moment . . ." or: "I don't feel very inspired today", and down tools. It seems beyond doubting that, as he grew older, he became increasingly subject to that peculiar malaise which attacks certain writers: a positive resistance to the act of grappling with the terrible demands of the unwritten page.

And yet he struggled on. Again, for the raw stuff of *Shepherdess*, he cast his net far and wide. His own experience inspired the American and Moroccan interludes. For the Coventry chapters he went to the mother of Sheila, his son Robert's wife — Rose Prescott. Rose told Diccon of her experiences as a mender in a Coventry mill, earning nine shillings and sixpence a week. She was allowed only one needle at a time; if it broke, she had to take all the separate fragments back to the supervisor in order to be granted a replacement, since a sliver lost in a piece of cloth might ruin it. Many of her experiences went into the making of Norah. 'Slaughterhouse Yard' was a row of seven terrace houses, so called because of the butcher's shop on the corner. Rose had been brought up in the end house, which had a larger garden than the others. Here she had fallen through the ceiling, as Norah does, because it had long been neglected. Rose told Diccon that she felt that Brian, whom he had invented, did not belong to the novel; but Diccon retained him.

His willingness to accept, and act upon, criticism is, however, shown by the history of those parts of *Shepherdess* which portray Mitzi, the Postulant nun. In 1969 or 1970 he sent versions of these chapters to his friend the novelist Caroline Glyn, who had some experience of convents, and asked her to criticize them. He had, it seems, taken Mitzi through the gamut of Carmelite experience in a single night. Caroline Glyn told Michael Bakewell that she found this

> terrifying . . . absolutely terrifying. It was much too much, the impact of it. No human soul could have lived through such a night — I didn't believe it, I had to tell him so; especially not a seventeen year-old girl entering the convent for the first day. . .

Hughes accepted her criticism and re-wrote accordingly, spinning out Mitzi's experience over a period of years, and saving what he regarded as the most important part of it for the book's final pages. But Caroline Glyn was almost sorry that she gave the advice she did, for she felt that the original version, though it strained belief, was "the most devastating piece of prose" she had ever read: and the published version had not the same power.

As with *Fox*, Hughes relied much, for his German scenes, upon the written record. By this time his source-books took up a significant portion of his study floor. Ranked spine uppermost for easy access, they resembled a phalanx of soldiers on permanent parade. Hughes's painstaking desire for factual accuracy is illustrated by his writing to Alan Bullock in January 1971, requesting enlightenment on a number of "conundrums" which were troubling him: these were uncertainties or contradictions that he had detected in the written record. A single example will suffice. His chief source for his Hotel Dreesen chapter was the Memoirs of Walter Schellenberg, who as a young S.S. man had stood guard on the afternoon in question. Schellenberg claimed to have recognized, through the French windows that opened out onto the terrace from the dining-room, not only Hitler and Göbbels, who were certainly present amongst other Nazi leaders, but Göring. Hughes wished to keep faith with Schellenberg, but had a problem. Schellenberg reported that Hitler and his companions were driven off in black Mercedes cars to Hangelar airport, near Bonn, from where waiting aircraft ferried them to Munich. Without doubt Göring was in Berlin for the purge, which he co-directed with Himmler. How then did he get there? Was he really at Bad Godesberg with the others? Or had he returned to Berlin after attending, with Hitler, a wedding at Essen on June 28th? Bullock in his biography of Hitler had written as if Göring was in Berlin on June 29th. His response to Hughes's query was to write: "Goering, I believe, returned to Berlin (he could have gone by train or car)". This pretty loose formulation (did Göring return after Essen or after Bad Godesberg?) rather left matters in Hughes's hands. His solution of the problem was not to solve it — he maintains the ambiguity of his sources. First, we read that Hitler's three chief henchmen are thrown into consternation by their leader's announcement that he is going to Essen:

> The Führer's excuses for going were both so flimsy they feared some diabolical trick if they let him out of their sight. Yet *someone* must stay in Berlin at the helm — with somebody else 'to lend him a hand', since none of these three conspirators wholly trusted the others. . . . Finally, Göbbels got his way. Let Himmler and him remain in Berlin while Göring attended the wedding and then returned poste-haste . . . (p. 343)

Later, when the two young S.S. guards peer into the ground-floor windows of the Hotel Dreesen:

> the Fuhrer was certainly there, striding the length of the room and biting the nail of his little finger. At Hitler's elbow was Göbbels, and. . .
> Was that or wasn't it Göring, away at the back there with all those others?
> "Göring was with him at Essen," said Hans: "After, they said he'd gone back to Berlin. . ." (p. 349)

Later still, when they watch Hitler, Göbbels and their party board an aircraft which flies off in the direction of Munich, there is no mention of Göring. Thus does a deft novelist negotiate a somewhat thorny patch of historical ground.

In early 1967 Hughes and Frances went out, at the invitation of the British Council, to Eastern Africa: a part of the continent he had not visited previously. On the same tour was the writer Edward Blishen, who had been supposed to interview Hughes formally for the International P.E.N. at precisely this time. In Kenya and Uganda the Hugheses took in the local colour, and Frances, who spent many of her later years painting waterfalls, had an opportunity to see some splendid ones. Hughes gave three lectures and placed an article, 'African Authors: Read your Contracts!' in the *Nairobi Nation*.

When in 1969 he was voted a member of the American Academy of Arts and Letters (membership of which is confined to the fifty most distinguished non-American writers, painters and musicians in the world!), he went to New York to give the Blashfield Address. It was forty years since he had last been there. He told *The New Yorker*:

> I am very pleased to be back in New York, because it is the one city I have visited that hasn't changed at all in forty years. It is still the same city of dreaming spires towering over medieval hovels that it was in 1929. People who live here will tell you that New York is changing all the time, but that is because their eyes are focussed on the details, and it is only the details that change. *This* building has gone up, and *that* building has come down. The city itself is exactly the same.[22]

He had a strange experience in a taxi. He had not long been sitting in the back seat when he found that his feet were getting wet. When he reported this to the driver, the driver denied that his taxi could be damp. But the wetness got worse, so that Hughes asked to be set down. He then found his shoes sticky with blood.

Hughes's desire for experience did not abate as he grew older, though the scope for adventurous travel contracted with age. He used to tell Ieuan Hughes, the Warden of Coleg Harlech, who had lived in Eastern Africa, "When I'm seventy we'll climb Kilimanjaro." But this was an intention they never fulfilled.

The Wooden Shepherdess appeared in 1973. It was not so well received as its predecessor, coming in for praise and criticism in roughly equal amounts. Derwent May discovered "extraordinary riches" in it, and declared that it offered "a wonderfully acute portrait of England and Germany between the wars". Hughes was again compared with great Russian novelists: by Olivia Manning, who thought his Hitler "more convincing than Tolstoy's Napoleon"; by Goronwy Rees, who, evoking the name of Solzhenitsyn, wrote: "like Solzhenitsyn, [Hughes] has as deep a passion for history as he has for literature, and he records it with the same accuracy and respect for truth as Solzhenitsyn himself"; and by Paul Theroux, who described *Shepherdess* as "a novel of Russian dimensions, written with serene English patience". The German portions of the book drew in general a more enthusiastic response than the English ones. Olivia Manning asserted that "the very power of the German scenes makes the intervening English and American ones seem, by contrast, flat and pallid". Goronwy Rees thought Hughes's portrayal of the Night of the Long Knives "wholly convincing", and his Hitler "unforgettable". Stephen Spender wrote: "Hitler and his gang . . . run away with the show". Although Spender felt that Hughes had "never done anything better" than his picture of "New England hard-drinking sex-titillating girls and boys", his was something of a dissenting voice. He criticised the Nazi sections of the novel as "awfully 'worked up'"; Hughes's omission of the reactions of the German working-class to the Nazis made "the clash between Nazis and aristocrats seem one between demons and puppets". Paul Theroux complained that Hughes's mixture of fact and fiction — a quality much-praised in *Fox* — was prone to "a curiously simplifying lopsidedness . . .; the fiction engages, and the fact — these mean, sham people with recognizable names — seems unsubtle, 'public', and without force". Augustine now came in for his share of criticism — a reflection, perhaps, of the feelings of those close to Hughes who believed the character 'wet'. Olivia Manning said that Augustine lacked development, was "as hero . . . a disappointment", while Stephen Spender was reminded "of Henry James's complaint that the hero of Flaubert's *L'Education Sentimentale* is altogether too slight a figure to carry the weight of so much circumstance". The critic of the *Times Literary Supplement*, in an unfavourable review, thought the book monotonous, lacking in variety of tone, and less comprehensive than its predecessor. Even Peter Thomas, writing in *Planet*, expressed doubts: "Whereas *The Fox* was able to linger upon and authenticate biography, *The Wooden Shepherdess* covers too much ground to be always able to convey the development of personality".

On December 3rd 1974 Diccon and Frances set off in their new Renault for Llandudno Junction. They were to catch the train for London, where Hughes was broadcasting on A.E. Coppard. Hughes turned the car over. Rescuers found the travellers hanging from their seat-belts, and hastened to cut them down. But the seat-belts had saved them: somewhat shocked, they seemed otherwise unhurt and, after spending the night at Conway, carried on to London the following morning. Hughes's secretary, Lucy McEntee, remains convinced that this crash contributed to Hughes's fatal illness.

Between July 1974 and November 1975, he completed twelve chapters — say a seventh of a book the size of *Fox* or *Shepherdess* — of his third volume. It was never given a working title. Hughes's search for perfection may be illustrated by the following statistic: his fifty-page foolscap typescript is backed by 911 pages of drafts. Since these chapters haven't yet been published, I give a synopsis of them in my Afterword, below.

The latest significant addition to Hughes's text was made on November 29th 1975, when he wrote the first tentative paragraph of chapter thirteen. After that he was able to go no further with the book: the disease which was to kill him rendered sustained work impossible. In October 1975 he and Frances flew to Ottawa, where they stayed with their daughter Kate and her husband Colin Wells, the classical historian, before going south to New York to stay with their son Owain. When Hughes arrived back in England, he was reduced to crossing the airport tarmac in a wheelchair. Hospital tests revealed that he was suffering from leukaemia. Between December 1975 and February 1976 he was still able to keep appointments outside Wales: these included attending a Foyle's lunch in honour of Edward Heath and a Candlemas Dinner at his old college, Oriel. In January or February, when he knew he was dying, he watched in company with his son Robert a TV programme which presented a fundamentalist view of heaven and hell. He made no comment, but Robert afterwards saw that he was crying. In March he was hospitalized; April he spent partly in hospital and partly at Môr Edrin. His family read to him a lot, and he seemed to find *The Odyssey* and *Anna Karenina* better medicine than the painkillers which were prescribed for his condition. From his bed at Môr Edrin he dictated a conclusion to his Introduction to *The Wonder Dog*, his Collected Stories for children. But had he not dictated to his mother, before he learnt how to write, his earliest literary efforts?

He died on the 28th of April.

PART TWO

Richard Hughes: Novelist

"The lyric poem comes like the flash of lightning, the novel comes much more like steady, low-candle-power electric light, but they are both electricity." — Richard Hughes

Chapter Five: The Early Work

I. *Gipsy-Night* (1922)

The poems included in Hughes's first book were for the most part written during the last four years of his minority: that is, from 1917 to 1921. 1922, the year of its publication, is of course, for literary historians, a date bristling with significance, its imagined skies still clouded with the smoke of poetical battles. On the one hand it was the year in which the last in the series of Edward Marsh's anthologies of Georgian Poetry appeared. On the other, it saw the appearance of *The Waste Land*. Between pages 97 and 103 of *Georgian Poetry 1920-1922*, four of Hughes's *Gipsy-Night* poems can be found: 'The Singing Furies', 'Moonstruck',[1] 'Vagrancy' and 'Poets, Painters, Puddings'. If I were asked whether the verse in *Gipsy-Night* is closer in style and concerns to that of the Georgians or to that of Eliot and Pound, I would certainly answer: the former. The young Hughes appears to have been influenced not at all by the poets of that historical 'movement' now known as Modernism. His poems do not possess, nor do they aim to possess, the witty sophistication cultivated by Eliot in his 'Love Song' or Pound in *Lustra*. Eliot's and Pound's searches for a fresh and contemporary idiom had taken them beyond both 'English' and 'American' traditions: Eliot went to the French *symbolistes*, Pound to the Latin epigrammatists. The two most important influences on Hughes's verse were native English poets: John Skelton and John Keats.

To name these two forbears immediately enables me to point up the very different styles and textures, the contrasting moods, to be found in Hughes's verse. On the one hand there is this:

> Robin stark-dead on twig,
>   Song stiffened in it;
> Fluffed feathers may not warm
>   Bone-thin linnet:
>   ('Winter')[2]

or this:

> Eight years of penury,
> Whining and beggary,
> Famine and cursing,
> Hunger and sharp theft:
> Death comes to such as these
> Under the sobbing trees:
> The cold stars nursing
> Those that are left.
> ('Martha')[3]

On the other hand, there is this:

> The kindly green and rounded trunks, that meet
> Under the soil with twinings of their feet
> And in the sky with twinings of their arms:
> The yellow stools: the still ungathered charms
> Of berry, woodland herb, and bryony,
> And mid-wood's changeling child, Anemone
> ('Vagrancy')[4]

with its direct reminiscences of 'Ode to a Nightingale' and 'Ode on a Grecian Urn'; or this:

> The silver mist that slumbers in the hollow
> Dreams of a breeze, and turns upon its side
> ('Weald')[5]

which may recall Prufrock's yellow fog, but is romantic-pastoral where the other is Laforguean-urban. There are two styles — or voices — in Hughes, then, both of which may be characterized as lyrical. One is expansive, sensuous, mellifluous, a style for the celebration of natural beauty. The other is clipped, compressed, harsh, a style for the expression of suffering. It is tempting to call one Romantic, the other anti-Romantic (though there is suffering aplenty in Blake, Coleridge, Wordsworth). The second dominates.

In his Prefatory Note to the first of his anthologies, *Georgian Poetry 1911-1912*, Marsh declared his belief "that English poetry is now once again putting on new strength and beauty". James Reeves[6] characterizes the typical reader of Marsh's anthologies — "as often as not a professional man or woman with only a week-end interest in the arts" — as one who "would prefer short, self-contained lyrical pieces with the accent on 'beauty' rather than 'strength'", and who was "mistrustful of sordid imagery and shaky syntax". Whilst Marsh's selections favoured 'beauty' rather than 'strength', he certainly published poets whose work possessed the latter virtue: W.H. Davies, for instance; and in the work of the war poets Owen and Sassoon, whom he also published, there was certainly "sordid imagery". Hughes's two styles can be related to the qualities valued by Marsh himself, then, even if they were not equally acceptable to many of those who bought and read *Georgian Poetry.*

To say this, however, is only to reflect on Hughes's two styles from an external and literary-historical viewpoint. *Gipsy-Night* reveals a sensibility that is keenly and sensuously aware of natural beauty and, in Wordsworth's words, "The pleasure that there is in life itself"; yet it also sees the privations, brutalities and miseries which some people must endure: either at the hands of other people, or at the whim of nature itself.

> It is a pleasant thing to dream at ease
> On sun-warmed thyme, not far from beechen trees.
> ('Vagrancy')[7]

Well yes. Trouble begins when human beings cease to be passive in face of nature or one another — or nature itself ceases to be benign. 'A Man'[8] briefly explores the first of these alternatives. The man (in an opening line of memorable simplicity) is "in love with grass", with trees, animals and birds. Suddenly, for no apparent reason, he offends against nature — which is to offend against his own nature:

> *Why did he break that small wing?*
> The sun looks hollowly:
> Mocking's where the water goes;
> The breeze bitter in his nose:
> Mocking eyes wide burning
> — Lost, lost is he!

Slight though his crime is in cosmic terms, it has dire consequences for the doer. He undergoes a kind of fall from natural grace which causes him to forfeit all his erstwhile delight. No reason is offered for his act: it is, perhaps, as irrational, as gratuitous, as the Ancient Mariner's killing of the albatross. The attitude of the poet to his 'man' is one of empathetic detachment. By this I mean that the poet is sufficiently inward with his subject's feelings to create and present them without *either* identifying with the man in his joy *or* implying sympathy for him in his wretchedness. Indeed, that exclamatory "Lost, lost is he!" risks suggesting something like exultancy in the man's lostness. To be, at need, inward with his characters and yet to remain emotionally detached from them is characteristic of Hughes as both poet and novelist: it is his version of Negative Capability. That 'A Man' turns upon a violent act, and that the violent act is registered unemotionally by the poet, make it a typical Hughes poem.

In 'The Rolling Saint'[9] the violent act is described at greater length with a studied, circumstantial detachment that is almost scientific. Seizing upon the ancient, shrivelled saint, "wild hill robbers"

> cramped her in a barrel
> (All but her bobbing head)
> And rolled her down from Teiriwch
> Until she was dead:
> They took her out, and buried her
> — Broken bits of bone
> And rags and skin — and over her
> Set one small stone:

That we feel no pity for the victim is due in part to the objectivity of the treatment, in part to the fact that she herself makes no complaint. As in 'A Man' the crime is motiveless — or, at least, left unexplained. This, the implication is, is simply how wild hill robbers behave when they happen upon ugly, apparently crazy old women. Again the victim exacts a certain price, if in this instance it is not paid by her murderers only: for, goes the legend, unless a passer-by adds a stone to her sepulchre, her ghost will roll in front of him "The whole night through". The story is absurd, but the device of enclosing it in passages of atmospheric descriptive writing lends sufficient weight to enable a reader to respect the poet/narrator's own residual superstitiousness:

> Dare I pass the place by
> And cast not a stone?

In 'The Singing Furies'[10] the violent act is nature's — though it is personified (? furified?) in "thirty singing furies" (which rather prevents me from characterizing it as an act of God). As the storm nears, Hughes gives us the responses of certain creatures:

> Slow bullocks stand with stinging feet,
> And naked fishes scarcely stir, for heat.

The epithets "stinging" and "naked" in their momentary succinct empathies would not disgrace Shakespeare or Keats (I think of Keats's appreciation of Shakespeare's snail, and his own minnows, for example[11]). The storm breaks — and dies away; the furies ride "muted . . . Down wet and slippery roads to hell":

> And, silent in their captors' train
> Two fishers, storm-caught on the main;

A shepherd, battered with his flocks;
A pit-boy tumbled from the rocks;
A dozen back-broke gulls, and hosts
Of shadowy, small, pathetic ghosts;
Of mice and leverets caught by flood,
Their beauty shrouded in cold mud.

It's characteristic of Hughes that he moves in this catalogue from human to animal victims wholly naturally, without allowing a reader to register any sense of incongruity. "Back-broke" is particularly blunt and unsqueamish, and already looks ahead in a small way to the broken necks of *A High Wind in Jamaica*. But Hughes does, on this occasion, sound a sympathetic note: it is there in the phrase "Of shadowy, small, pathetic ghosts". But coming as late as it does, this has the effect of extending pity only to the mice and leverets. I have quoted the version from *Confessio Juvenis*; in *Gipsy-Night* there is a semi-colon after "flood", which allows the predication of "beauty" to every victim of the storm. The comma of the revised version allows beauty only to the mice and leverets, and I print this feeling it to be more in tune with the tenor of Hughes's youthful imagination — as, retrospectively, I imagine it.

In 'The Horse Trough'[12] the violent act is the killing of a fly. (I thought of writing "no more than" the killing of a fly, but Blake prevented me.) The killer is a little girl, a mere tot. The poem opens seemingly as a celebration of children at play — children splashing and clattering in the sun round a horse-trough — but the closing lines shift unexpectedly into quite another key:

> who can be this silent one,
> This dimpled, pensive, baby one?
> — She sits the sunny steps so still
> For hours, trying hard to kill
> One fly at least of those that buzz
> So cannily . . . .
> And then she does.

This skilful closure — with its inevitable and clinching rhyme — possesses a resonance which might, on the face of it, seem out of proportion to the slightness of the act. But the effect is worked for by "silent", "so still/For hours", "trying hard" which establish her separateness, her concentration, her single-mindedness: qualities at apparent odds with her "dimpled" babyhood. Hughes restricts himself to externals, to observing and reporting, yet in such a way as to provoke questions in a reader's mind: Why should this one child be so absorbed in this particular activity? Is such behaviour natural or unnatural? The poem opens up a fascinating area of psychological interest which it simply refuses to explore. At the time of writing 'The Horse Trough' (which I take to be in his late teens), Hughes, perhaps, could go no further than he did. But both his first play and his first novel would return to the theme of the child (indeed, the *girl*-child) and the violent act: then, of course, with a real ambition to probe his subjects' minds.

The only other poem in the collection to look closely at a child is 'Martha' (subtitled 'Gipsies on Tilberstowe: 1917'). It is among the weaker inclusions, and was not reprinted in *Confessio Juvenis*. When in 'The Horse Trough' Hughes invites unarticulated questions to accumulate around a simple situation, the poem works very well; when in 'Martha' he tries to go beyond detached presentation, he produces something suspiciously like a higher-case rhetoric:

> Child of the Wide Earth,
> Born at the World's Birth,
> Grave with the World's pain,
> Mirthless and tearless:

and so on. The poem is strongest when, simply but insistently, it directs us to look at this small, pinched-faced child who stares and stares "as if/Stare she must". Or when, towards the end, he suddenly reflects:

> My God is overhead:
> Yours must be cold. Or dead.

— lines which set Martha's wretchedness *sub specie aeternitatis*, and strike harshly at the all-embracing loving deity of Christianity.

God, in fact, is a problem for the author of *Gipsy-Night*. In the relaxed, celebratory 'Vagrancy', it seems natural for Hughes to invoke Him when expressing his uncomplicated pleasure in the "beechen hollow" in which he's encamped:

> — There are more shadows in this loamy cup
> Than God could count: and oh, but it is fair . . . .

When he looks at pinched-faced Martha, however, it is, as we have seen, a different story: Hughes's God comes apart in his hands — or at least in his words. And when, in 'Dirge'[13], he speaks on behalf of those who inhabit mouldering dwellings in the twisted streets of crowded cities, where lives are constricted and harsh, "God the Creator" is One to be invoked only in "Quick oaths — terse blasphemous thoughts". For such people, dying involves no destiny so pat as Heaven or Hell: rather,

Death is a quiet and deep reliever, where soul upon soul
And wizened and thwarted body on body are loosed from their
 duty
Of living, and sink in a bottomless, edgeless impalpable hole.

Dead, they can see far above them, as if from the depth of a pit,
Black on the glare small figures that twist and are shrivelled in it.

For a critic to declare these lines overadjectived and overwritten would not
be a matter for surprise. Today as I write, I am inclined rather to register the
freight of powerful — and, so it seems to me, sincere — feeling that they
carry. This, perhaps, makes 'Dirge' a young poet's poem: for along with the
actual violence of the human world it contains the literary violence of its
author's mind. When Hughes sits down to write a poem specifically about
death, 'Felo de Se',[14] he produces something that is only marginally more
Christian than Hamlet's most famous soliloquy. He asks whether Mind
survives the death of the body: and if so, does it continue to exist in the state
of doubt which characterized its bodily existence, or is it granted Certainty
about all issues which in life were shrouded in mystery? If the former is the
case, there seems little point in dying:

The back, Death, till I call thee!
Hast come too soon.
— Thou silly worm, gnaw not
Yet thine intricate cocoon.

The "silly worm" is Hughes himself, biting futilely and prematurely at the
physical frame which both restricts and preserves him — and which,
'intricate' seems to suggest, it is worth staying alive to explore. 'Felo de Se' is
the most intellectually ambitious of the poems in *Gipsy-Night*, but in it
Hughes is compelled to recognize the limitations of his intellect. Did he also
recognize the limitations of its poetic language — well-illustrated in the
stanza I have quoted? Here, indeed, is an "intricate cocoon" — one that in a
number of poems threatens to suspend the poet in the cage of an idiom
already gone under the hill.

 The poems I have glanced at represent fairly, I think, Hughes's strengths
and weaknesses as a verse-maker. He tends to write most effectively where
he is attempting less: ambitiousness leads him into strained effects and
strained ideas. His poetic language is not at all times his own, and his idiom
is not a modern one. Except occasionally, he does not give the impression of
being *inevitably* a writer of poems — that he was born to write poetry first and
last. Hindsight, perhaps. But there are effective and attractive poems and
parts of poems in *Gipsy-Night*, and the mind behind them is unmistakable.
Hughes had still to discover what kind of writer he was meant to be.

II. *Plays* (1924)

His first play, *'The Sisters' Tragedy'*, is resolutely a drama of ideas. Hughes, indeed, was able to invest his one-act structure with a more complex, and more teasing, sum of ideas than any poem or short story he'd written before it. Although the play appeared in the London Grand Guignol, he stipulated that it should not be acted in the Grand Guignol manner: it needs to be acted naturalistically, and the part of Lowrie, in particular, "taken with great restraint" (*Plays* p. 3).

Philippa, Charlotte and Lowrie, three apparently parentless sisters aged twenty-eight, nineteen and thirteen respectively, live in an early-Victorian mansion in the Welsh hills. Together they look after their brother Owen, a blind deaf-mute of twenty-four. Charlotte has a fiancé, John, but feels unable to marry, since that will throw the burden of caring for Owen upon Philippa. Philippa declares her readiness to devote her life to Owen, "and so make an offering acceptable unto the Lord" (p. 12), but her self-martyring stance only irritates her younger sister, increasing Charlotte's reluctance to leave him. She expresses their predicament in these succinct words:

> Why should you and I and John have our lives spoilt for the sake of Owen, whose life really isn't worth living? (p. 14)

Events reveal, however, that the third and youngest sister, Lowrie, is not prepared to allow the situation to continue indefinitely.

The play opens with Charlotte killing, at Philippa's insistence, a rabbit whose back has been broken by a cat. Lowrie wildly accuses her of being a murderer, but apologises when Philippa explains that "it's right to put a thing out of its pain .... when living is only a burden to it" (p. 9). Immediately, by way of the violent act, Hughes engages a lifelong preoccupation: the inabsolute, shifting nature of good and evil. Tragedy is to be generated out of the difference between an 'adult' but unimaginative understanding of what constitutes good, and an imaginative child's understanding of what constitutes good: between experienced and conventional, and innocent and unconventional views. Charlotte's and Philippa's minds accept that paradoxes and ambiguities complicate moral issues: for them pragmatism sits down with idealism, so that they practise a form of double-think. Lowrie's mind is at first dogmatic: but Hughes shows it developing as she struggles to assimilate new and disturbing notions. If it can be right to put a badly-damaged *animal* out of his pain, she reasons, why not a badly-damaged human being? — if a rabbit, why not Owen? Of course there are differences between rabbits and men, and it is these that she now begins to contemplate. When Philippa tells her that animals do not go to heaven, as humans do, the way is open for her to ask John, with a child's order of logic, if it isn't "really much more killing to kill an animal than to kill a person?" (p. 19). Surely it would be better for Owen to die and go to heaven, where his eyes and ears would be restored? Then, of course, Charlotte and Philippa would be free to live their own lives.

The twofold good that killing Owen appears to proffer is, however, offset by one certain evil. For whilst killing Owen would be good for Charlotte, Philippa and John, it would be bad for Lowrie herself, since she is convinced of the truth of the Christian doctrine that the souls of murderers go to hell.

Hughes thus opens up a debate about the nature of the truly selfless act. The persons of the three sisters offer ironically contrasting perspectives upon self-sacrifice. Charlotte and Philippa find themselves in a situation which their sense of rectitude requires them to endure: self-sacrifice is *exacted* from them by circumstance. Charlotte chafes bitterly against her bondage: but whilst Philippa can, in theory, release Charlotte from her duty (doing which may be no more than an outward show), she cannot release her from her conscience (which inwardly requires a standard of behaviour from her, and will punish her if she falls short of it). Charlotte feels that she has not been cut out for martyrdom. For her part, Philippa accepts the self-sacrificial role which life — or God — has thrust upon her, and is prepared to look after Owen single-handedly and indefinitely. But, viewed askance, her selflessness comes to resemble self-interest: for she is convinced that by performing her Christian duty in *this* world she will be rewarded — reimbursed — in the next: her saintly labours will guarantee her a place in heaven. Is true selflessness compatible with calculation? The household, in effect, constitutes a web of mutual sacrifice: Philippa can only take on a self-sacrificial role because Owen exists. Lowrie comes to see that "he is being sacrificed to her, not her to him" (p. 20): but it would be truer to say that Owen and Philippa are being sacrificed to one another. In comparison with that of her sisters, and in spite of the fact that it involves murder, Lowrie's order of self-sacrifice appears wholly virtuous. She considers her own interests not at all: in order to act in the best interests of Owen, Charlotte, Philippa and John, she is prepared to be damned. Her only anxiety lies in her awareness that she may not be strong enough to carry out the necessary act. Thus, before attempting to smother Owen — her first strategy — she is driven to utter this curious prayer:

> Oh, God, help me to do it! I'm very young and weak to wilfully give my soul to be damned, but help me to have strength to do it, for Phil's sake and Chattie's, Amen — (p. 24)

This is the kind of teasing formulation Hughes delights in: doing good and doing evil are revealed to be one and the same thing. Hughes has succeeded in identifying the selfless act and the violent act. What Lowrie does not understand, of course, is that earthly sufferings are not, for Christians, to be relieved by positive action, but passively to be endured.

When she finds that she cannot bring herself to suffocate Owen, she conceives the idea of letting him out of the house in the hope that he will fall in the pond and drown: a stratagem which succeeds. The chief irony in this is that only Lowrie truly loves Owen — as the responses of the various characters to his death make plain. Charlotte and John are "quite composed" (p. 28) as they bear in his body; and when later Charlotte dabs her eyes, there is a suspicion that she is merely going through the motions of sorrow. Philippa breaks down, but her self-accusation that she has been "a cruel sister" (p. 28) to Owen, and treated him unkindly, suggests that her reaction is partially prompted by a guilt that is not merely imaginary. Lowrie's love for Owen is plain throughout: her words as she strives to bring herself to smother him pathetically mingle her care and hope for him with her growing terror at herself. When she asks him to forgive her, and declares that it is only because she loves him that she can kill him, we see that the paradox conveys an extraordinary truth. Her reaction to his death is suddenly to collapse, from a dry-eyed silence, in loud weeping upon the floor.

Quite early in the play, Philippa has expressed the notion that God

> may already have decided to take Owen to Him in His own way, by His own instrument unknown and even unguessed at by us. (p. 15)

The play invites us to see Lowrie as precisely this instrument without ever allowing us to feel secure in this identification. Immediately after the drowning, everyone says that it is for the best, and Philippa recalls her earlier speech by declaring:

> It was God's kind will to take him from his suffering . . . God's purpose is worked out in His own time, and though He may use the weakest of us sometimes as His instruments, it is not for us to anticipate His will: He accomplishes it without any help from us. (p. 29)

But when Charlotte and Philippa begin to consider how it was that Owen got out of the house, they see that Lowrie must be questioned. Breaking down, she admits her guilt. What was acceptable to her sisters and John when it could be seen as an act of God (God can kill as and when He likes), is not acceptable as a human act. Philippa hurries out, appalled. John knocks Lowrie down, declares that he cannot possibly marry a murderess's sister, and leaves. Charlotte pursues him. Abandoned on the stage, Lowrie must now suffer the psychic consequences of her act. Her mind, which all along has been literal and intensely moral, no longer able to hold in some sort of equilibrium the contending abstractions which press upon her, no longer able to bear the heavy responsibility of bringing her world to irretrievable ruin, implodes into madness. The ironic, and dreadful, price of her mind's survival, is to imagine Owen to be alive, that she never killed him.

'The Sisters' Tragedy' is quintessential Richard Hughes. It is wholly successful in its attempt to generate complex and irresolvable moral questions out of limited dramatic elements. What is love? — can it be caring for another person so much that you are prepared to kill him? What is true selflessness? — can its proper reward be an eternity of torment? What are good and evil? — can they sometimes be one and the same thing? What is God's purpose? — is it to be understood as working itself out through human actions, or do human actions exist to subvert it? That *The Sisters' Tragedy* turns on the violent act, and that the violent act is the act of child, stamp it with the undeniable stamp of Hughes's mind.

It is more difficult to pronouce on the *Tragedy* as dramatic mechanism. I have not seen it acted — nor, for that matter, Hughes's two other plays for the stage. My impression is that its closing pages, in their desire to clinch the play, may err on the side of the melodramatic. Is John's response —

> Murderer! Murderer! You, to kill your own blind brother! [*She clings to his foot.*] You snake, give up crawling around me! [*Heaves her off his foot.*] (p. 33)

— Is John's response too emphatic, too overstated? Lowrie's concluding soliloquy strikes me as a very difficult matter to bring off for as young an actress as the text requires. Whatever the case may be, the *Tragedy* is a play that has been sorely neglected: its text reads so freshly that I imagine a performance would prove it to have dated far less than the many drawing-room pieces which the Twenties and Thirties unleashed upon the British public.

As Hughes himself remarks of his other one-act stage play, '*The Man Born to be Hanged*', "The principle of its construction is quite simple" (p.145). Nevertheless, to talk about the play's structure (as Hughes does in his Prefatory Note) is to talk pointedly about the play; for whilst in '*The Sisters' Tragedy*' the characters flesh out ideas which constitute the play's heart, in '*The Man Born to be Hanged*' the characters flesh out the play's form. The '*Tragedy*' is conventional in form: characters appear on stage in groupings that vary as the action requires. But in the later play the presence of the characters on stage (and the shifting values accorded to those characters) is the means by which the play works as a piece of drama. '*The Man Born to be Hanged*', then, is scarcely a naturalistic play at all: and intrinsically of less interest as a vehicle for ideas than its predecessor. Structurally, however, it is of considerable interest: in it Hughes succeeds in translating shock tactics and trickery into dramatic form.

This little play, I suggest, has two centres: an apparent one and an actual one. The apparent centre is Bill, whose large narrative contribution seems to confirm his dominant and eccentric physical presence as the focus of dramatic interest. The true centre is Nell: despite her small speaking part, it is Nell who generates all the action, Nell around whom the other characters may be seen, from the vantage-point of the play's dénouement, to have revolved. It is in relation to her that their dramatic significance is defined: Bill the absconding husband, Davey the would-be romantic lover, Mr. Spencer the brief companion, and Mr. Lenora — the man "born to be hanged" who, we speculate, will be accused and convicted of killing her: the one man, ironically, with whom she has had nothing to do.

The mystery at the play's centre is the mystery of a woman's love for a man: a love in this instance so powerful as to lead to one attempted murder and an actual suicide. As Nell is revealed, so is the power of her love: it surprises everyone, and it terrifies them. Bill, who claims to know her thoroughly, is seen to know her hardly at all. Her reality shows the men up for the pasteboard they are: they flee from her fierceness.

Reality is love, says the play; and thwarted love can be violent. So far so good. The play's weakness lies in the incongruity of the love and its object. Hughes, I suppose, wanted to make the point that love *is* incongruous, irrational. In making Bill a larger-than-life comic grotesque, however, he seems to go out of his way to strain the credulity of an audience: could such a woman love so passionately such a man? If one doubts this, one may feel that the play's two centres conflict with each other. But it is tempting to see '*The Man Born to be Hanged*' as a very early example of the Theatre of the Absurd. Its structure, its interpretation of character as form, renders such a reading attractive. Nell's love may then be seen as a residual naturalist power, a romantic anachronism which the absurd world cannot accommodate because it cannot recognize it for what it is. To suggest that an audience familiar with Ionesco, Pinter or Tom Stoppard would take this particular play of Hughes in its stride is one way of suggesting the determinedly modern cast of its author's mind in the early 1920's. '*The Man Born to be Hanged*' is very much experimental drama. It was, I suspect, ahead of its time.

A Comedy of Good and Evil, Hughes's only full-length play for the stage, picks up a number of the themes of *The Sisters' Tragedy*. Again it seeks to demonstrate — though this time in a comic context — the complex interdependence, and even the indivisibility, of good and evil. Again it is decidedly a drama of ideas.

Its main theme is quickly and plainly announced:

> MR. WILLIAMS . . . . It is a grand, terrible thing to be a humble soldier, fighting the shadowy battles of the Lord: fighting for the forces Good against the forces Evil. Yes. But there are times when it is not easy to tell which is which. (p. 46)

And again, by way of variation:

> MR. WILLIAMS. There are times when I say to my soul: Life is simple: do that which is right. Then my soul answers within me: What is Right? — How shall I answer my soul? (p. 47)

The difficulty which Mr. Williams recognizes here in the abstract becomes a concrete problem to be faced up to when he realizes that he has unwittingly admitted a devil into his house. He has a choice of two courses of action: should he cast the devil out, or should he continue to show it kindness and hospitality (it is injured), and so imperil his soul? His answer is unequivocal; indeed he has also given it theoretical expression before the devil arrives: since "the virtue of the act does not lie in the divine nature of the stranger but in the hospitable intention of the giver" (p. 58), it is one's duty to show hospitality to a guest — whatever the nature of the guest. In practice, then, he finds himself in the curious position of doing good to an emissary of hell. As with Lowrie in *The Sisters' Tragedy*, the doing of good to another (or others) brings evil consequences: Mr. Williams, in consorting with a devil, damns himself in law — as Lowrie feels herself to be damned for killing her brother. In the *Comedy*, as in the *Tragedy*, the nature of the truly selfless act is defined when Mr. Williams insists than an act is virtuous in so far as the doer ignores his own best interests. His statement that "It's good with no hope of gratitude, no hope of return, no thought of danger to ourselves that is the good really!" (p. 67) can stand as a retrospective criticism of the 'selflessness' of a Philippa — who thinks by good deeds to reap a tangible reward.

But Lowrie was a child — albeit an intelligent child — and Mr. Williams is an adult. From the start he is conscious of the infinitely complex nature of the moral world — a truth which Lowrie discovers painfully as *The Sisters' Tragedy* develops. In the *Comedy* it is Minnie, Mr. Williams's wife, whom Hughes invests with the moral absolutism that we find in Lowrie at the opening of the *Tragedy*: events will break down Minnie's simple absolutism as relentlessly as they do Lowrie's — but with comic, rather than tragic, results.

If, to play with a theological metaphor, Mr. Williams may be said to be the soul of Hughes's comic perception in this play, Minnie is its heart. Her comedy arises as much out of language as out of stage business (i.e. the antics of her new leg). Hughes says in his Note that his characters' accent is that of the South Snowdon district; and that their dialect represents not a translation of Welsh idiom, but English as it is spoken there. In Minnie's mouth the dialect is emphasized by the fact that she speaks English with some difficulty. (Hughes dramatically accounts for her use of English by saying that Mr. Williams demands that she speak it every other month in order to keep it up.) The delight Hughes takes in her speech is everywhere to be felt: it is comparable to the delight felt by Synge in the speech of the rural Irish of the Western Isles. If Hughes heightens Minnie's English (and I don't believe the heightening to be great), it is for the same reason that Synge heightened the language of his Arran Irish: Hughes seeks to bring out its felicitous and poetic qualities — the qualities of an English that is not a regional variant, but an English come at by way of the grammatical structures of a very different language. Hughes's comic intention in the *Comedy* is far distant from that of Caradoc Evans — for whose stories he expressed sharp dislike in an article published in 1924.[15] Hughes is not a satirist with a personal animus to express; he does not employ a strongly Welsh English as a means of suggesting a narrow mentality and a narrow morality; nor is his interest in Minnie anything to do with quaintness. Her character is celebratory: Hughes, quite simply, is in love with the English she speaks: he relishes her every word. It therefore follows — as the night does the day — that a production which cannot make an audience feel the rich poeticality of Minnie's speech must necessarily fail.

At the beginning of the play, Minnie sees good and evil as simple and obvious opposites. She cannot comprehend her husband's disquisition on the difficulty, sometimes, of telling them apart. Her Christianity is fundamental and, in a sense which I mean to be literal, and not perjorative, childlike: "Isn't the love of Heaven will save you, whatever?" (p. 46) The play will go on to show, in this instance, precisely the opposite to be the case: for Mr. Williams will be saved by the love of Hell. For Minnie, at the beginning of the play, evil is evil and good is good; angels are angelic and devils devilish. Hughes, in order to chip away at the notion that things must be, in their natures, what their physical appearance implies (a recurrent preoccupation in his early novels), gives his devil (Gladys) the form of a blue-eyed, golden-haired girl-child, and his angel (Owain Flatfish) the form of a repulsive fishmonger. When Minnie first sees Gladys, the child's beauty leads her to think she may be an angel. Minnie's exclamation: "There isn't no human innocence had the eyes like that, bless him!" (p. 64) is soon shown to be true in a sense she cannot at that moment suspect. Then the child, in burning her fingers on a bible, reveals her provenance, and Minnie's natural response is to treat her cruelly: until, that is, Mr. Williams reminds her that true Christianity lies in loving one's enemies. Minnie's education has begun in earnest.

Hughes's decision to clothe his devil in the shape of a beautiful little girl who is the epitome of 'innocence' is characteristic. (In 'The Stranger', the story from which the play was developed, the devil is, more conventionally, "a grotesque thing, with misshapen ears and a broad, flat nose", with knotted limbs and "crumpled wings, as fine as petrol upon water".[16]) Gladys is the third station on that early Hughesian line which runs from the fly-killing tot in 'The Horse Trough', through Lowrie, and on to Emily in *A High Wind in Jamaica*. As Gladys is conceived in the spirit of Hughes's love of inversion, so she operates. Her *raison d'être* is a precise inversion of Mr. Williams's (given above):

> Oh Mr. Williams, can't you *see* that the only thing in life which matters is the glorious struggle against the forces of good? To drive good out of the world, and so at the Last Day to receive the glorious crown of Victory! (p. 79)

And she is every bit as subtle as devils are traditionally famed to be. Not for her blatant evil-doing — no! Rather than seeking to deceive through falsehoods, she almost always tells the truth. And when she says, "I mean, you can do ever so much more harm by telling the truth than you ever could by lies, surely" (p.103), we may be reminded of Banquo's unheeded warning to Macbeth:

> And oftentimes to win us to our harm,
> The instruments of darkness tell us truths,
> Win us with honest trifles, to betray's
> In deepest consequence.
> (I.iii)

In causing Minnie to grow a new leg to replace her wooden one, she answers one problematical good by another one. Since miracles are traditionally ascribed to the forces of good, Minnie finds her brain going into a spin: her old certainties, upon which her simple faith was based, have collapsed. In what kind of moral world do devils do good? — "now my old conscience she going round in my head like a wheel, till I don't know God from the Devil" (p.103). Gladys has, by doing good, achieved evil results: for, Minnie is so distressed that she is tempted to kill the girl — an action which would drop her straight in Satan's lap. Yet when the devil-like Owain Flatfish appears and exorcises Gladys with bell, book and candle, Minnie bursts into tears.

The third Act of *The Comedy* takes place a year later. Mr. Williams is dead, and dramatic interest centres on the fate of his soul (we do not see him in person in this Act, only hearing his voice). Gladys, reappearing, announces· that he is bound to be damned for consorting with a devil. She is pleased with her achievement in performing an act "with no trace of good in it anywhere, either of motive or effect" (p.125). If the essentially good are tempted to do evil, the essentially evil are tempted to do good: and this temptation she has, in this instance, triumphantly withstood. For his part, Mr. Williams is unsurprised at her prognostication: to be damned, he feels, is no more than his desserts. This she vehemently denies: had she not interfered in his life, he would certainly have gone to heaven. It is now that the play arrives at its central affirmation of the necessary interdependence of evil and good:

> GLADYS. Returning evil for evil doesn't really count, you know: it's only in returning evil for good that we can show ourselves really worthy of our great master. But it was hard, hard.
> MR. WILLIAMS. Good gracious me! Then good was the mother of evil, for if I had not first done good to you, you could never have done true evil! Dear, dear! But I see no other conclusion possible in this dualistic universe! (p.126)

We thus find ourselves to have been present at a good-humoured demonstration of the necessity of what Blake called contraries — without which there is no progression. Good is dependent for its profitable existence upon evil, and evil upon good. Only evil makes good possible, and only good evil. Neither can exist without the other.

Owain Flatfish, "the plain-clothes angel for the district" (p.126), now enters formally to debate with Gladys the destiny of Mr. Williams's soul. No sooner has Gladys made good her claim for him, however, than she finds it impossible to hold to her duty.

> There was never a better saint in Wales, I swear it, and I ought to know. It was pure charity got him damned! (p.128)

Justice, she says, demands that Mr. Williams go to heaven. Owain counters that Justice has nothing to do with it: what condemns Mr. Williams is Law: Law is Truth, Justice Opinion. Ironically, at this point in the play, it seems that evil wears a charitable face and good an uncharitable one: but Hughes still has further twists up his sleeve. Mr. Williams interrupts the dialogue to demand to be sent to hell: for what is irrepressible Gladys doing but tempting an angel? — the impudence of the girl! Her apparent good conceals an evil purpose: again the two are inseparable. Owain exits, leaving Mr. Williams's soul with Gladys. The spirit of comedy now demands that she conduct him to heaven: for he is quite unsuitable for hell, where he'd be "like a square peg in a round hole" (p.133).

Hughes's comic dualism, like Blake's in *The Marriage of Heaven and Hell*, is thoroughgoing. The two champions — the saintly Mr. Williams and the devilish Gladys — are brought in the play to recognize the power of what each is up against. So, Mr. Williams admits that Gladys's "very existence is dependent upon the conception of evil as a positive" (p. 80), while Gladys has to realize that Good is no less a 'faith' (p.139) than evil is. Although, in the last movement of the play, Gladys is tempted — by, of all people, Minnie — to abandon her master Lucifer, she does not give way, and the contraries remain tense. Wit and good humour rule in *The Comedy*, yet Gladys's parting cry — "If I'm not bad — I'm nothing!" (p.140) crystallizes an idea that would gather some adherents in the new century. When, almost fifty years later in *The Wooden Shepherdess*, Hughes returned to contemplating evil as a positive, as a faith, it would necessarily be without the lightheartedness of youth.

In *Danger*, his first and only published play for radio, Hughes turned to a different theme, but one that is no less characteristic. A brief exploration of fear, this little play looks ahead to *In Hazard*. A young man, a young woman, and an elderly man, who have become separated from the main party, find themselves in darkness when the lights fail in the coal-mine they are touring. At first there seems to be no danger, and the young people, Mary and Jack, pretend, for the thrill of it, that they are caught in a real pit disaster. Their false security is punctured, however, by two explosions followed by the sound of water: the mine is flooding. Mary is the first to lose control in face of death, but Jack calms her. When Bax, the older man, comments sardonically that it will be better for them to die together, in one another's arms, than at different times, Jack retorts that it's all very well for Bax to be stoical — he's had his life, they are still young. Bax's response represents a typical Hughesian inversion of conventional wisdom:

> D'you think it is any easier for the old to die than the young? I tell you it's harder, sir, harder! Life is like a trusted friend, he grows more precious as the years go by. What's your life to mine? A shadow, sir! Yours, twenty-odd years of imbecile childhood, lunatic youth; the rest a mere rosy presumption of the future! Mine, sixty solid years of solid, real living; no mere rosy dream! Do you think it is easy for me to leave my solid substance as you to leave your trumpery shadow? (p.182)

Jack counters that another person depends on him: who depends on Bax? Jack is the next to show signs of cracking up, but it is Bax who panics as the water-level rises up their bodies; Jack and Mary remain calm. If, as Bax claims, the young people scarcely appreciate what, with life, they are losing, it seems also that they have little sense of what death is. Mary expresses a simple Christian belief in the immortality of the soul. Bax counters violently: "Death's being nothing — not even a dratted ghost clanking its chains on the staircase." (p.189) But a tapping of hammers above their heads brings hope; and, with the water threatening to engulf them, the rescuers break through. As Mary is lifted clear, Hughes perpetrates his final twist: Jack and Bax vie to be the last to be hauled up. Each has accepted the other's argument as to the comparative value of their lives; Jack is hauled protestingly upwards; Bax is swept away.

The Sisters' Tragedy and *The Man Born to be Hanged* are constructed around the murder-act; *Danger* makes use of the extreme situation. Violence human and natural then — the two faces of a coin of great value to Hughes's imagination. He is obsessively drawn to explore the psychological states of those who find themselves in such situations. *A High Wind in Jamaica* and *In Hazard* will employ the same imaginative language as these early plays, but developing and refining it as an analytical instrument.

III. *Confessio Juvenis* (1926)

Confessio Juvenis, Hughes's Collected Poems, consists for the most part of poems which appear in *Gipsy-Night*: twenty-seven of them, some lightly revised and some retitled. To this foundation are added four early poems and ten later ones. By way of approaching the question: Why did Hughes give up verse at so early an age? (which, whilst it isn't the only question raised by the book, is one that a critical biographer can hardly duck) it will be instructive to glance at the fate which he himself visited upon one of these poems. 'Lover Finds Something Out' (p. 59) takes the form of an extended simile: fish in a river are compared to the notions in a girl's mind — at one moment clearly seen; the next, obscured by the action of the wind. The fish themselves, which

> Dart here and there as if they were afraid,
> Or hang above the golden gravel-bed
> In rings of lovely light to view displayed;

are heavily in debt to Keats's minnows in 'I stood tip-toe upon a little hill'. Sadly, the whole thing is rather twee. Its conclusion —

> Ah! sad young man, this moral here you find:
> Touch not her heart if you would know her mind.

— goes so far beyond the terms allowed for by the fish-simile as to seem tacked almost arbitrarily on to the poem, The first four lines of the second paragraph run:

> So have I often stood, as by a brim,
> In girls' clear minds to watch the fishes swim;
> Which bubble to their eyes, or dive into places
> Deep, yet visible still 'neath crystal faces . . .

These, in *The Fox in the Attic* (p.154), become the opening lines of a poem composed by Augustine Penry-Herbert as he lies in bed in Schloss Lorienburg:

> *Oft have I stood as at a river's brim*
> *In girls' clear minds to watch the fishes swim:*
> *Rise bubbling to their eyes, or dive into places*
> *Deep, yet visible still through crystal faces . . .*

He was rather pleased with that beginning, at first — its detached attitude was so adult. But then he grew disgruntled with its idiom. Why didn't his few poems, when they came, arrive spontaneously in modern idiom — the idiom of Eliot, or the Sitwells? They never did . . . 'Oft . . .' *This* idiom was positively Victorian. *Victorian* idiom . . .? "Idiom Makyth Man", Douglas Moss had once said; and the recollection gave him now a most uneasy feeling.

"Oft" doesn't appear in the original; but pedants may be satisfied to balance it against the equally grisly "neath", which does (the differences, Hughes told me, are accounted for by the fact that he was quoting from memory). While it would be presuming too much to interpret Augustine's self-critical response as Hughes's own at the time he wrote it (he did, after all, finish the poem and publish it), there are enough signs of dissatisfaction among the other later pieces in *Confessio Juvenis* to suggest that disgruntlement with 'Lover Finds Something Out' may not have been long in arriving. (It is interesting to compare the whole poem with the three paragraphs of the novel (p.151) in which Augustine conceives the terms of the comparison: these prose paragraphs are in every way superior to the complete poem, and forfeit nothing in beauty of poetic language.) Hughes was conscious of what in one poem he terms "the decadence of the pseudo-revolutionary Georgian Age", and Passus IV contains a number of determined efforts to liberate himself from Victorian and Georgian idiom. The poem from which this phrase comes, 'Lines Written Upon First Observing an Elephant Devoured by a Roc' (pp. 71-6), so determinedly mixes absurd and metaphysical elements as to wear the features of an early piece of literary dadaism. 'Lines' begins, tongue-in-cheek, as a pastiche of Wordsworth: we find ourselves in a landscape of summery laziness along with a complacent poet-narrator. Soon enough, however, the poet starts to play tricks on us:

> I saw a beetle in the cress
> Tangled, his voyage scarce begun:
> And where — pink tongue, and tusks agleam —
> In yellow meadows by the stream
> The lovely elephants made play,
> I saw the fire-winged king-fisher
> Like light in light dispread, appear
> And bear a bream away.

Now comes the sound of heavy wings: it is the roc of the poem's title: the herd scatters — except for one doe, which is caught up and borne away. The remainder of the poem takes the form of an Epilogue in which a number of Voices (parodying *The Ancient Mariner*) debate the significance of what has just happened. The first Voice deprecates what it sees as a "prank" played by Heaven, in mixing naturalistic and fantastic elements in so frivolous a manner. The second Voice applauds it: for it detests "Mimetic Nature . . . . Forever playing one dull trick/Of reproduction". The third Voice finds the event "clever" but purposeless. The fifth, sixth, seventh and eighth Voices offer various symbolic interpretations. It is not until the fourth Voice makes itself heard that Hughes gives us a clue as to what he is about:

> How stale
> That 'sunny day': and all the tale
> Of flower and beast and usual bird
> Before the miracle occurred?
> By this event would Heaven impart
> Views on contemporary art,
> That some new wonder — plainly doth it show it —
> Shall disturb the indolent regurgitations of the nature-poet.

This is half-way to the truth: substitute Hughes for heaven and one is there. 'Elephant and Roc' is a self-conscious poem: it sets up an outworn style, parodies it, and then, in proffering a series of self-interpretations, pokes fun at critics' ability to dissolve a text into meaninglessness by over-interpretation. The trouble with the poem is that it is whimsical rather than witty: its self-consciousness is in turn self-conscious. Alongside Eliot's 'The Hippopotamus', 'Elephant and Roc' looks and feels heavy-handed, clumsy. Hughes was, by 1925, kicking a man who was down, and worse, he was attacking a tradition from which he himself seemed unable to extricate himself: for it strikes me that the best writing in the poem occurs when Hughes, setting the scene, forgets that his intention is one of pastiche:

> The tiny rumbling of the mole
> Answered the treading of the lark,
> And circling ripples showed the vole
> On oarage of swift feet embark.

Hughes, theoretically, might disparage descriptive nature-poetry, but it is one of his stronger suits in *Confessio Juvenis*.

The most ambitious poem in the book is 'Vision' (pp. 82-8). It divides into 'Meditative Ode' and 'Ecstatic Ode'. The first Ode is spoken by *animus* — mind or spirit — the second by *corpus* — body. Hughes sets out to contrast intellectual vision with sensual vision, and to show the adequacy or inadequacy of language to the expression of what, respectively, the two perceive. Nature, *animus* finds, is fine, but spirit is finer. As Keats found "ditties of no tone" superior to any music composed by men, so *animus* finds "sad tones/Unsounded .... More beautiful than stones". Fully to experience such spiritual music, man must pass out of nature into a realm which can only be adduced by means of paradoxes. *Animus* declares that the realm of spiritual vision exists beyond language: at which point Hughes, caught in an old Romantic trap, is left with only language to lament its own inadequacy — a symbolist language that remains stubbornly attached to the natural objects it signifies even as it denies them:

> Naked of words we enter in
> Where formless beauties walk in threes,
> And soundless music stirs no trees,
> And thoughtless knowledge bursts no mind,
> And uneyed senses thin as wind
> Swim on the darkness with no fin,
> No light wing-fall . . .

Returning from trance or reverie to the waking world, *animus* finds it as drab and debilitating as did Endymion when waking out of dream: "sticks and mud", no more: True poetry becomes an impossibility. The poet (who now appears to speak in his own person, rather than from behind the mask of *animus*) wishes

> to be free
> Of formless beauty! To make a jewelry,
> To write with sweet meticulous ease
> Of barn-door fowl, pattering chestnut:
> Or conjure scent of lime-flowers on the breeze:
> Or tell what Irony hid in a shepherd's hut,

What Passion solved itself in the pond's ooze:
So, to be saved: to be no soul forlorn,
But without soul to lose . . .

This is the second occasion on which the phrase "formless beauty" (or
"beauties") has occurred. Spiritual vision, it seems, is vision without
pattern: it is the sensual mind which perceives *form* in nature and natural
objects. Even as the poet expresses the sense of oppression which his soul
now feels, however, he is released from it: "a god" bursts his heart "like a pod
of peas".

The force that frees him is a spontaneous upsurge of repressed sensual
energy. Body has liberated itself. Blake comes to mind when I read:

— Lo, the immortal shadow in me,
That pale incubus the Soul,
Faints and fades, and I am free:
Saved are my five senses whole.

The natural world, perceived with visionary intensity by sense, is more than
sufficient unto the poet: at its centre, a hare seems to act as a focus for all
creation's energies:

What wild fury filled that hare!
His blazing eye! Electric fur!
The fearful flashing of his paws!
The patting of his sparkling claws!

The hare's furious splendour comes by way of 'Kubla Khan'; around it the
whole of the material realm is in motion, energized by the brute force at its
core. Now that it is emancipated from the opaque questings of spirit, body
finds language wholly adequate to its needs. Words are again equal to the
task of invoking things; the complex structure of the world has its analogue
in the complex structure of a language: more, it is because words make
sense that we can make sense of the world:

I saw the World's arches,
The spreading roots of light,
The high wordy pillars
That hold all upright,
The deep verbal fundament
Whereon rests sure
The world on thoughtful vaulting,
Interlocked, secure.

It is interesting to speculate on the reasons for Hughes's choice of the hare as his central image-symbol. Had he read that the Algonquin Indians worshipped the Great Hare, believing it to have brought the Earth into being? or that the Romans declared the hare's flesh sacred and divined the future from its motions? or that in pre-Christian Europe the hare was a fertility symbol? Certainly the poet's advance from melancholy to intoxication makes the hare an appropriate choice: for it is a folk-tradition that the hare's melancholy turns to madness in the Spring. Finally one may note the pun at the end of the penultimate stanza:

> I saw the limbs of Vision
> Outstretched in Form, where
> Intoxicant Vision lay couchant,
> Motionless as a hare.

Hughes denied form to the ineffable beauties glimpsed by spiritual vision: but it is impossible to deny a hare its form! In this one word idea and thing come neatly and wittily together to clinch one another. The Vision fades, and Hughes becomes, ironically, "mere bodied spirit" once more: a 'whole man' less than whole.

The extracts I have given from this poem should be enough to suggest that Hughes's language in it is no less Romantic than in many of his other poems: Blake, Coleridge, Shelley, Keats are palpable presences. It is as if Yeats, in the 1920s, were writing a dialogue of self and soul in the poetic idiom of a century and more before. When this is said, however, it seems to me that 'Vision' is still an important act of clarification, embodying, as it does, both negative and positive lessons. In 'Meditative Ode' Hughes sees the futility of the Romantic versifier's desire for transcendent experience: it cannot be rescued for poetry. In 'Ecstatic Ode' he celebrates sensual things and sensual perception and affirms the power of the word.

The penultimate poem in *Confessio Juvenis*, 'When Shall I See Gold?' (p. 90), trembles at once with uncertainty and with a sense of imminence. It is one of Hughes's most sensuous and satisfying poems. Flowers ask of half-ripe corn:

> 'Why do you disguise yourself, drinker of darkness?
> Put on your golden robes.'

But the corn cries

> 'I have come to the place where the roads meet.
> Where shall I go? Which way shall I now take?
> It may be that I shall go hence and perish.
> My heart is all green jade:
> When shall I see gold?'

The poem invites interpretation as personal allegory: the as yet immature Hughes has come to a critical fork in his artistic life: to what literary form should he commit himself? Will he succeed or fail? His heart is made of the right stuff — but will he produce the real thing? The last poem, 'Travel-Piece' (pp. 91-3), is autobiographical: it alludes to, among other experiences, his Danubian journey, and subsequent flirtation with politics in Croatia, and his steerage-passage to America. From none of this, however, substantial living though it may be, can he take satisfaction:

> Now, coming to manhood, I know I have plunged no deeper
> Into thought or doing than a kitten
> Trying to dare to pat an electric fan.

And he exclaims:

> Surely it's high time that something happened,
> Something snapped somewhere, and I entered in;
> — Ceased to be like the man who painted in the dark
> Then called for a light to see what he had painted?

What was to happen with regard to poems was that Hughes was virtually[17] to cease writing them. In retrospect, 'Travel-Piece' looks like a reckoning and a farewell. "Entering in" involved the abandonment of a craft in which, for all his efforts, Hughes had not succeeded in breaking out of romantic language into a style which was securely of the century. Could poems have abandoned Hughes rather than Hughes poems? I am not inclined to believe it: his abandonment of the theatre was deliberate and summary — why not, then, his abandonment of verse? Indeed it seems to me that his achievement in drama is more secure (if not intrinsically more interesting) than his achievement in poetry. As a piece of self-criticism, his ceasing to write poems is characteristically ruthless: If I cannot make the top flight, I will not be an also-ran. But if Hughes stopped writing poems, he did not stop being a poet.

IV *A Moment of Time* (1926)

Hughes's early volume of stories for adults is a mixed bag of a book. Its twenty-two inclusions feature a high proportion of fantasies, ghost stories and fables, none of which is longer than seven pages. These pieces, thirteen in all, reveal a youthful, quirky imagination: it has glimpsed a quick idea passing and snatched it for the page. But few of these stories — if any — would inevitably call up the name of the author of *A High Wind in Jamaica* if put unsigned under a well-read reader's nose. I shall restrict myself to commenting on just a couple of them, giving no more reason for my choice than the fact that these are the two I find most memorable.

'Jungle' is a tantalizing extract from some epic fantasy, an exotic nugget, a piece of barbaric image-making and a piece of verbal music which its composer could well have marked *crescendo*. The act of violence it ends with remains unexplained — though we may wish to take it as a sacrifice of sorts. Freudian critics will have few problems with the imagery of pillars and knives in a story whose eroticism is unconcealed, if undeveloped. I will content myself with suggesting that Jasan, magnificent and primitive but enslaved, represents something which Mellicles of Cos can dominate only by destroying. It is curious to consider that the instrument with which Mellicles kills the slave is made of the same splendid metal which decorates Jasan's uncivilized nakedness. Having conceived his scenario, Hughes simply follows its self-generated rhythm through to the point of climax. Whether that climax is perverse or inevitable is a matter of opinion.

'Monoculism: a Fable' is just that. It has much in common with Hughes's children's stories — except that it is not a children's story. (His marvellous children's story 'The Spider's Palace', a fable about the gains and losses of growing up, is one that adults could read with profit as well as pleasure.) The Queen of a certain country wears a monocle — a symbol of Constitutional authority sometimes addressed as "His Majesty the King". It magnifies very slightly. Discovering that there is an Ambassadress in her court who in secret wears *pince-nez* — an act at once immoral and illegal — the Queen demands that she be recalled. The Ambassadress's Queen defends the practice of wearing two lenses and suggests that since, in her opinion, they are superior, the monocular Queen should become binocular. This irritates the latter until she perceives its absurdity:

> for did she not know that her own eyeglass, for all his roundedness and transparency, nevertheless hampered her vision somewhat by his exaggerating tendencies? How, then, could a series of glasses do other than destroy vision altogether? (p.122)

Hughes's fable implies the conventional nature of human values. Whether political, religious or sexual, they are culturally determined and relative. The general truth that 'Monoculism' wittily proposes is one which Hughes would go on to explore in some particularity in his novels.

Several of the stories in *A Moment of Time* have a Welsh setting. Two — 'The Stranger' and 'Poor Man's Inn' — were the basis for the plays *A Comedy of Good and Evil* and *The Man Born to be Hanged*. 'The Stranger' has been included in more than one anthology of Welsh Short Stories, but I believe 'Llwyd', which Welsh anthologists have passed over, to be a finer tale. Hughes never wrote of the Welsh mountains with more evocative power than he displays in the story's opening paragraph:

> The mountains seemed knotted, and climbing on one another's backs; stretching their rocky fingers up to Heaven, who sat mockingly like a vast Blue Boy astride the roof-ridge of the world. their backs were rugged, lumpy, with rough patches of bilberry; their heads were grey, hairy with distant chutes of shale; but their black, gnarled fingers clutched among the white, unsubstantial clouds, straining up, without movement. And the clouds sailed quietly over like silent argosies, ballasted with thunder, sounding the plain with a long shadow, or anchored with a silver chain of rain; then the thin breeze would fill their mainsail and foretopsail, and they would slide quietly on, breasting the crested hill. (p.78)

These anthropomorphic mountains seem to express the inevitable failure of earthbound aspiration. They are conceived in terms of motion-in-stillness. One might say that Hughes writes with a painter's eye were it not equally the case that he writes with the eyes of a poet.

Llwyd is a boy who does not go to school because he is too "mazed". The story deals with his enforced passage from innocence to experience. Although its setting is naturalistic, it is a mythic statement that recalls Blake's *Songs*. Llwyd, insulated by his mazedness, dwells inwardly in a realm of feminine imagination: his mind is a region of "diamond-like" lucidity across which move the Ellyllon, three fairies whom he knows from folk-legend. Becoming dissatisfied with the inarticulate wisdom whispered by Maned, the foremost of the three, he makes the grievous mistake of applying to his father for enlightenment about the meaning of natural objects — buzzards, say, hunting high above a stream that "glitters like spilt mercury". His question, then, is age-old: What is the meaning of violent death in a world of such beauty? His father's answer is to preach a sermon of dreadful eloquence, mapping out the Universe, "and God, and Hell, and the Why and the Wherefore, and idols, and punishment, and Amalekites, and the Beast, and the angels out of Ezekiel" (p.83): he clouds forever the clear spaces of his son's mind. The story ends:

> The three fairies were lost for ever in the fiery murk of Ezekiel, and the black thunderclouds from Sinai grew solid as rock, crushing in with their weight the three-cornered cave in the hills, blocking him from his imaginations with their eternal adamant. (p.84)

Masculine law, one may say, crushes feminine imagination: in Blakeian terms, Urizen drives out Los, and Llwyd falls from grace. The story is succinct, cogent, and completely satisfying.

'Llwyd' is one of several stories which focus upon children. Two others —
'Cornelius Katie' and 'Martha' — take for theme the discovery of
artistically-talented children in unlikely places. In 'Martha' the talented
child is a twelve-year-old illegitimate girl, half-Chinese half-English. Wal
Henderson, a failed painter, discovers her drawing pictures for the clients of
a Chinese restaurant where her mother, Lottie, is a waitress. Under the
guise of employing the child to 'do' for him, he teaches her the use of oils
and encourages her to draw and paint. At the heart of the story lies the
complex relationship between Wal and Martha. His first intention is to
exhibit her as his discovery, but he cannot resist the temptation to pass her
work off as his own — work in which she loses interest as soon as she has
finished it. Martha appears indifferent to him, but it is a surface appearance
only: a deep attachment to him is in fact growing in her. When Lottie loses
her job and forbids Martha to go to Wal's, matters come to a head. Lottie
and Wal struggle for Martha, who prefers the painter to her mother. No
sooner has Wal emerged victorious, however, than "All the pains of Judas"
take hold of him. His double-guilt — at betraying the child and seducing
her from her mother — is a "net of cords" from which he can liberate himself
only by renouncing Martha. In a rage he ejects her from his room, tossing a
bundle of paints and brushes after her. This conclusion is quietly resonant.
Wal's act of self-liberation is also an act of self-sacrifice — for in the person of
Martha he has finally renounced all his artistic pretensions. For Martha,
who knows nothing of Wal's appropriation of her work, the rejection must
appear unmitigable and inexplicable. It is tempting to see in the pathetic
figure of the cast-out Martha an emblem of the curious sufferings that
artists may be compelled to endure. Certainly 'Martha', 'Cornelius Katie'
and 'Llwyd' are agreed in their determination to illustrate the harsh
unaccommodatingness of life to children.

A fourth story, 'The Cart', is no less uncompromising. Ursula Wortley is
the child of middle-class parents — a father who is often away from home,
and a neurotic mother. Mrs. Wortley's habit of disparaging her daughter in
front of her (Mrs. Wortley's) guests while the girl is present, causes Ursula
considerable pain. When Mrs. Wortley comes upon Ursula crying into her
pillow on the night of her father's departure on a long absence, her
exclamation: "Fancy crying like this! Anyone would think your father was
dead!" (p.129) immediately calls up in the child's mind the image of a dead
mole she has seen that day in the garden. Mrs. Wortley herself, we are told,
is "constantly afraid of death", but this fear is a part of her general histrionic
affectedness. Two days later, suffering an attack of the megrims, Mrs.
Wortley becomes hysterical, cries out that she is dying, and faints. Ursula

screams and runs from the house. Death "like a huge mole" runs at her side. She jumps on to the back of a cart "full of long, irregular packages done up in sacking". The story concludes:

> She felt that Death was with her somewhere in the cart, but did not dare to look for him. She was afraid of those packages, even before she saw what they were. They were sheep's carcasses. The sacking burst on one: she could see right into its gutted belly. She moved, and her hand slipped on a piece of suet. (p.134)

As in 'Jungle', Hughes rides the rhythm of his story to its inevitable end. It is not enough that Ursula experience the counterfeit death of her mother: she must be brought face to face with — even into squirming bodily contact with — an authentic piece of death. By comparison with 'Jungle', which is effortless, 'The Cart' is a little contrived, a trifle wilful. Nevertheless, Ursula's apprehension of death as a mole is psychologically convincing — quite as complete in its way as any adult apprehension of death, and beyond anything that her mother is capable of. As so often for Hughes, childhood guarantees a sensitivity which growing up merely seems to deaden: adulthood deadens the nerve-ends which in children are so raw. Ursula Wortley is a predecessor of Emily Bas-Thornton.

Hughes's story-telling technique in *A Moment of Time* varies in accordance with the needs of his material. In the shorter pieces which make up a good portion of the book, it is unpretentious. In 'Jungle' and 'Llwyd' we look directly into the clear stream of the narrative — the coloured pebbles on its bed are made over to us with sensuous immediacy. When Hughes wants to create a more complex narrative surface, a surface capable of generating irony, when he wants to manipulate his reader, he opts for first-person narrative. His narrator may be entirely detached from the events described (as in the longest story 'Lochinvárovič'), or implicated in them to some degree. The latter is the case in 'Poor Man's Inn' and 'The Diary of a Steerage Passenger'. The 'Diary' I take to be documentary, not fiction: Hughes's narrative procedure in it is similar to that in the longer 'A Diary in Eastern Europe', which was no doubt thought too diffuse to be reprinted in a collection of stories. In both diaries Hughes's persona is involved in the flow of events, but he writes much of the time as if he is mentally detached from them. The effect is to suggest a presence so cool as to be utterly indifferent to the physical indignities it is itself compelled to experience:

> This morning . . . we were all officially bathed and searched for lice; it took most of the day. Our bodies were carefully examined with a strong light, and our heads supposed to be scrubbed with soft-soap and

paraffin. Meanwhile the men who did it told us terrible tales of the horrors of Ellis Island. (p.222)

Such a narrator, one imagines, might describe his own death with perfect insouciance. His detachment, of course, is strategic. Nothing, it seems, can surprise him, nothing disturb his habitual poise. But suddenly something *does* happen that disturbs him — and it is all the more effective for puncturing so resistant a surface. In order to draw the reader 'into' a situation — to encourage, as it were, a reader to throw in his lot with the narrator, Hughes begins in these stories to make use of a second person. (It is Eliot's technique in, for example, 'Portrait of a Lady': "You will see me any morning in the park/Reading the comics and the sporting page.") Thus, on the opening page of 'Poor Man's Inn', we find:

> You will tell these places of shelter, probably, by seeing a few lousy rags hanging on bushes near . . . you are at the bottom of a sort of shaft, roofed very far up with dripping oak-leaves . . . (p.85)

The narrator takes it for granted that our experience is similar to his own: and by taking it for granted, he makes it so: for now we *have* seen those "lousy rags", *have* reached "the bottom of a sort of shaft". There is no going back, though we may object to being railroaded in this manner: if, that is, we can resist the authority of the written word in the first place!

In 'Lochinvárovič', Hughes tried out the ploy of the detached narrator in a story of some length. The piece is co-titled 'A Romantic Story', and so, in a number of ways, it is. But there runs throughout an ironic current which undercuts romance. Hughes-as-narrator cannot take Mitar Lochinvárovič seriously as a romantic lover, for the simple reason that Mitar himself cannot sustain the role. Mitar is self-divided: in him there is both a romantic who egotistically desires to become a folk-hero, and a realist who argues that the game isn't worth the candle (by a typical, if somewhat strained inversion, Hughes identifies the romantic in him with Head, and the realist in him with Heart). Much of the comedy of the tale then derives from Mitar's unstable identification as romantic hero: he advances towards and recedes from the ideal like a random human tide, and, without the promptings of Natya's friend Zdenka, would have lapsed into inertia at an early point in the proceedings. His most daring exploit is performed when he is drunk: on the way back from Natya's wedding he stops the car which, incognito, he is driving, pulls out a couple of automatics, reduces the families of the bride and groom by half, and then drives his car (which contains the groom's four younger brothers together with two gross of eggs) over the edge of a cliff. The Romantic egoist is violent as well as absurd.

Such an incident tests credibility, of course. But Hughes as narrator takes it in his stride — and, what is more, insists that the two families do. Throughout the story he handles the banal and the fantastic in the same level, unperturbable tones. From a stance of amoral detachment, he treats violence as an everyday occurrence. No doubt there is in this a deliberate attempt to shock, *épater le bourgeois*, with acts that seem gratuitous. *Le style, c'est l'homme*: and certainly it seems to have been Hughes's style to go "jumping out at you from behind a door armed with a fire-cracker"[18] not only in his youthful writing, but in his youthful conversation.[19] Now it is easier to dismiss this as the strategy of an immature trickster, but to do so unreservedly is to demonstrate the complacency — the very British complacency — that Hughes was aiming to unsettle. The society which Hughes describes in 'Lochinvárovič' is one that lives much closer to violence than the one he is writing for — and it is a violence sanctioned by moral and social codes. Once Natya has run away from her husband Srdič,

> immemorial etiquette dictated that in a case like this the injured husband should telegraph for his wife's nearest male relations; and on their arrival should avenge the insult that had been offered him by shooting them dead. Etiquette was equally firm that the unhappy father and brother should accept the invitation, as if they were ignorant of its import: and allow themselves to be shot with expressions of polite, if fictitious, surprise. Then, and not till then, the ball was open, and that mortal catch-as-catch-can called a blood-feud would begin between the two families until one or other was exterminated. (pp. 47-8)

That killing one's in-laws is conventional merely, and a convention within which the reluctant Srdič feels miserably trapped, is only a further twist — yet another of those ironies of violence which Hughes set himself to tease out over a lifetime.

All this, however, is something of a bonus for him. This main theme is passionate love, its absurdity and its vagaries:

> Love at first sight is a strange and beautiful invention of the Deity. It is curiously discrete: that is to say, it bears little relation or resemblance to anything else in the Universe: a kind of hint that God is not reasonable by necessity but because He prefers to be: an everlasting reminder of the sort of Universe He could have created had He preferred to be absurd. (p. 5)

Now, although these sentences are concerned specifically with the phenomenon of love, I cannot resist the temptation to extract from them a statement revelatory of Hughes's creative pursuit in his two pre-war novels. His imagination, I suggest, is one characteristically in search of the "strange and beautiful". The universe he seeks to uncover is not the charted, mundane, familiar place, but that "absurd" realm which God, had He been so minded, "could" have created in preference to a realm governed by reason. In Hughes's world we see what transpires when human reason fails, or nature's benevolent mask slips.

Chapter Six: Theory (1)

I

In his early twenties, Richard Hughes spent some time thinking about the nature of poetic creativity. This thinking I wish to describe. A reader may find it strange that I have not made the first chapter of Part Two of this book such a description. My reasons for not doing so will, I hope, be seen to be good ones. But before I give them I must describe the documents which contain as much of his theoretical thinking as has come down to us from this period.

The first takes the form of an eleven-page letter, typed on sheets of foolscap and dated October 7th 1921, which Hughes addressed to Amabel Williams-Ellis but apparently never sent her. The second is a Preface, probably written late in 1921 for *Gipsy-Night*, but not included in the book. The third is a lecture, 'Technique of Poetry', written some time in 1922: this is made up largely of little-changed material from the Preface, but adds to it some new matter. (The piece entitled 'A Preface to his Poetry' in *Fiction as Truth* consists of the Preface intercut with a paragraph or two from the lecture.)

Hughes published none of these documents in his lifetime: and this is the first reason for not opening the critical part of this book with an account of them. The last thing I wish to do is to establish some sort of critical grid — even a grid derived from Hughes himself — through which to peer at his creative work. And then, as Hughes himself says in his Preface, the opinions expressed there were not the opinions he held when he wrote the bulk of the verse that makes up *Gipsy-Night*. Lastly, I hope to capitalize retrospectively upon the ground covered in the previous chapter: as we examine Hughes's theories, we may be able to see without straining how the creative work implies the theory — as well as vice versa.

II

That Hughes's mind was developing rapidly in his early twenties, and bubbling with ideas, can be seen from the most obvious difference between the letter and the Preface. In the letter he puts forward a single theory to account for the existence of art in general and poetry in particular: Man is a pattern-making animal. In the Preface, however, he writes — and the credal force of the expression is deliberate:

> I believe that there is not, and never can be, any single holy catholic faith in poetics: that the phenomenon of poetry cannot be traced to any single source, any more than the Universe or Truth can be reduced to any single principle. I must confess to being a polytheist both in religion and art.[1]

Certainly there is more than a savour of heterodoxy about this "poetic Athanasian Creed". It is not a case of *credo in unum deum*, but of *credo in multos deos*. Immediately we recognize the stamp of Richard Hughes. We are about to encounter a theory that is not one theory, but many theories: a theory, indeed, that looks like nothing so much as an anti-theory. The anti-theorist is one who can see the virtue in a variety of explanations of a particular phenomenon, and will not compromise his integrity for the sake of making a splash with a particular hypothesis. So, in his Preface, Hughes declares that he is going to outline *three* psychological sources of poetry whilst allowing that many more may exist.

He finds it convenient to refer to his three sources as "plausible though inexact definition[s] of Man".[2] The first derives from Robert Graves's thesis in *On English Poetry*.[3] Man is a Neurotic Animal, and poetry is auto-therapeutic, being

> to the poet what dreams are to the ordinary man; a symbolical way, that is, of resolving those complexes which deadlock of emotion have produced: but with this difference. That while dreams resolve a man's private neuroses only, it is the universal nature of poetry to be able to resolve the reader's too. . .[4]

Whether Hughes, in later years, would have been entirely satisfied with the word "resolve" I am inclined to doubt. Coming back to Graves's theory in an Introduction written in the mid-sixties for a new American edition of *In Hazard*, he declares it to be essential that the poet remains unaware of what his poem is about in the act of writing it. It must be the case that the writing of a poem may obscurely relieve a poet whilst "resolving", in poetic terms, nothing. Hughes quotes the example of 'La Belle Dame Sans Merci':

[Keats's] agonized mind has palpably fused Fanny Brawne and Consumption in a single image, yet his own comments at the time (and his revisions are even more symptomatic) seem to show him quite unaware of this at a conscious level.[5]

The pale knight is as much in thrall to his beautiful enchantress at the poem's end as is Keats to his: nothing is "resolved". But this does not affect the strength of Graves's proposition, which had a major contribution to make in elucidating the genesis and meaning of *In Hazard* — as we shall, in due course, see.

Hughes's second theory is indebted to Aristotle, whose politikon zoon (political animal) Hughes reinterprets by saying that Man is a Communicative Animal. This is a notion which immediately suggests the partiality of Graves's thesis.

> For if the sole function of poetry were to resolve the poet's neuroses, there would be no earthly need for him to show his poems to anyone else . . . and yet that poet is not yet born who was content to put his poems in the fire as soon as he had written them.[6]

The necessity of intelligible communication requires that a poet acquaint himself with the tradition, and study the techniques of his craft.

Hughes's third theory is the one which he canvassed in the earlier letter: Man is a Pattern-making Animal. By way of glossing "pattern" he goes on to write: "Pattern is a crude form of rhythm, a skeleton of rhythm."[7] Pattern-making and rhythm-making are means by which the artist creates the beautiful: "it is not possible to divorce Beauty from some kind of rhythm or pattern". If we think of painting, it seems that Hughes is not a million miles distant from Clive Bell's 'Significant Form' — and indeed, he had been reading Bell. (In *The Fox in the Attic*, Augustine has to go to Germany to discover the idea!) In *Art* (first published in 1917), Bell writes:

> What quality is shared by all objects that provoke our aesthetic emotions? What quality is common to Sta. Sophia and the windows at Chartres, Mexican sculpture, a Persian bowl, Chinese carpets, Giotto's frescoes at Padua, and the masterpieces of Poussin, Piero della Francesca, and Cézanne? Only one answer seems possible — significant form. In each, lines and colours combined in a particular way, certain forms and relations of forms, stir our aesthetic emotions.[8]

Later Bell anticipates Hughes still more closely when he writes:

> with those who judge it more exact to call these combinations and arrangements of form that provoke our aesthetic emotions, not 'significant form', but 'significant relations of form', and then try to

make the best of two worlds, the aesthetic and the metaphysical, by calling these relations 'rhythm', I have no quarrel whatever.[9]

Hughes, of course, is a writer not a painter, and Bell himself denied literature the status of 'pure art' on account of its intellectuality. 'Form', 'pattern' and 'rhythm', however, are all terms common to art-criticism and literary criticism. Hughes himself seems to harbour a preference for 'rhythm' above 'pattern'. That it *is* preferable may be suggested by glancing at the Marxist critic Arnold Kettle. Kettle begins his book on the English novel by suggesting that "there are in all novels which are successful works of art two elements"[10] — 'life' and 'pattern'. The first of these words remains vague. Kettle can find no adequate synonym for it: novels that possess 'life' are 'life-communicating', convey a "sense of life" which quickens our faculties. As for the second:

> Pattern is not something narrowly 'aesthetic', something which critics like Clive Bell used to talk about as 'form' (as opposed to life or content). Pattern is the quality in a book which gives it wholeness and meaning, makes the reading of it a complete and satisfying experience.[11]

Now Kettle's problem, and one he's well aware of, is that these elements "are not, in truth, separable. Pattern is the way life develops."[12] The great writer perceives life in terms of pattern, imposes a vision upon it which rescues it from chaos and gives it significance. Yet Kettle, like so many other critics (and I cannot myself have escaped this pitfall), is compelled to proceed as if, to some extent, 'life' and 'pattern' are separable entities. Hughes's term 'rhythm' is one way of resisting this dichotomy. Rhythm may be found in abstract language as well as in visual shapes: "What is logic itself," asks Hughes, "but a kind of rhythmic thought, patterned conclusion?"[13] Rhythm, to coin a metaphor that counters Kettle's division, is the life of literature. In a poem it may be felt everywhere, both as a *physical* presence which regulates the speed at which words enter a reader's consciousness and declares itself in the sound-pattern of the language, and as a *supra-physical* (or intellectual) presence implied by the interplay of images, symbols and ideas.

Hughes now arrives at a conception which seems to me to illuminate his own practice as a writer. The business of the poet, he says, is

> to excite vivid impressions of colour, of sound, of shape, smell, touch, taste: moreover, vivid conviction of the truth of more abstract things.[14]

— Hardly a programme which Keats would have disagreed with. To that characteristic product of intellectual imagination, of the felicitous marriage of thing and notion, Hughes gives the name *eidolon* or, in his letter, 'Idea-image'. Idea-images, as might be expected, vary in constitution from those in which the imagistic element is dominant — where what is presented is a definite sensory image — through weaker gradations of image to those in which the ideational element is dominant — where what is purveyed is an abstraction. The idea-image with the fullest capacity for life is one that simultaneously excites sensual and intellectual responses in a reader.

Someone familiar with Ezra Pound's definition of the image may well feel that Hughes's 'idea-image' is a more elaborate name for the same thing. Pound speaks of the image as "that which presents an emotional and intellectual complex in an instant of time."[15] But while Pound's image is as complete an expression of mind as Hughes's idea-image, there is I think a difference between the two — and it is adumbrated in that temporal clause: Pound's "complex" must be presented "in an instant of time". Immediacy of impact is essential to his conception, and the Imagists took it as an article of faith that the image itself must flare up and be brief. Not so Richard Hughes.

When Hughes stopped writing poems in his mid-twenties he did not stop writing poetry. Indeed, I would want to stay that he only matured poetically after he'd ceased to write poems. The crucial truth here is that he wrote prose as poets write verse. In perceiving no disjunction between the genesis of poetry and the genesis of prose, he disagreed fundamentally with Robert Graves. Graves regarded novel-writing as a separate discipline from poetry-writing, and an inferior one — as a poet he served the White Goddess, but as a novelist Mammon. He might regard his own *I, Claudius* as a potboiler, but Hughes did not. *He* believed that prose could be fed from the same unconscious streams as poetry, and saw no reason why the verbal resources of the poet shouldn't be drawn on by the prose-writer. In his humbler way, he suggested in a favourite simile, the novelist lays his novel as a hen lays an egg — answering the same irresistible call as the poet. Elsewhere, he said:

> It's rather like the difference between electric light and a flash of lightning. The lyric poem comes like the flash of lightning, the novel comes much more like steady, low-candle-power electric light, but they are both electricity.[16]

Among the means at his disposal was the extended eidolon; and Hughes developed it into one of the most powerful weapons in his fiction-making armoury.

His later poems have already begun to nurture it. In retrospect we can see that the hare in 'Ecstatic Ode' is a case in point: Vision is incarnated in a living animal: the eidolon is both sensory and intellectual. 'Lover Finds

Something Out' provides an example of an idea-image which works imperfectly because Hughes has tried to set it out in too schematic a context. But its prose version in *The Fox in the Attic* is entirely satisfactory, and memorable. When in 'When Shall I See Gold?' Hughes does not force the imagery blatantly to declare its idea, but allows the idea slowly to rise up to the surface of the verse, the poem works very well.

To see how Hughes makes a poetic eidolon available for prose, we can look first at 'On Time':[17]

> Unhurried as a snake I saw Time glide
> Out of the shape of his material frame:
> I, who am part of Time's material name,
> Saw that unhurried serpent quietly slide
> Through a strait crack in his material side
> Between a prince and a stone: flicker, and presently coil,
> A small bright worm about a stalk of fennel;
> While light stood still as spar, and smell
> Spread like a fan, sound hung festooned, and toil
> Rose balanced and patterned like a storeyed palace
> Whose wild tons grapple in immovable grace;
> While laughter sat on a rustic seat with tears
> And watched the corn-sheaves lean across the plough:
> Ah! then what wind across the nodding years!
> What ecstasies upon the bough
> Sang, like a fountain to its peers:
> And in the meadows what deep-rooted men
> Flowered their lovely faces in the grass,
> Where death, like a butterfly of dark-coloured glass
> Flitted and sipped, and sipped again!

This is another poem about vision — an attempt, I would guess, to bridge the space between 'Meditative Ode' and 'Ecstatic Ode'. The idea behind the poem might prosaically be expressed as 'The timelessness of the visionary state'. The poem seeks throughout to clothe abstractions in physical garments — so that Time is a serpent and death a butterfly. The poem's opening is complex, with the main complication arising from the ambiguity in the first line, whose syntax allows us to attach the phrase "Unhurried as a snake" to both "Time" and "I". If we think of vision here as inward, as taking the form of imaginative trance, then the poet himself provides both its material framework and its inner constituents. His body is the Time-frame out of a crack in whose side the serpent slides. The whole metaphor implies a curious revision of *Genesis*, with the serpent emerging from the gap in Adam's side from where God took the rib to create Eve. The timeless moment is presented in a series of sensory expansions — of "light", "smell", "sound", "toil". Lines 2-16 are the weakest part of the poem: the personification of "laughter" suggests a momentary slackening of imagination, a falling-back upon Keats, and the fountain singing "to its peers" involves an unconvincing rhyme. The poem ends strongly, however: death as a butterfly sipping at the faces of the human flowers is a remarkable conception. Hughes's "fearful hare/With fur of bright glass" and his "butterfly of dark-coloured glass" are recognizably denizens of the same image-world: his lucent imagination invests them both with a certain crystalline quality. Both are beautiful, both might be feared, but one is "bright" and one "dark" — one incarnates energy and one feeds upon it. Characteristically, Hughes ends 'On Time' with death — but not, I think, wilfully. According to Milton, it was "Man's first disobedience", at the serpent's behest, which brought time and death into the world. For Hughes, however, the visionary moment transcends despair, and any 'disagreeables' dissolve to leave only a faint aftertang of disturbance in the air.

Writing *A Comedy of Good and Evil* in 1923-4, Hughes drew upon his Time poem for Mr. Williams's vision of death.

> I saw Death in a garden, like a butterfly of dark-coloured glass. She sips at our hearts, drawing from us with her curving lip the strong honey of mortal life, quickening in us the seeds of life immortal. Ah! . . . Now she alights so gently upon a frail child as scarcely to bend its head with her weight, now with her feathered thighs brushes the yellow dust of fear from the flaming petals of the tiger: blowing apparently aimlessly upon the wind, yet there is no flower that she fails to visit.[18]

This prose eidolon takes off where the verse one ends. 'On Time' has no religious or theological content, but passing the sipping butterfly through the sensibility of the Rector of Cylfant provoked Hughes into extending the idea-image in a quite new way. The butterfly is now seen to give as it takes, making possible life eternal even as it sucks up life temporal. The prose eidolon is in no way inferior in intensity or eloquence to 'On Time'; and, writing prose — or prose-poetry — Hughes is able completely to assimilate the influence of Keats. The foreshortening of tiger-lily into "tiger" is particularly felicitous: it leaves the sentence posed suggestively between plant and animal. To Mr. Williams, Death is not a sternly masculine power, a pale rider upon a horse, but a feminine presence:

> Ah! Mother Death! Mother Death! And out of the dark blossom of Golgotha I see one bright stamen rising. Ah! since Death folded her wings and crept to the heart of that flower, the seed of life has clung ever about her sides.[19]

Hughes has now re-imagined the "blossoms" which in his poem were the faces of men. Now there is *one* flower, Christ: Hughes audaciously imagines the butterfly death entering the body of crucified Christ and picking up inadvertently the pollen which, carried abroad, will grant men immortal life.

In his Preface, it seems, Hughes requires three things of the good poem. These are: that the idea-images be vivid and quickening; that they be organized into an orderly and satisfying structural whole by a governing "rhythmic conception"; and that "the conception in all these dimensions be influenced by their own interplay". The eidolon of the butterfly death is an isolated instance in the *Comedy*, and, though I wouldn't want to lose it from the play, it doesn't strike me as being indispensable to it. There are in *A Moment of Time*, however, one or two pieces which might be interpreted as attempts on Hughes's part to write prose as he believes poetry should be written. It isn't difficult to apply Hughes's three requirements to 'Jungle',[20] which is perhaps best characterized as a prose-poem. I have already spoken of the 'rhythm' of this 'story', a rhythm that initially derives from one of its constituent elements — Jasan, the slave — communicates its imperatives to another — Syrono — and finally provokes a violent response from a third — Mellicles. The triangular relationship established between the three figures at the moment of climax has about it the diagrammatic motion-in-stillness, or tension, of a painting poised between representation and abstraction. It might well be described as an attempt to apply the conception of 'Significant Form' to the prose-poem. The dead mole in 'The Cart' and the three fairies in 'Llwyd' are other examples of eidola: important in context, if less than the whole story in which they feature. Far from being mere bits of decoration, they exist at the psychological and imaginative centres of these tales.

In the wake of these experiments, we may well imagine that the question Hughes asked himself was: Might a *novel* be constructed in accordance with the requirements which he had proposed for the good poem? Reviewing *Mrs. Dalloway*[21] in 1925, he opened with a favourite quotation from Gautier: "To the poet the visible world exists: it shines with an intense brilliance, not only to the eye but to the touch, ear, smell, inward vision." Clearly, he was describing the kind of poet he was himself. The creation that, for him, made Virginia Woolf a poet of the novel, is her London. "It emerges, shining like crystal, out of the fog in which all the merely material universe is ordinarily enveloped in his mind: it emerges, and stays." *Mrs. Dalloway* may be taken as a gloss on Hughes's declaration of faith in his letter: "Art is not imitative: it is creative: creative of beauty." A brief excursion into philosophy will give depth to the point. The Scottish philosopher David Hume divides human perceptions into two distinct kinds. To "sensations, passions, emotions" he gives the name 'impressions'. To "the faint images of these in thinking and reasoning" he gives the name 'ideas'. Ideas themselves are of two kinds: of imagination, or memory. Between these again he asserts a difference to lie, ideas of memory possessing a greater degree of vivacity than ideas of imagination.[22] When Hume comes to consider how imagination is employed in poetry, he continues to maintain that poetic ideas ("poetical fictions") differ from ideas belonging to memory or judgment in the comparative weakness or imperfectness of the feelings they engender.[23] For him, "Imagination, then, consists in *having* (seeing, hearing, tasting, etc.) weak experiences."[24] Richard Hughes inverts Hume's teaching: for him an artist cannot be truly creative unless he or she has the ability to invest objects with a vividness, a paradoxical reality, that they lack in objective perception or in memory. The images created by the poet may be more intense than those we receive from the outside world.

Thus Hughes can say apropos of *Mrs. Dalloway*: "To Mrs. Woolf London exists, and to Mrs. Woolf's readers anywhere and at any time London will exist with a reality it can never have for those who merely live there." As he had argued several years before, however, vividness in itself is not enough: it is the material of art, not art itself. Virginia Woolf creates, "behind the eye of the reader", a mental *pattern* "composed directly of mental processes, ideas, sensory evocation": so that it is "not by its vividness that her writing ultimately stays in the mind, but by the coherent and processional form which is composed of, and transcends, that vividness". *Mrs. Dalloway*, then, is a novel which fulfils Hughes's prescription for a good poem. Whether the publication of Virginia Woolf's novel fuelled his own ambition to write a poetic novel I do not know. In the event, though *A High Wind in Jamaica* makes splendid use of the resources of the poet, and contains some memorable idea-images, it is not, I think, informed by a dominant eidolon which can dictate a rhythm to the whole story. *In Hazard*, however, *does* possess such a dominant eidolon: and as a result possesses a more satisfying shape, and approaches more nearly his theoretical ideal, than any of his other novels.

III

A number of the reviewers of Hughes's pre-war novels spoke of the callousness or inhumanity of his imagination. Hugh Walpole described *A High Wind* as a "sinister work and often cruel"; *Time and Tide's* reviewer found it a "cruel and disillusioned book". Coming to specifics, J.E.S. Arrowsmith asked:

why, for instance, does [Hughes] step beyond the bounds of all that is credible, decent, thinkable, and have his perfectly human pirates commit the villainy of first betraying poor Margaret and then throwing her over-board? (That she is picked up by a boat is incidental.) This event in the story is a shock that turns the blood to ice.[25]

When *In Hazard* appeared, Edwin Muir commented that "Mr. Hughes's imagination has a touch of inhumanity". V.S. Pritchett criticized him on the grounds "that in writing with childlike simplicity he takes on the simple cruelty of the child's-eye view." L.P. Hartley connected the two novels by finding "the same callousness" that characterized the first in the second also: "much modified, it is true, but unmistakeable [sic]". Now whilst a novel-reader accustomed to the strong meat of the 1960s, 1970s and 1980s may wonder what all this fuss was about, may indeed dismiss such comments out of hand as having to do more with moral taste than literary criticism, it is worth considering the point of view of those readers of 1929 and 1938 for whom the critics I have quoted voiced genuine misgivings about Hughes's books; worth it because Hughes himself was well aware of the risk he took of offending readers in writing as he did. In *A High Wind* the problematical quality may be said to reveal itself in the nonchalance with which the Miss Parkers, Sam the negro, the boy John (not to mention a host of creatures not *homo sapiens*) are consigned to perdition. In *In Hazard* one thinks of the injury to the Chinese bosun at the height of the storm, of the fate of the birds during and after the lull, and above all the drowning of Mr. MacDonald.

Writing to Mrs. Williams-Ellis in 1921, Hughes recognized that "a rather interesting philosophical question" arose out of his belief that the artist must pursue the beautiful:

> Roughly, it is this: if beauty is an absolute end in itself, as I believe, then one must distinguish two meanings of this word 'ought'. There is the ordinary moral 'ought' and the aesthetic 'ought': you can say that an artist 'ought' to have used more red, less green, where there is plainly no moral significance. Now: if there are two 'oughts' why should they not clash: why 'ought' not the artist to be feeding his wife, and so [on]? And if two 'oughts' can clash — for there can be no ballancing [sic] of pros and cons when there is a definite difference in kind: you can't value acts of parliament in relation to glue — if they clash, where is Kant's Categorical Imperative? Nursing its shins somewhere in the Ewigkeit, I am afraid: there is no absolute standard of right and wrong, and Morality has to pass down the car.

A couple of paragraphs later, Hughes relents a little:

> my own creed is to follow beauty as my real aim, and to be moral not as

an end in itself, but (a) because, all things considered, it is one's natural inclination, (b) because it is the line of least resistance, and (c) because it is impossible to be immoral without hurting other people, which is very rarely justifiable, and then only for the sake of some very great beauty . . .

Such beauties for Hughes the novelist, of course, mean death for his characters — those tissues of language who seem to us to be no less real, and sometimes more real, than real people. The aesthetic ought is a demanding master-mistress, and is to be appeased at times by not less than everything.

Here is the end of Mr. MacDonald in *In Hazard*:

Now that he had firmly resolved to leave the sea, that little hard, feverish knot in his mind, whose continual spinning had kept him for five days and nights from even a wink of sleep, seemed to dissolve. There was a pool of sleep in his mind, in which it melted fast. Suddenly — with no warning at all — deep sleep overcame him: and he fell off the rail backwards into the sea.

The shock of the water, of course, woke him, and he swam for quite a time. (p.248)

Of this, L.P. Hartley wrote in his review:

Without, apparently, a quiver of regret, Mr. Hughes gives over the chief engineer, Mr. MacDonald, to a watery death without justification or purpose in the story, except to demonstrate that Fate is no respecter of persons.[26]

Hartley we may take as a disciple of the moral ought. "Justification" for him is related — or fails to be related — to ethical imperatives: the novelist, looking down at his creations from an Olympian height, ought to be a just divinity. Hartley, it would seem, is incapable of experiencing the aesthetic emotion which spontaneously arises from the ironic perception that simple physical weariness has precipitated what a storm beyond all previous recorded human experience has, over a period of four interminable days, signally failed to precipitate: the death of a single crew-member of *Archimedes*. To round upon such an emotion as 'callous' or 'inhuman' is to fail to see that art sanctions a range of experiences which in life would be open to moral question.

In his letter Hughes consigns, with a mildly rueful jauntiness, Kant's Categorical Imperative to Eternity. Had he read Kant's *Critique of Judgment*, however (and perhaps he had, for some of Kant's ideas chime exactly with his — as, for example, the notion that we find Nature beautiful because it looks like Art), had he read this *Critique* he would have found in it the following statement regarding "the intellectual interest in the Beautiful":

it would seem that the feeling for the Beautiful is not only (as actually is the case) specifically different from the Moral feeling; but that the interest which can be bound up with it is hardly compatible with moral interest, and certainly has no inner affinity therewith.[27]

Such a passage suggests that Kant would more rigorously separate Art and Life than would Hughes himself.

Another defence against the charge of cruelty of imagination may be sought elsewhere. The poet and critic Vernon Scannell finds in Keith Douglas's war book *Alamein to Zem Zem*

something, too, of the ruthlessness, the apparent heartlessness that many, if not all, artists to some extent possess, a quality which is in fact less ruthlessness than detachment, a suspension of involvement which is necessary if an event is to be observed clearly and objectively, an experience absorbed and transmuted into art.[28]

A High Wind in Jamaica and *In Hazard* provide abundant evidence to suggest that Richard Hughes possesses this heartlessness which is artistic detachment. It is the creative mind's defence against the bogus consolations of sentimentality. But it would be absurd to suggest that Hughes's imagination in its 'cruelty' even begins to approach Shakespeare's — to go no further. For Hughes's reviewers appear to have nothing against the blinding of Gloucester or the madness of Ophelia. When that has been said, however, it must also be said, and emphatically, that Hughes is not a novelist whose imagination is quickened only by death — for he brings precisely the same art, the same unquenchable vitality, to his presentation of life.

IV

It is a truism to say that no two people read the same poem or novel or, despite being present at the same performance, see the same play. As we bring different sensibilities to bear upon a particular object, so it excites in us different responses. The mind of a great writer — Shakespeare, let us again say — is so large that his creativity is liable to overflow the banks of the stream it has, on any given occasion, chosen to fill. It is possible to define Shakespeare's greatness in a variety of ways, says Hughes in his letter:

he is great as a dramatist, a realist, an idealist, a philosopher, a psychologist, a teller of tales, and a mine of general knowledge. Whatever your particular criterion of judgment, you will put him in the first class. So, to think Shakespeare a great poet does not mean that you mean the same thing as I do, or that either of us mean[s] the same thing as Middleton Murry, or Ben Jonson.

Such a genius will always show above "the fluctuating waves of critical theory" because he is 'hydra-headed'. Later, Hughes adopted the term 'club-sandwich' for a work of art capable of appealing to people on a multitude of levels.[29] Imagine a contemporary audience watching a performance of *Hamlet* at the Globe: a groundling sees a ghost story, a courtier a revenge tragedy, a doctor a play about madness, a young woman a tragedy of love, a statesman a political play, a poet gluts himself on a feast of images — and so on, each taking from the play in accordance with his or her sensibility. This is a simplification, no doubt, but the point remains that Shakespeare was able to satisfy an audience composed of people from every level of Elizabethan society: there is something in *Hamlet* for everybody.

Now it seems to me that in his novels Hughes was attempting to write for a variety of tastes, to bridge the gap between the popular novel and the literary novel. To choose only three of the qualities common to *A High Wind in Jamaica* and *In Hazard*: they are yarns, adventure stories; they are novels of ideas; they are the fictions of a poet, and crammed with sensuous images: to Hughes the visible world exists. Despite the fact that certain surveyors of the field of twentieth century literature have valued them highly (e.g. Walter Allen, Martin Seymour Smith[30]), they have in my opinion received less critical attention than they merit. In accounting for this fact, I am inclined to feel that their status as yarns has tended to obscure their interest as novels of ideas: so that they have paid a price for their very readability and breadth of appeal. Hughes's 'strength' has too readily been identified as — and limited to — his story-telling ability, and it is a part of my purpose in the following chapters to correct that misconception.

If little critical attention has been paid to *A High Wind in Jamaica* and *In Hazard*, much has been paid to two books which, at a quick glance, look very like them — *Lord of the Flies* and *Typhoon*. The inference may then be drawn that, *of their kind*, these books are superior to Hughes's. Now it is not a part of my programme to enter into evaluative comparisons, so that what emerge are 'winners' and 'losers'. It seems to me — and it seemed to Hughes — that comparisons between his novels and Golding's and Conrad's can only help, in pointing out their notable differences, to define their individual character. Hughes himself, for example, was always puzzled when people saw resemblances between *A High Wind* and *Lord of the Flies*: Golding, he felt, had been concerned with what children and adults had in common, while he had been concerned with the differences between them: "Golding's children were the instruments of an allegory about the whole human race and its history."[31]

I have suggested that Hughes's gathering up of his plays, poems and stories in three definitive editions between 1924 and 1926 cleared the decks for the writing of *A High Wind in Jamaica*. I have little doubt that it also made him think critically about his achievement so far, about the strengths and weaknesses of his previous writings. If I were asked to choose one notable quality from each book, I would opt for the following: from the plays, a sinewy freshness of idea; from the poems, a sensuous vividness of imagery; from the stories, a drily ironic quality of artistic detachment. The task now before Hughes was to combine and body forth these strengths in a single sustained work.

Chapter Seven: *A High Wind in Jamaica*

I

The shimmering surface of Hughes's first novel brilliantly testifies to his giftedness as storyteller and poet. Looking down through this translucency, however, one perceives a boulder-strewn bottom — a conglomeration of formidable questions. Some of these we recall from his earlier work; others define themselves for the first time.

In *The Sisters' Tragedy* and *A Comedy of Good and Evil*, Hughes demonstrated the inabsoluteness of good and evil, showing that one person's good is another's evil, and that to do good to another may be to do evil to oneself. These recognitions now animate the world of *A High Wind in Jamaica*, and provoke the questions: Is moral behaviour conventional merely, are moral codes purely relative? And, in a world which appears increasingly necessitarian and deterministic: Are the much-vaunted human freedoms of action and choice any more than chimerical?

Against the complex but compromised moral sensibilities of young adults, Hughes in his *Tragedy* set the immature but imaginative sensibility of a pubescent girl. Now, instead of one child, he takes seven, giving himself the opportunity to study children's minds at a number of points in their development. Thus he can ask: When does a person became a person? In what circumstances and with what implications does self-consciousness emerge in the individual? What are the imperatives of identity?

Hughes's early writings reveal an imagination fascinated by violence — violence in both the human and the natural realms. The action of *A High Wind* turns on both kinds of violence — on, most importantly, a murder and a hurricane — and provides a question which I will frame like this: Is human justice — the product of reason institutionally embodied — superior to natural justice — the product of undirected elemental forces?

In Chapter 19 of *The Fox in the Attic*, Augustine Penry-Herbert and Jeremy Dibden find Mary Wadamy reading Lytton Strachey's *Eminent*

Victorians. This prompts Jeremy to remark that the only really eminent Victorians were Marx, Freud and Einstein (that none of them were *English* doesn't trouble him in the least!), with Freud the greatest of the three. Augustine agrees, declaring Marx to be the least of them and "the one most eminently Victorian", since Victorian science was "dogmatic" in its character: "its aim, systems of valid answers". Einstein, he feels, has "lifted modern science onto the altogether higher level of systems of valid questions". Augustine overlooks the fact that Einstein, unlike himself, believes in God. Despite this, however, Augustine's distinction touches on Hughes's own conviction — borne out fully in his practice as a novelist — that creative writers should ask questions, not seek answers to them. The Einsteinian principle of relativity may be admitted to be at work in Hughes's fiction if one transfers its application from the realm of physics to that of ethics — from cosmic to human bodies. But when this has been said, it remains, I think, true that of the two eminent Victorians whose influence is most palpable in *A High Wind in Jamaica,* only one appears in Jeremy's triad. That one is Sigmund Freud. The other is Charles Darwin.

II

To begin *A High Wind in Jamaica* is to encounter both a story and a storyteller. No doubt, like the dancer and the dance, they are difficult to separate, but the narrator's presence and style (his presence *is* his style) so direct and shape the reader's response to his narrative as to make time spent reflecting upon him time well spent. If first of all we ask what the narrator's *interest* in the story is, it is not easy to say. It is not the interest of someone who has a stake in events: Hughes's narrator is certainly not at the centre of the narrative, as is Pip in *Great Expectations* or Jane in *Jane Eyre;* he lacks even the peripheral involvement of a Lockwood — who, in *Wuthering Heights,* fancies himself a little in love with Catherine Linton. On the other hand, *High Wind*'s narrator is not Richard Hughes *in propria persona:* for Hughes is not present in his own novel as Thackeray is in *Vanity Fair* or George Eliot in *Middlemarch.* To distinguish between these last-named cases will help us, however. George Eliot's 'I' is omniscient: she is a moral guide through the judgmental minefield that is the novel, and it is crucial that a reader trust her. Thackeray's first person is a more problematical entity: self-conscious and slippery, and liable to shifts of attitude and allegiance. Importantly, it is not omniscient: one thinks of its ignorance of the depth of Becky's involvement with Lord Steyne. Becky remains, at a climactic moment, elusive, opaque. Hughes's narrator will, in a similar ploy, declare himself at a late point in the proceedings unable to "read Emily's deeper thoughts, or handle their cords" (p.276). He is not omniscient.

Hughes has put himself to the trouble of adopting a mask, or persona. His narrator's revelation (p. 4) that it is "a long time ago now" since he visited the island — 1860, to be precise (so that, for example, he is ignorant of modern methods of distilling rum) — suggests that we should imagine a Victorian gentleman in late middle or old age. Doubtless this persona is strategic, since Hughes himself had no first-hand knowledge of Jamaica when he wrote the book. To say so much, however, is only to scratch the surface of this narrator. Let us listen to his voice:

> The two old Miss Parkers lived in bed, for the negroes had taken away all their clothes: they were nearly starved. Drinking water was brought, in two cracked Worcester cups and three coconut shells on a silver salver. Presently one of the heiresses persuaded her tyrants to lend her an old print dress, and came and pottered about in the mess half-heartedly: tried to wipe the old blood and feathers of slaughtered chickens from a gilt and marble table: tried to talk sensibly: tried to wind an ormolu clock: and then gave it up and mooned away back to bed. Not long after this, I believe, they were both starved altogether to death. Or, if that were hardly possible in so prolific a country, perhaps given ground glass — rumour varied. At any rate, they died.
>
> That is the sort of scene which makes a deep impression on the mind; far deeper than the ordinary, less romantic, everyday thing which shows the real state of an island in the statistical sense. Of course, even in the transition period one only found melodrama like this in rare patches. (pp. 2-3)

This incident is one recalled by the narrator from personal experience. Yet while it appears to have stirred his imagination, it seems not in the least to have aroused his sympathy (or if it did, he does not trouble himself to recreate it). His presence at the Miss Parkers' is scarcely a bodily presence: unacknowledged by the old ladies, he is not *involved* in the least in what he describes: like an invisible eye he sees and reports, reducing what he has seen to a series of events connected by colons and forwarded by ineffectual verbs: "tried . . . tried . . . then gave it up and mooned away . . .". His dead-pan style has its peculiarities, however, which are held off from whimsicality only by their grotesqueness. Consider the odd emphasis that "altogether" gives to "starved altogether to death"! The possibility that the Miss Parkers might have been given "ground glass" signally fails to disturb his equanimity. Murder is par for the Jamaican course, an event to be taken in one's stride. If this "sort of scene" — "romantic" (!) and melodramatic — "makes a deep impression on the mind" (not *my* mind but *the* mind —

holding the experience at an impersonal distance), it seems, in the case of the narrator, that it has provoked no response that might be said to be grounded in moral consciousness. Our Victorian narrator is an unsentimental man of the world who remains unsurprised by the fantastic, unperturbed by the grotesque, and unmoved by the pathetic.

In his *Anatomy of Criticism*, Northrop Frye remarks, apropos of the ironic fiction-writer:

> Complete objectivity and suppression of all explicit moral judgements are essential to his method. Thus pity and fear are not raised in ironic art, they are reflected to the reader from the art.[1]

This nicely encapsulates Hughes's method in the novel — as well as indicating a third line of defence (if one is needed) against the charge that Hughes's imagination is inhuman needlessly.[2]

If we search nineteenth-century British fiction for an ironic narrator like Hughes's, we will not, I think, find one. But consider:

> As it was growing dark we passed under one of the massive, bare, and steep hills of granite which are so common in this country. This spot is notorious from having been, for a long time, the residence of some runaway slaves, who, by cultivating a little ground near the top, contrived to eke out a subsistence. At length they were discovered, and a party of soldiers being sent, the whole were seized with the exception of one old woman, who, sooner than again be led into slavery, dashed herself to pieces from the summit of the mountain. In a Roman matron this would have been called the noble love of freedom: in a poor negress it is mere brutal obstinacy.

Reading this closing sentence, I find it impossible to decide on the speaker's attitude to the negress. Is his irony directed at those humans who enslave others — or at the negress herself? The ambiguity must exist because of the omission of "called" from the last-quoted clause: had the writer written "it is *called* mere brutal obstinacy", it would be impossible to find him in collusion with the general opinion of the negress's behaviour. Again, consider:

> My companion, the day before, had shot two large bearded monkeys. These animals have prehensile tails, the extremity of which, even after death, can support the whole weight of the body. One of them thus remained fast to a branch, and it was necessary to cut down a large tree to procure it. This was soon effected, and down came tree and monkey with an awful crash. Our day's sport, besides the monkey, was confined to sundry small green parrots and a few toucans.

The liveliness of this description is not in the least infected by any sentiment regarding the victims of the day's sport. How can one possibly feel sympathy for "*sundry* small green parrots"? The monkey which comes down to earth "with an awful crash" can hardly fail to call to mind Hughes's Jacko, who "fell plump on the deck and broke his neck". What stimulates the writer's curiosity is the fact that after death the monkey's tail stays determinedly wrapped around its branch!

Since the author of these passages is Darwin,[3] we should hardly be surprised that his interest is the interest of a naturalist. Now it seems to me that the curiosity of Hughes's narrator is of the same order: he writes like a Darwinian naturalist, with precisely the same interest in the idiosyncratic, with a comparable objectivity and a comparable absence of moral concern. And indeed, such a narrator is exactly right for a novel which asks to be read as an ironic post-Darwinian fable.

In *The Origin of Species*, Darwin proposes that evolution proceeds by means of the competition of species. Those species which develop characteristics that give them an advantage over the species with which they are in competition will be *naturally selected*. The less fit species will dwindle until they become extinct. For our own purpose it is crucial to note that competition is a principle that governs not only the lives of competing species — existing, that is, "between organism and organism" — but applies to the life of a single species — existing, that is, "between child and parent". In a chapter entitled 'Extinction', Darwin writes:

> The competition will generally be most severe . . . between the forms which are most like each other in all respects. Hence the improved and modified descendants of a species will generally cause the extermination of the parent-species; and if many new forms have been developed from any one species, the nearest allies of that species, *i.e.* the species of the same genus, will be the most liable to extermination. Thus, as I believe, a number of new species descended from one species, that is a new genus, comes to supplant an old genus, belonging to the same family.[4]

What struck Hughes when he began to read up on latterday pirates was their surprising softness, their lack of savagery, their unwillingness to indulge in acts of violence. They seemed, indeed, the lingering survivors of a dwindling species. Still, Darwin himself makes provision for the survival of anachronisms:

> But whether it be species belonging to the same or to a distinct class, which have yielded their places to other modified and improved species, a few of the sufferers may often be preserved for a long time,

from being fitted to some other peculiar line of life, or from inhabiting some distant and isolated station, where they will have escaped severe competition.

"Some distant and isolated station . . .": precisely. If Hughes's pirates are, in Darwin's words, "the parent-species", then their "improved and modified descendants" are, of course, the children. Children and pirates are, in one passage in which Hughes has his cake and eats it, both "different" and "the same":

> — How small the children all looked, on a ship, when you saw them beside the sailors! It was as if they were a different order of beings! Yet they were living creatures just the same, full of promise. (p. 65)

Darwin, it's worth noting, refers to his anachronisms as "sufferers". It is hardly possible for a reader not to feel that Hughes's pirates suffer from their freight of children: and there is a general awkwardness about their behaviour at times which suggests their own half-consciousness of their ill-adjustment to their century. Do the children then 'put them out of their misery', in a manner of speaking?

Hughes makes it possible for a reader to take in — consciously or unconsciously — his strategy by a number of means, two of which I will comment on. First, he seizes every opportunity to undermine the distinction between humans and animals. I do not mean that he takes advantage of the simple truth that human beings are 'higher animals'. It is here that the poet in him combines with the naturalist. His humans are animal-like, his animals human-like. On the one hand there are, for example, Mr. Bas-Thornton, who is "quite as temperamental as a mule" (p. 3), and the blacks who, in the bouncing rain of the hurricane, "wallowed like porpoises" (p. 37). On the other there is, for example, the big white pig: "he was not entirely inhuman, that pig" (p.115). When the ship's monkey snatches a banana from between his very trotters:

> You would never have thought that the immobile mask of a pig could wear a look of such astonishment, such dismay, such piteous injury.

And when, "taking an airing on deck", he is carried overboard in a sudden squall, he vanishes to windward, "his snout (sometimes) sticking up manfully out of the water" (pp.116-17). God, alas, has "required his soul of him".

A considerable part of Hughes's Darwinian stategy is invested in ironic comparisons between humans and apes. In the case of the pirates, we get overt similes: Captain Jonsen, we are told, "carried the backs of his hands forward like an orang-outang" (p. 72), and his general shambling clumsiness suggests a creature at a modest point on the evolutionary ladder; José, the little sailor who befriends the children, is referred to on several occasions as "monkeyfied". The children are compared to a small zoo of creatures — turtles, tadpoles and frogs, pigs, an octopus, a mole, polecats, dogs and cats — as well as "pink predatory monkeys" (p. 7). But the novel's prize exhibit here is both elaborate and subtle. On the *Clorinda*, young John comes upon the sailors doping the ship's monkey with rum in an attempt to anaesthetize him before they chop off his gangrenous tail. Each time the monkey escapes, they catch him: "As for John, he could no more have left the scene now than Jacko the monkey could." (p. 68) John and Jacko: the one is a diminutive of the other. But, just as the operation is about to begin, Jacko escapes again, "drunk as a lord, and sick as a cat" (!) into the rigging. Hughes now contrives, with insidious wit, to play metaphor against reality:

> . . .the children, now, stood open-mouthed and open-eyed on the deck beneath in the sun till their necks nearly broke. . .
> (p. 69)   Poor little Jacko missed his hold at last: fell plump on the deck and broke his neck. That was the end of him — (p.70)

"Poor" here is conventional merely: the singsong nursery-rhyme of the pay-off and the laconic (or is it amused?) brutality of "That was the end of him" ensure that not the slightest trace of sympathy exists in the text for the dead animal. A reader may either go with the narrator's humorous response; or, rebounding off his callousness, be prompted to feel what the narrator cannot. Later, however, for John, the metaphor will jerk into stark reality. Leaning too far out of the doorway of the warehouse at Santa Lucia, he loses his balance and falls "clear to the ground, forty feet, right on his head" (p.110). The crowd below does nothing until José has descended, when:

> they stood back and let him have a good look at it, and shake it, and so on. But the neck was quite plainly broken.

How quickly the boy has become a lifeless *thing*, an "it". The narrator takes the happening in his stride, expending no more sympathy on John than he did on Jacko. Death to him is a fact of life, and, whether or not it occurs in absurd circumstances, an inevitable one. We may recall Mr. Bax's assertion in *Danger* that the young, in death, lose comparatively little — since it is the past, not the future, which one loses in death: a "mere rosy dream", a "trumpery shadow".[5] The narrator's dispassionate treatment of John implies that a human life is no more or less significant than a monkey's.

If both children and pirates at times put Hughes's Darwinian narrator in mind of monkeys, they share a more obvious quality: predatoriness. Piracy is a predatory trade, and we see Captain Jonsen and his crew practising it. The question Hughes poses is: Do the pirates possess the ruthlessness which in nature predators need to survive? It is not, perhaps, so easy to see children as predators, but Hughes sets out to seed the idea in the reader's mind from the very start. In the trees which surround John and Emily's bathing-pool, they set tree-springes:

> Lame-foot Sam taught them how. Cut a bendy stick, and tie a string to one end. Then sharpen the other, so that it can impale a fruit as bait. Just at the base of this point flatten it a little, and bore a hole through the flat part. Cut a little peg that will just stick in the mouth of this hole. Then make a loop in the end of the string: bend the stick, as in stringing a bow, till the loop will thread through the little hole, and jam it with the peg, along which the loop should lie spread. Bait the point, and hang it in a tree among the twigs: the bird alights on the peg to peck the fruit, the peg falls out, the loop whips tight round its ankles: then away up out of the water like pink predatory monkeys, and decide by 'Eena, deena, dina, do,' or some such rigmarole, whether to twist its neck or let it go free — thus the excitement and suspense, both for child and bird, can be prolonged beyond the moment of capture. (p. 7)

The passage is a splendid example of how Hughes persuades a reader to adopt the child's-eye view (if you have forgotten what it was like to be a child, you rediscover it, willy-nilly, in this novel). Here the notion that human beings are ape-like and the notion that they are predators come together in the phrase "pink predatory monkeys": over the captured bird John and Emily exercise the power of life and death, but whether the bird lives or dies is in the lap of the random gods of rigmarole. So it will be at the end of the novel: upon Emily's testimony depend the lives of the captured pirates. Now it is another rigmarole — "a sort of Shorter Catechism" (p.277) — which is to decide whether these birds are to hang — to have their necks twisted — or go free. Birds and pirates form the first and last terms in Hughes's ironic sequence. The children's attitude to their victims at the pool is perfectly amoral, but in the case of John an equal amorality will be turned upon a child: the narrator entertains just as much sympathy for dead John as John and Emily for the birds they strangle — or, for that matter, as the court entertains for the condemned pirates. At the last, it is not the cruelty and insensitivity of the narrator that is "reflected to the reader from the art", but the cruelty and insensitivity of human justice.

Before we leave monkeys altogether (and they seem to have carried us a considerable distance), one further passage demands quotation. Otto, the mate, is at the wheel of the schooner when his eye is caught by the ship's monkey:

That animal, with the same ingenious adaptability to circumstance which has produced the human race, had now solved the playmate question. As a gambler will play left hand against right, so he fought back legs against front. His extraordinary lissomness made the dissociation most lifelike: he might not have been joined at the waist at all, for all the junction discommoded him. The battle, if good-tempered on both sides, was quite a serious one: now, while his hind feet were doing their best to pick out his eyes, his sharp little teeth closed viciously on his own private parts.

From below the skylight, too, came tears and cries for help that one might easily have taken for real if they had not been occasionally interrupted by such phrases as 'It's no good: I shall cut off your head just the same!' (pp.192-3)

The first paragraph here is surely a Hughesian eidolon, and could be savoured with or without a context. It shows the Darwinian ironist in perfect symbiosis with the poet. The monkey's "dissociation", I suggest, is by extension that of the human race, whose various limbs are still light years away from mastering the temptation to play vicious games with one another. Hughes is not the first writer to build an idea-image around monkeys: Blake in *The Marriage of Heaven and Hell* employs them to suggest the self-consuming character of analytical rationalism. Blake's purpose is more strictly satiric than Hughes's, however, and his description correspondingly nauseous. Hughes succeeds in suggesting at once the playfulness and viciousness of the apparently schizoid animal. The second paragraph then glances at the ambiguous nature of play in the human realm: that the real-sounding "tears and cries" of children are pretend ones is borne out by the exaggerated nature of the words which punctuate them. Them children, it seems, are playing pirates again: the piratical children deal mercilessly with their captives. Again we are thrown ironically forward to the novel's closing pages.

III

Hughes always professed himself astonished by the furore provoked by his depiction of children in *A High Wind*. He had not set out with any intention of changing the way adults perceive children: "I thought it was just what everybody must think about them," he told Alasdair Clayre in 1975.[6] But once he had assumed the voice of a Darwinist ironist, it was inevitable that his novel would deal a severe blow against the tradition which held children to be possessed, at birth, of "original innocence". This tradition, which originated in the writings of Rousseau and was fostered by Wordsworth and memorably enshrined in Blake's *Songs of Innocence* (but not his *Songs of Experience*), was the creation of literary Romanticism. Rousseau had performed a necessary service in insisting that children be seen as children, and not as miniature adults. In equating "original innocence" with childhood virtue, however, and proposing that "all deviations from virtue derive from environment", he fostered a myth which would take some time to lose its appeal. The Victorian period saw this tradition age into senility: in the hands of popular novelists such as Marie Corelli, Mrs Henry Wood and J.M. Barrie, the child-innocent carried a freight of sentimental piety, or transferred neurosis.[7] What these novelists conveniently ignored — if they ever noticed it — was the view of children which Blake expressed in his second set of *Songs*. It took Freud to rediscover — and to propound in crude and schematic terms — what Blake had understood with incomparable subtlety a hundred years earlier: that the child is a sexual being from infancy, a being equipped with an intense capacity to will and to desire, and a being capable of deep secrecy.

By way of presenting a group of portraits of children between the ages of three and thirteen, Hughes builds up a picture of child-development of a range and subtlety such as no previous novelist had attempted. In *The Brothers Karamazov*, Ivan Karamazov declares:

> Children when they are quite little — up to seven, for instance — are so remote from grown-up people: they are different creatures, as it were, of a different species.[8]

Hughes's narrator certainly accepts that babies are a separate species. Children they may be, but *human* they are not:

> they are animals, and have a very ancient and ramified culture, as cats have, and fishes, and even snakes: the same in kind as these, but much more complicated and vivid, since babies are, after all, one of the most developed species of the lower vertebrates. (p. 158)

The authority of this is the authority of the natural scientist. Children's minds "work in terms and categories of their own which cannot be translated into the terms and categories of the human mind". To think, then, as Laura thinks (she is approaching four), is quite impossible. In order to express her otherness, his sense that she inhabits a realm so removed from that inhabited by adults as effectively to exclude them, he develops the most audacious eidolon in the novel:

> When swimming under water, it is a very sobering thing suddenly to look a large octopus in the face. One never forgets it: one's respect, yet

one's feeling of the hopelessness of any real intellectual sympathy. One is soon reduced to mere physical admiration, like any silly painter, of the cow-like tenderness of the eye, of the beautiful and infinitesimal mobility of that large and toothless mouth, which accepts as a matter of course that very water against which you, for your life's sake, must be holding your breath. There he reposes in a fold of rock, apparently weightless in the clear green medium but very large, his long arms, suppler than silk, coiled in repose, or stirring in recognition of your presence. Far above, everything is bounded by the surface of the air, like a bright window of glass. Contact with a small baby can conjure at least an echo of that feeling in those who are not obscured by an uprush of maternity to the brain. (p.159)

Hughes's simile-within-the-metaphor — "the cow-like tenderness of the eye" of his octopus — is worth a moment's pause. It is a detail which agains attests the oneness of observing poet and observing naturalist. Hughes, no doubt, had looked closely at octopi. So had Darwin, who, having written in *The Origin of Species* that "the eye of the cephalopods or cuttle-fish and of vertebrate animals appear wonderfully alike", goes on to say that beyond this "superficial resemblance, there is hardly any real similarity".[9] Hughes also goes into reverse after his dash at the self-deceiving sentimentality that can be expended on small children:

Of course it is not really so cut-and-dried as all this; but often the only way of attempting to express the truth is to build it up, like a card-house, of a pack of lies. (p.160)

Much is made, nowadays, of 'self-conscious' novelists who deliberately break the illusion that their stories treat of life, and remind us that we are reading a work of fiction. Here, I suggest, we glimpse behind the Darwinian ironist a more recessive Hughesian persona: that of the relativist who believes that contraries, viewed askance, melt into one another — good into evil, lies into truth. It is this persona which is aware, ultimately, that 'omniscience' is a confidence-trick: the novelist can only 'know' what he can imagine: and the otherness of Laura, which strains imagination to the utmost, can only be expressed by a brilliant sleight-of-hand.

What we call childhood 'innocence' is a kind of ignorance: it is the condition of Adam and Eve — those primordial children — in Eden before the eating of the apple of knowledge. Laura has barely yet been scratched with the burdensome pin of moral awareness. To make use of a convenient Freudian term, she exists in that animal, pre-social state characterised by the free play of the id — a "primeval conglomeration" or "seething mass of impulses or instinctual desires entirely lacking in any directing or guiding consciousness".[10] Or, as Hughes wittily puts it, "Laura's mind was as humoursome an instrument to play as the Twenty-three-stringed Lute"(p. 162).

The children between the ages of five and nine possess a rudimentary moral awareness. Stamped by the stamp of their parents, they reproduce the conventional attitudes of their class, culture and age in their opinions, judgments and prejudices. Thus, collectively, they are appalled when Jonsen, moved to unusual exasperation by their tobogganings, asks them who they think is going to mend their drawers for them if they develop holes. When he adds: "'And I'll not have you going about my ship without them! See?'" they retreat, outraged and embarrassed, to the bows, "their joy . . . dashed for the day" (p.120). Rachel, the only girl in this age-group, is said to have two over-riding interests — the first domestic, the second moral. Liable to appropriate any moveable article as her property, she will metamorphose it by an act of imagination into a baby or a household item. Her sense of rectitude is as infallible as her property-rights are absolute and unnegotiable:

> She had an extraordinary vivid, *simple* sense, that child, of Right and Wrong — it almost amounted to a precocious ethical genius. Every action, her own or any one else's, was immediately judged good or bad, and uncompromisingly praised or blamed. She was never in doubt. (p.156)

Her world is one of simple categories, by which the individual is tarred with the brush of the genus:

> it was now tacitly admitted that all these men were pirates. That is, they were wicked. It therefore devolved on her to convert them: and she entered on her plans for this without a shadow either of misgiving or reluctance. (p.157)

(Her judgment here, of course, anticipates that of the court which sentences the pirates to death.) She has a conscience, but it is powerless to cause her suffering. It is rudimentary, perhaps, because her egotism is based on a complete sense of security: the world has not yet revealed to her her vulnerability. Conscience, that is, is contingent upon self-consciousness: and *that*, as yet, Rachel has not developed. With Emily it is otherwise.

Emily is the live core of *A High Wind in Jamaica*. Her realization that she is a separate being constitutes the pre-eminent psychological event in the book and is, for that reason, placed at its mathematical centre. It is out of (in both senses of the adjective) her *personal* crisis that Hughes establishes what I have called "the imperatives of identity".

Emily's realization "that she was *she*" (p. 134) is quite gratuitous. It might have happened, says the narrator, five years earlier or five years later. Essentially it takes the form of the mind's recognition of the separateness of the body it inhabits.

> She slipped a shoulder out of the top of her frock; and having peeped in to make sure she really was continuous under her clothes, she shrugged it up to touch her cheek. The contact of her face and the warm bare hollow of her shoulder gave her a comfortable thrill, as if it was the caress of some kind friend. But whether the feeling came to her through her cheek or her shoulder, which was the caresser and which the caressed, that no analysis could tell her. (pp.135-6)

Despite its pleasurableness (it is identity which makes possible narcissism!), Emily's discovery is a kind of Fall, for it involves the gaining of knowledge that cannot be erased. Out of the holistic condition of the child-as-animal, she passes into the dualistic condition of the child-as-person. This is the Blakeian transition from the realm of innocence into the realm of experience.

Having woken up to her separateness, Emily begins to reckon the consequences of her awakening. Reduced to the simplest terms, the imperatives of identity are three: vulnerability, secrecy and survival. Bound up with her new sense of self is a sense of others — that her family, the pirates, "the whole fabric of a daily life" exists beyond herself. Freshly perceived in this way, the world appears "vaguely disquieting":

> Were there disasters running about loose, disasters which her rash marriage to the body of Emily Thornton made her vulnerable to? (p. 138)

The mind's discovery that the body to which it is wedded is vulnerable makes its defence the first priority. That survival is a necessity is an instinctual recognition. But how does a child defend what is so slight and, in a physical sense, so defence*less*? The answer is secrecy. If people don't *know* that Emily is a "particular person" or, even, that she is God (Who for a time she suspects she is), surely they will leave her alone? Thus she embarks, like the infant in Blake's Notebook version of 'Infant Sorrow', "on a life of deception" with no misgivings: for, says the narrator, "A child can hide the most appalling secret without the least effort, and is practically secure against detection." (p.139) Hughes's portrayal of Emily's emergence into identity articulates acutely the ambiguous nature of freedom. Without selfhood there can be no first person to declare its separateness and individuality; but the emergence of the self-conscious 'I' brings with it the experience of existential fear: what can the fledgling awareness be but fearful for its survival? Here again Hughes was ahead of the psychologists.

Erich Fromm, who quotes a part of Emily's self-realization in *The Fear of Freedom* with the comment that it is "A remarkably keen description", writes:

> The primary ties offer security and basic unity with the world outside oneself. To the extent to which the child emerges from that world it becomes aware of being alone, of being an entity separate from all others. This separation from a world, which in comparison with one's own individual existence is overwhelmingly strong and powerful, and often threatening and dangerous, creates a feeling of powerlessness and anxiety. As long as one was an integral part of that world, unaware of the possibilities and responsibilities of individual action, one did not need to be afraid of it. When one has become an individual, one stands alone and faces the world in all its perilous and overpowering aspects. [11]

What Fromm takes several sentences to say is succinctly stated at a later point by Hughes in less than twenty words: "As a piece of Nature, she was practically invulnerable. But as *Emily*, she was absolutely naked, tender." (p.186) Fromm believes the antidote to aloneness and anxiety to lie in "spontaneous relationship to man and nature", relationship made possible by productive work and love. But long before Emily is old enough to undertake so positive a strategy, she will be driven to kill a man.

This killing proved too much for a fair percentage of the early readers of the novel. Hughes, however, takes care thoroughly to prepare the psychological ground for Emily's act, so that whether or not one accepts or rejects that act becomes a question of whether or not one accepts the psychological context in which it is perpetrated. Her existential fear for the "rather pleasing little casket of flesh" (p. 136) that contains her identity is wrought to crisis-point when, already feverish from the leg-wound caused by Laura's dropped marlin-spike, she is left alone, in Jonsen's stuffy cabin, with the fearsome Dutchman:

> Emily was terrified of him. There is something much more frightening about a man who is tied up than a man who is not tied up — I suppose it is the fear he may get loose.
> The feeling of not being able to get out of the bunk and escape added the true nightmare panic. (pp. 173-4)

When Vandervoort begins to roll towards the knife on the floor, Emily begins to scream. Instinctively she recognizes the situation as one of kill or be killed. Despair lends her strength, and she stabs him again and again: so that, quite simply, he bleeds to death from the number of his wounds.

The emphasis on Emily's *terror* — she "was terrified of him", she is "beside herself with terror" (p. 175) — should be enough to call up to a reader Emily's second most significant experience in the novel: the death of her cat Tabby. On the night after the hurricane which has seen Tabby pursued from the house by a horde of wild cats, Emily experiences dreams in which he is "torn to pieces by those fiends" (p.39). In the days that follow —

> If she was silent, and inclined to brood over some inward terror, it was not the hurricane she was thinking of, it was the death of Tabby. That, at times, seemed a horror beyond all bearing. It was her first intimate contact with death — and a death of violence, too. (p. 42)

The cat's death has sunk deep into her imagination. But what *is* death, what does it involve? An answer is implicit in her discovery of her identity: death is the end of self. The look which she has seen upon the doomed cat's face — a look far more human and terrible than that on the face of the negro Sam in the storm — enters into her mind, and stays there vividly. When, later, she bites Jonsen's thumb to hold him at bay, his look (it is his sense of horror at himself) recalls Tabby's (p.150); so that when in the courtroom she sees the now doomed Jonsen, she is seeing Jonsen, Tabby, and death inextricably mingled:

> The terrible look on Jonsen's face as his eye met hers, what was it that it reminded her of? (p.281)

and

> 'Father, *what* happened to Tabby in the end, that dreadful windy night in Jamaica?' (p.282)

Here, darkly, her 'innocence' reveals itself. Is she groping towards the realization that she herself is Jonsen's death, that she is his "wild cat"? Has she glimpsed the cost of her own survival: the lives of a number of others? We cannot be sure. But with the turning of fate's wheel she herself has become an agent of that same "terror" which she herself so savagely imagined as Tabby's lot.

After the murder, Emily's neurotic fear intensifies. In her madness — for children's minds "differ from adults' in kind of thinking (are *mad*, in fact)" (p.158) — she believes that everyone is thinking of killing her:

> When she heard the captain's step on the stairs, it might be that he was bringing her a plate of soup, or it might be that he had come to kill her — suddenly, with no warning change of expression on his amiable face even at the very end. (pp.189-90)

Her fear, the narrator supposes, is "the reflection of her own instinct for secretiveness". She can confide in no one: self-preservation demands it: for everyone is a potential enemy. Still later we are told: "She feared everybody, she hated everybody." (p.225) So that, even when she returns, in England, to the bosom of her family, her fear ensures that she will not confess what she has done: until, that is, she finally and disastrously breaks down in court.

IV

It is in its last movement — from the killing of Vandervoort to the hanging of the pirates — that *A High Wind in Jamaica* most plainly invites reading as an ironic Darwinian fable: or, if you will, as a comedy of natural selection.

> As natural selection acts solely by the preservation of profitable modifications, each new form will tend in a fully-stocked country to take the place of, and finally to exterminate, its own less improved parent-form and other less-favoured forms with which it comes into competition. Thus extinction and natural selection go hand in hand.[12]

"Natural selection" is a neutral, scientific term. It suggests a less conscious process than the clichéd 'struggle for survival'. Neither children nor pirates crudely perceive their predicament as an 'us or them' situation. The events which determine which of the two groups are most fitted to survive will be shaped by a combination of involuntary actions and conscious choices.

To put it simply, the imperative of survival proves most pure, most uncomprised, in Emily. It is unthinkable that she should confess and jeopardize her newly-discovered self: every precaution must be taken to preserve it. In her, "self-love and social", far from being in agreement, as Pope in *The Essay on Man* finds them, are utterly at odds. Emily is not old enough to have perceived that others possess selves whose needs are as imperative as her own. She has not, one may say, yet been 'infected' by civilised values. With the pirates, of course, it is otherwise. The very weakness of their self-preservative instinct is a crucial factor in their downfall. They are, ironically, 'corrupted' by the humanitarian values of the civilisation on which they prey.

It is tempting to express the Hughesian inversion as: diabolical children — tender-hefted pirates. The killing of the Dutch Captain appals the pirates: bloodshed, even in the way of business, is anathema to them:

> The way it had been shed left the pirates profoundly shocked, their eyes opened to a depravity of human nature they had not dreamt of . . . (p.181)

Now, the pirates' earlier feelings of tenderness towards the children, their sense that the children are "a sort of holy novelty" (p.133) has entirely disappeared — to be replaced by, of all things, fear:

> [The children] were treated with a detached severity not wholly divorced from fear — as if these unfortunate men at last realised what diabolic yeast had been introduced into their lump. (pp.182-3)

They perceive that they must get rid of the children. The securest option is to kill them, to "sew them up in little bags" and drop them over the side (p.222): to dispose of the evidence of kidnap. But Jonsen and Otto can only conceive of this option jokingly: in fact, as the narrator says, it shows up Jonsen's "latent sentimentality". Since it is too far to their base, Santa Lucia, the alternative is to put the children on to another ship. This involves great risk, however, — the risk of being given away by the children, pursued, and captured: which is precisely what happens, for Emily betrays them as soon as she finds herself in the *gunaikeion* (women's quarters). The pirates' altruism, then, proves their evil: killing the children — doing evil — would have constituted their good. The inversion is familiar from the plays.

But in truth *A High Wind in Jamaica* is too complex a book to be reduced to so neat a formula as: diabolical children — tender-hefted pirates. It is not, like *Lord of the Flies*, allegorical; Hughes's children are individuals richly defined, not representations of human types; his creativity does not flow in a predetermined channel; it is not a book that illustrates a thesis. Though Emily is a murderess, she can hardly be said to be wicked: we do not, I think, concur with her own conviction that she is "the wickedest person who [has] ever been born" (p.188).[13] In a very real way her murder-act *is* a product of innocence — innocence defined in psychological rather than moral terms as a child's partial or distorted perception of 'reality': 'reality' as it is constituted for an adult. Her murder is also a product of circumstance, and Emily herself prompts us as to how to view her destiny when she concludes: "Some appalling Power has determined it: it was no good struggling against it." (p.188) If we ask the question: Could she have done other than she did in the predicament she perceived? we must surely answer No: she is no less a victim of circumstance than the man she kills. We may wish to say that no appalling (and arbitrary) Power is responsible for what happens to her: but it is difficult to resist the proposition that her behaviour follows what one might call 'the logic of nature', a logic which is relentlessly deterministic. When Emily entertains the notion that she is God, she is in effect claiming the ultimate in existential freedom; but to perceive, then, that she is damned, is to perceive the opposite — that she is a driven and fated creature — the plaything of Hardyesque gods.

To whitewash the pirates is equally unacceptable. Consider their summary treatment of Margaret, whom they spontaneously and collectively assume to be the murderess. As the children conventionally assume the pirates to be wicked, the pirates conventionally assume the children to be pure. Both groups perceive in accordance with cultural stereotypes. Far from constituting for the pirates mitigating factors, Margaret's age and sex serve only the more absolutely to condemn her. Only the mate, as she vanishes to windward (like the pig, as the narrator reminds us), seems to feel other than a righteous horror: "the expression on her face . . . left a picture in Otto's mind he never forgot". The very lack of specificity in this makes for a certain power of emphasis. Margaret, like Nabokov's Lolita, may connive at her own seduction, but that this is so prevents neither Otto nor Humbert from feeling guilt: has not Otto recognizied his own complicity in a process of corruption which has led her to this act? if Margaret is guilty, isn't he also?

The reader who asks him or herself the question: Are the pirates the playthings of a deterministic universe? may conclude that in their case freedom is not distinguishable from necessity. They *choose* to safeguard the children rather than kill them: as in *The Sisters' Tragedy*, the altruistic act which puts the doer at risk declares the freedom of the doer. Voluntarily to endanger the self enables one to break out of the biological rat-trap. But if one then asks: Could the pirates have acted other than they did — *could* they have dropped the children overboard in little sacks? I think the likely answer is No. The pirates are no less subject to 'the logic of nature' than the children. It is to the point here to recognize the deterministic impulse which runs through both Darwinism and Freudism: Freudism accepts no mental happenings as accidental,[14] and the theory of natural selection inevitably dooms those species which cannot compete to diminishment and extinction. When, at the very end of the book, the negro cook declares: " *You* know that I die innocent: anything I have done, I was forced to do by the rest of you", that "you" implicates everyone (p.283). He sees himself as a creature enmeshed in a web of events he can neither alter nor escape. In freely embracing his fate, he bows to necessity. Emily the murderess, and the martyred pirates, are all fools of nature — but some, in this world, are more fools than others.

V

The limitations to which human rationality is subject is shown most forcefully — and absurdly — at the trial which closes the novel. The comedy takes on satirical tones as the inadequacy of the judicial system is laid bare. Human beings seek through collaborative activity to create institutions which will make possible a clarity of judgment which it is difficult for them as individuals to attain: but the court in *A High Wind* signally fails to free itself from the assumptions and prejudices of its constituent individuals, and its attempt to administer justice is a grimly ironic travesty.

The trial is prefigured, in different ways, by two earlier occurrences. I have already mentioned the "rigmarole" by which the "pink predatory" monkey-children decide whether to twist the necks of their bird-victims, or to let them go free. The birds, of course, are innocent. Then there is Lame-foot Sam's finding of one of Mr. Bas-Thornton's handkerchiefs in the compound: he steals it, ignoring the angry growls of the thunder — and this in spite of the fact that it is Sunday. Later, after the storm has erupted, he bursts in upon the family at supper, flings the handkerchief on the table, and stumps out. This attempt at appeasement, however, comes too late:

> Shortly after that Sam's hut burst into flames. They saw, from the dining-room, the old negro stagger dramatically out into the darkness. He was throwing stones at the sky. In a lull they heard him cry: 'I gib it back, didn't I? I gib de nasty t'ing back?'
> Then there was another blinding flash, and Sam fell where he stood.
> (p. 34)

Looking forward from the comic platform provided by these incidents, we may ask: first, whether the proceedings of the English court are any improvement on those which decide the fate of the birds; and second, whether the 'natural' justice meted out to Sam by the Powers of the Air (or the Power beyond the Air) is any less summary than that meted out to the pirates by the court (it may be noted that, as Sam gibs back the handkerchief, the pirates give back the children . . .). In addition we must bear in mind the rough justice meted out to Margaret, who is condemned without trial and 'executed' on the spot by being dropped overboard. Will the judge and jury that try the pirates prove any more enlightened than the pirates are themselves?

Mr. Mathias, the counsel for the prosecution, believes that

> the natural and proper witnesses are the children. There is a kind of beauty in making them, who have suffered so much at these men's hands, the instruments of justice upon them. (p.271)

That the children have suffered at the hands of the pirates is, of course, no more than an assumption (the privileged reader may feel that the pirates have suffered at the hands of the children): it is directly contradicted by Mr. Thornton's belief that the children became "very fond" of Jonsen and Otto. But then, Mr. Mathias, as a criminal lawyer, is concerned not with "facts" but "probabilities", and as Mr. Thornton's insight is not one which can help his case, he lays it aside. His notion of making the children into "instruments of justice" amounts to a kind of poetic justice: for he, along with the rest of the court, can see only one explanation of the disappearance of John and Captain Vandervoort: the pirates have murdered them. But since young children, as Mathias himself says, are notoriously unreliable witnesses, nothing must be left to chance. Emily, therefore, must be 'programmed' to say exactly what the prosecution wants her to say. Since she has no comprehension of the nature of the theatricals in which she is the star performer, the "catechism" in which Mathias instructs her can be to her no more or less than a "rigmarole" — a meaningless ritual sequence of words — than that which she and John used to decide the fate of the captured birds.

Hughes ensures that we perceive the absurdity of making a child the chief weapon in the armoury of the prosecution by compelling us to see the court through her eyes. Her comic inability to evaluate what she sees sharpens the edge of Hughes's satiric intention. The face of the Clerk of the Court catches her eye:

> It was an old and very beautiful face, cultured, unearthly, refined. His head laid back, his mouth slightly open, his eyes closed, he was gently sleeping. (p.278)

No sooner is the Clerk ennobled than the illusion is punctured: Justice sleeps throughout the trial. The whole thing amounts to a sort of fancy-dress tableau. The Judge appears to Emily "like some benign old wizard who spent his magic on doing good" (p.279) — humankind's parody of God. It is only when Watkyn, the defending counsel, begins his cross-examination of Emily that we begin to see the proceedings as a serious matter of life and death. Watkyn's direct approach breaks the comfortable shell of rigmarole in which Mathias has encased the girl, and something monstrously real is fleetingly, if incoherently, revealed:

> Those who were watching the self-contained Emily saw her turn very white and begin to tremble. Suddenly she gave a shriek: then after a second's pause she began to sob. Every one listened in an icy stillness, their hearts in their mouths. Through her tears they heard, they all heard, the words: '. . . He was all lying in his blood . . . he was awful! He . . . he died, he said something and then he *died*!' (pp.280-81)

It is shortly before the trial that the narrator admits that he "can no longer read Emily's deeper thoughts, or handle their cords" (p.276) — so dark and elusive have they become. Emily's broken utterance, then, stands unglossed: we do not know whether it represents a confession (and the final collapse of her effort to protect her new self), or the final nail knocked by an imperfectly comprehending child-betrayer into the gallows of her victims. If this latter possibility seems a little far-fetched, we should remember not only that her defence of her identity is at all times more instinctive than consciously-contrived (so that her doings remain mysterious to herself as well as others), but that her own father shrinks from touching her after the trial — as if she were some sort of monster. Has Emily passed out of 'innocence' into 'experience'? where does one end and the other begin? or, if she has not, must we recognise that 'innocence' is capable of spawning monstrosities in their way quite as savage as those born to 'experience'? This fearsome Emily is the little girl who, in another of Hughes's splendid eidola, first communes, and then sleeps with, an alligator:

> The eye of an alligator is large, protruding, and of a brilliant yellow, with a slit pupil like a cat's. A cat's eye, to the casual observer, is expressionless: though with attention one can distinguish in it many changes of emotion. But the eye of an alligator is infinitely more stony and brilliant-reptilian.
>
> What possible meaning could Emily find in such an eye? Yet she lay there, and stared, and stared: and the alligator stared too. If there had been an observer it might have given him a shiver to see them so — well, eye to eye like that. (p.238)

It is the novelist as naturalist again, as dedicated observer of all animal species. If Laura's otherness is conveyed in the eidolon of the octopus, Emily the alienated murderess's is conveyed in that of the alligator, and in both passages Hughes focusses on the eyes of his subjects. Emily and the alligator are "two children": she has more in common with a cold-blooded reptile than with any of the adults in the book. The association is recalled when, much later, Mr. Thornton first discovers that he is afraid of his daughter:

> But surely it was some trick of the candle-light, or of her indisposition, that gave her face momentarily that inhuman, stony, basilisk look? (pp.275-6)

Upon what resources might such a creature call in a last-minute attempt to protect herself?

The court, at any rate, can read in her broken utterance only the pirates' death warrant. Hughes writes off its pretence of administering justice in a couple of sardonic sentences:

> Trials are quickly over, once they begin. It was no time before the judge had condemned these prisoners to death and was trying some one else with the same concentrated, benevolent, individual attention. (p.283)

The irony of this is of the order of Pope's

> And wretches hang that jurymen may dine.

If nature's 'justice' is rough (to Lame-foot Sam), that dispensed by this civilized court is no improvement.

VI

Romantic art is expansive: the Romantic poet declares the infinite potential of human individuals and human societies. The art of the ironist is constrictive, classicist. Hughes in *A High Wind* threw off the spirit of Romanticism which haunted his poetry. Whatever his intention, his novel challenged a conception of the child which was sentimental and categorical. The lush island of Jamaica may have a look of Eden, but it is a deceptive appearance. The Emily who finds "abominable" that "sort of expressionless light kissing" administered to her submerged body by hundreds of infant fish is a recognizable denizen of a post-Freudian world. In this teasing garden, innocence is a problematical entity, and the individual ego the paramount fact. 'Civilization', the ironist sees, is a garment human beings adopt to cover the bare skin of primitive imperatives. The War had revealed to a generation just how flimsy that garment was, and the war years were the formative years of Hughes's own adolescence. Afterwards, neither life nor art could be what they had been before.

When you have stripped away the old and worn veneer which covered your furniture, you see the wood as it really is. What will you do with the fresh, clean surface you have revealed? It is too stark, too raw perhaps, to be left as it is. *A High Wind*, a post-war novel, was more concerned with demolition than reconstruction; *In Hazard*, a pre-war novel, would reverse the metaphor.

Chapter Eight: *In Hazard*

I

Richard Hughes has left us two revealing statements about the meaning of *In Hazard*. They are very different. The first, written in 1938 in response to those reviewers who felt that the book "is 'about' a storm, and that the men in it hardly matter",[1] set forth part of his conscious purpose: to write "a book about fear". A thoughtful reader, he imagined, would see that "almost every possible effect of fear, good and bad," is represented in the various responses of *Archimedes*'s crewmen to prolonged danger.

> In Mr. Rabb and the Chinese crew you see the paralysing effect of panic. In the captain you see the opposite, the way fear can stimulate a man to do things beyond his ordinary powers. In the mate, Mr. Buxton, you see the disciplined reaction of a man who can so control fear that it does not affect his efficiency either way. In the others — in the elderly chief engineer and most of all in the junior officer Dick Watchett — you see (what would probably be your own case in an emergency) the interplay of all these different effects, now one now another holding sway. And you see the effect on fear of the imagination, and the effect on the imagination of conquering fear.[2]

Immediately we can see one way in which *In Hazard* continues where *A High Wind in Jamaica* left off: for in its latter half the earlier novel is also a study in fear — the fear felt by Emily for her newly-discovered self, and the strategy of survival dictated by that fear. Now, in *In Hazard*, we see how the fear of death affects a cross-section of individuals who vary in age and temperament — from the teenage junior officers, through the senior officers, to the Captain himself. Hughes felt in 1938 that he was stating no more that what should be obvious; and, indeed, his comments (though disposing most effectively of one particularly wayward 'objection' to the book) strike me as a perfectly straightforward piece of auto-interpretation. If we postulate that *In Hazard* possesses both an 'outward' meaning and an 'inward' meaning, a *literal* level of signification and a *symbolic* one, then his 1938 commentary illuminates what is outward and literal. By contrast, his Introduction to *In Hazard* of 1966, written almost thirty years later, concerns itself with what is inward and symbolic. In saying "Now . . .I do think I begin to see at least one reason" for the compulsion that gripped him, Hughes is not being entirely truthful.[3] Nevertheless, the Introduction demonstrates the persistence of his attachment to a particular theory, for, in drawing upon Robert Graves's ideas about the neurotic and therapeutic character of poetry, he picks up preoccupations of almost fifty years before. In order to explain the symbolic significance of the hurricane, he recalls the self-delusive political climate of Britain in the 1930s — a Britain that wished to believe, against the accumulating evidence of reality, that there would be no war.

> Right till the end all 10 parts of Reason went on telling us the final cataclysm would be dodged. Even in the summer of 1938, when Chamberlain waved 'Peace in Our Time' in our faces, most of us believed him — or thought we did. "Or *thought* we did" — for that is the point I am making, that all this time, the bottoms of our minds knew better; that in our bones we had foreseen from the very beginning this hurricane of preternatural power which no manoeuvering could dodge. Under this threshold of consciousness we were well aware that it would prove worse than even imagination could envisage but that we should endure, somehow reviving in ourselves that trust in stubbornness and Providence supposedly long since leached out.[4]

The hurricane, then, represents fears which the conscious mind has repressed: in it, imagination tackles what the diurnal mind couldn't bring itself to face.

It was only later, too, that Hughes recognized the 'clues' which lay scattered through his text. On its opening page we find that the chief engineer is a certain Mr. Ramsay MacDonald; and the narrator is "astonished"

> to see what appeared to be my Prime Minister, in a suit of overalls, crawling out of a piece of dismantled machinery with an air of real authority and knowledge and decision.

The subconscious, one sees, has a sense of irony. Then the narrator tells us that when its "guys were properly set up", the ship's funnel "was as safe as the Bank of England" (p. 4). Later, discussing the behaviour of hurricanes, he quips: "Ships (which can run) are safer in those latitudes than government offices (which cannot)" (p. 33). The Captain's surname, Edwardes, suggests a line of English kings — the last, by his own doing, a brief incumbent. Hughes writes that his choice of an American vessel as salvage ship might entitle him to be thought of as "a prophet of no mean rank" — but to read his book as an *allegory* would be to misread it:

> since this is not allegory at all but symbol; and symbol (in the dream sense) is never concerned primarily with the future *qua* future but with a much more timeless kind of truth.[5]

It would not be unduly difficult to construct an interpretation of *In Hazard* upon this line of thought. This is not my intention in this chapter, however. I shall return to the question of fear in due course; but in the meantime, I wish to erect upon the building-plot which Hughes himself has prepared a rather different kind of structure.

By way of preliminaries, we may note first the preoccupations carried over from Hughes's earlier writings. He is again concerned, as I've already noted, with the psychology of fear. His extended treatment of the Englishman Dick Watchett and the Chinaman Ao Ling enables him to build upon his achievement with Emily Bas-Thornton, and to explore the spiritual development of older children of very different races. His concern with biological and psychological necessity now broadens, and he explores the limitations of freedom in a more expansive context than *A High Wind* made possible. Now, against the dark ironies of chance, he finds himself able to set the luminous ironies of providence. Most obviously, we encounter the Hughesian violent act in its purest form: the elemental forces of nature, in the shape of the hurricane, gather the human world, in the form of *S. S. Archimedes*, up in its violent embrace and will not be gainsaid. A kind of warfare, an enormous test ensues — but it is warfare conducted entirely in terms defined by the storm. Whatever human violence occurs — Watchett's subduing of Ao Ling, for example — is utterly dwarfed by it: yet, as we have already seen from Hughes's own comments, natural violence renders human violence supererogatory — for the hurricane is a symbol of war.

Second, it is necessary to say something about the narrative voice in *In Hazard*. From the opening chapter it appears as if the *physical* relation of Hughes's narrative persona will be strictly comparable to the one he had adopted in *A High Wind*. Again the novel is set in the past — though now in the recent past: *Archimedes*'s voyage takes place in the late summer of 1929, whereas *Phemius*'s took place in November 1932. *In Hazard*'s narrator is given, like *A High Wind*'s, the status of a *visitor*: as the one had visited Jamaica some years before the events that form the main story (having

'business', we remember, with the Miss Parkers of Derby Hill), so the other
has visited *Archimedes* five years before her epic voyage, in 1924 — when the
chief engineer showed him round the engine-room. This stance, of "the
visitor to whom Mr. MacDonald is showing his regions" (p. 7), becomes a
means of acquainting the reader with a part of the ship which will play a
critical role in the book: as the narrator is introduced to the engine-room, so
is the reader. In the same way, the narrator gave us a first-hand impression
of Jamaica in the early pages of *A High Wind*. The withdrawal of *In Hazard*'s
narrator behind the third person —

> At Norfolk (Virginia) they took in some low-grade tobacco, also bound
> for China . . . (p. 14)
> The next night, the night before their departure for Colon and the
> Panama Canal. . . (p. 18)

— might lead a reader who stopped to consider the matter to assume that
the narrator is a person who, from a position of privilege, has pieced the
story together after the event (as indeed Hughes did), and who is prepared
to imagine what he could not know — as again is the case in *A High Wind*. It
then comes as something of a surprise to find that the narrator is actually on
board: "the dancing dolphins were the most beautiful thing I had ever
seen" (p. 22). This is the only occasion during the voyage on which the first
person insists upon its physical presence on *Archimedes* and is, I would say,
the only serious false note in the novel. First, it seems to me that it is
naturally Dick Watchett who should see the dolphins; second, and more
seriously, the narrator immediately drops back into a third person that
seems firmly to exclude him from participation in the events narrated:

> It took them four days to reach San Salvador.
> They seemed now to have passed through the little oasis of summer.
> (p. 24)

Had the narrator been on board, it would seem natural to say 'we'. And
would not an on-ship presence necessitate, in place of the effortless
objectivity of vision which we are given, a personal response to events — of
which there is no trace? It is true that the narrator frequently opts for a
second person which might be read as a sort of surrogate 'we':

> Except for occasional momentary lulls, you could not see the sea, or the
> deck even. It was only by the wincing of the ship you knew what huge
> waves were hitting her: by that, and the thunderous banging. You
> could not see anything. Standing in the damp chart-room, you could
> descry, through the glass between, the little Chinaman, on his mat, at
> the wheel; but nothing outside: and it was only by shouting close into
> each other's ears that they could hear, either. (p. 44)

This second person is a favourite recourse of Hughes, and is familiar from *A High Wind* (the octopus eidolon, for instance): he employs it as a means of reeling you, the hypocrite lecteur, in — of implicating you in experiences you have not had and imparting to you opinions you may not hold. Hughes is a novelist who likes to play with his reader, to tease, to disconcert — and his frequent changes of pronominal angle are a means of manipulation. At the end of the last-quoted passage there is an abrupt shift back to the impersonality of "they": it is as if, having been vouchsafed a close-up which has given us the illusion that we ourselves are on board the ship, the director has suddenly cut to a distance shot, pushing the action away from us. It is by such devices that Hughes keeps the reader on his toes too, refusing to allow him to settle into complacent relationship with the events unfolding before him. The narrator of *In Hazard* is not the Darwinian ironist of *A High Wind*, but he *is* an observer who imagines participation rather than a participator who observes and imagines. And, again like the earlier narrator, his persona is authoritative but not omniscient.

II

Richard Hughes believed *In Hazard* to be his most formally perfect novel, and it is a view I share. This is not, of course, to deny that *A High Wind* possesses a most satisfying formal symmetry. If novels can be likened to string quartets, *A High Wind* may be said to have five movements which may be represented thus:

```
                 The         The pirate       The
JAMAICA —                        —                         — ENGLAND
              Clorinda        schooner       steamer
```

Movements one and five balance one another (with the muddy Thames providing an ironic counterpoint to the idyllic bathing-pool), and so do two and four: rather as in Bartok's Fourth and Fifth Quartets. The first and last movements take place on land, the central three at sea — two and four being transitional in nature. Writers on Bartok have drawn on architectural metaphors to help them describe his five-movement quartets, calling them 'archlike': *A High Wind*'s dominant third movement may be described as the keystone in the novel's arch. *In Hazard*, by way of contrast, is in one movement — though here one might descry the elements of a sonata, and mark the piece accordingly

Andante;   Presto con moto;   Adagio

where *con moto* allows for the variations caused by *Archimedes* passing in and out of the centre of the hurricane, and the flanking slow markings represent the pre-storm and post-storm sections of the book.

It is, indeed, the integrated nature of *In Hazard* which makes for its formal perfection, and the wholly Hughesian — or fictive/poetic — character of this integration may be demonstrated by applying to it his three theoretical requirements for a good poem. These were: that its individual idea-images be vivid and quickening; that they be organised into an orderly and satisfying structural whole by a governing "rhythmic conception"; and that "the conception in all these dimensions be influenced by their own interplay".

I shall begin with the "rhythmic conception" which Hughes invests with the responsibility of organising all the constituent elements in the novel. This — especially if we have read Hughes's own Introduction — is not difficult to perceive: it is the conflict between the simultaneously real and symbolic entities of ship and weather — *Archimedes* and her crew on the one hand, and the hurricane on the other. To put it another way, the rhythm of the novel is the sea-rhythm of *Archimedes's* fantastic voyage. It begins in calm as the ship steams complacently towards Panama; but the wind gathers and the danger-signs accumulate, ship and book move *crescendo* towards the heart of the hurricane: the hatches are stripped, the funnel plucked out, and the ship left rolling helplessly in maddened seas. The rhythm of the main part of the novel is one of alternating buffetings and lulls as *Archimedes* is pushed in and out of the circular storm. Only when she is at last spewed out in the hurricane's rear does, upon exhausted sailors and readers alike, some semblance of calm descend. But they are not quite the same people they were when *Archimedes* set sail.

It is wholly proper that the novel ends where it does. Rather than "petering out", as some of the reviewers of 1938 suggested, it winds down. Aesthetic symmetry demands that it should close on a crippled ship limping in tow to port through a gradually diminishing swell. To include the matter of the Sage Line's enquiry into Captain Edwardes's handling of his vessel (Desmond MacCarthy's suggested conclusion) would be to embark upon a fresh sea of controversy, to introduce a distinct rhythmic element — and the balance of the tale would be impaired. The Owners' verdict upon their Master would be a secular affair, whereas the true matter of the storm-voyage has been spiritual.

Hughes's "rhythmic conception" holds two conflicting, two interacting (and to some paradoxical extent, as we shall see, co-operating) entities within its field of play. It would be natural to think of ship and storm as utterly different phenomena: the one a product of human science and technology, the other of elemental nature. But it soon becomes clear that Hughes is determined to dissolve these polarities in the solvent of his imagination. In a talk (whose original occasion has been lost) on 'The Poet and the Scientist', he argues that though the poet and the physicist project "upon the continuum" a very different "net-work", they must both, when they use the words "to say the unsayable ... equally use a translogical association of ideas".[6] In *In Hazard*, then, it seems natural that he should continually seek out ground upon which the scientist and the poet can meet and merge, language in which their interests may be reconciled. In a beautifully-judged series of transactions, the man-made and the natural effect an interchange of metaphors, so that in the resulting eidola what is mechanical is expressed in terms of what is natural, and vice-versa.

Our early visit to the engine-room of *Archimedes* in Chapter One climaxes in our discovery of the propellor-shaft: "a smooth column of steel, lying in cool and comfortable bearings and turning round and round with no sound". Now, in order that we shall imaginatively grasp the working of the ship's engine, nothing less than "a translogical association of ideas" is called for:

> Think of a tree. The roots of a tree spread in a most complicated manner through the ground, extracting all kinds of necessary things. This nourishment passes, unified, up the plain column of its trunk, and bursts out in the air into a countless multitude of leaves. So all the varying forces, the stresses and resistances, proceeding from that welter of machinery, are unified into the simple rotation of this horizontal column: are conducted calmly along its length into the sea: and there burgeon suddenly into the white and glass-green foliage of the swirls, the tumbling currents, the enormously powerful jostling of crowded water which is a ship's wake. (p. 8)

For myself, the effect of this Hughesian eidolon is something like that produced by an elaborate metaphysical conceit — though Hughes sustains his conceit to greater length than is normal in seventeenth-century verse. In the vivacious sensuousness of his English he is more akin to Marvell than to Donne. Heterogeneous things are yoked together, but there is no sense of violence in the yoking: Hughes's art is effortless and seamless, and I am conscious of no poetic gymnastics, no striving on the author's part to produce an effect. Organic and inorganic are audaciously interfused.

Against this passage we can set the following paragraphs from Chapter Two. As we must understand how a steamship is powered, so we must understand how a hurricane is powered.

> Air moving in from all round towards a central point: and in the

middle, air rising: that is the beginning. Then two things happen. The turning of the earth starts the system turning: not fast at first, but in a gentle spiral. And the warm air which has risen, saturated with moisture from the surface of the sea, cools. Cooling, high up there, its moisture spouts out of it in rain. Now, when the water in air condenses, it releases the energy that held it there, just as truly as the explosion of petrol releases energy. Millions of horse-power up there loose. As in a petrol motor, that energy is translated into motion; up rises the boundless balloon still higher, faster spins the vortex.

Thus the spin of the earth is only the turn of the crank-handle which starts it: the hurricane itself is a vast motor, revolved by the energy generated by the condensation of water from the rising air. (pp. 34-5)

The rhythm of the first of these paragraphs is that of the gradually intensifying motion which it describes. We begin calmly with air moving in and air rising; to which, then, the turning earth imparts a gentle spiral movement. The risen air cools, condenses, and releases its energy — for that energy itself to be translated into motion; and so to the urgent "faster spins the vortex". Hughes's passage about the propellor-shaft moves even more obviously from calmly reflective beginnings to an energetic conclusion. The second extract is less extravertly poetic than its counterpart, but again we see Hughes employing "a translogical association of ideas": he seeks to make the storm comprehensible through mechanical metaphors. The hurricane is "a vast motor" (or, a few lines later, an "extraordinary engine, fifty miles or more wide, built of speed-hardened air"): what will clash in the novel are man-made and natural *engines*, both of which comprise energy-creating rotatory systems. The ship's engine creates in the sea a vortex which drives it forward; the circular storm is also a vortex — wind spinning around a vacuous centre. When Hughes comes to write, of the latter: "Mere motion has formed a hollow *pipe*, as impervious as if it were made of something solid" (p. 35; my italics), we may recall that the narrator sees in Mr. MacDonald's engine-room "Large pipes of varying widths, some of them — cold — of shining bedewed copper, and others wrapped in thick white clothing to keep in their heat" (p. 5). The smallest word is grist to the poetic novelist's mill, to the business of creating the 'interplay' which Hughes believed essential between the distinct but metaphorically sympathetic elements of his "rhythmic conception". To see that the interplay between ship and storm is also an interplay between 'the scientific' and 'the poetic' in *In Hazard* is to see how completely John Brophy had misread the novel when he wrote in his review: "Mr. Hughes lectures well, about engine-rooms and meteorology, and so on, but these disquisitions irritate and hold up the story."[7] Hughes may be a fine story-teller, but his concern to create a patterned and image-rich whole is not subordinate to his desire to tell a good story: he seeks to satisfy more in the human imagination than that which enjoys a good yarn.

That individual idea-images in *In Hazard* are, as Hughes requires them to be in poetry, "vivid and quickening", will surely be admitted by anyone who has read and responded to the book. Eidola of an extended nature come most readily to mind; the haunting episode when birds land on the ship; Ao Ling's surreal dream; the dance of the dolphins — which Richard Church in his review likened to a triple fugue. I shall give just one example. Here is one of a number of descriptions (though 'descriptions' is an inadequate word) of the behaviour of the seas in the storm:

> The seas, huge lumps of water with a point on top, ran about in all directions in a purposeful way at immense speeds. They were as big as houses, and moved as fast as trains. Sometimes they ran into each other, hard, and threw themselves jointly into the air. At others they banged suddenly against the ship, and burst out into a rapid plumage of spray that for a moment hid everything. (pp. 41-42)

In saying that Hughes's storm is *beautiful* (as was the air-raid he experienced on the roof of the Empire Hotel in Bath[8]), I use the word deliberately. Eighteenth-century aesthetic philosophers distinguished between the beautiful and the sublime. Kant in his *Critique of Judgment*[9] proposes that our perception of beauty is connected with *form*, of sublimity with *the formless*; that satisfaction in the beautiful is bound up with the representation of *quality*, in the sublime with the representation of *quantity*;

> satisfaction in the sublime does not so much involve a positive pleasure as admiration or respect, which rather deserves to be called negative pleasure.

This distinction affords us an excellent means of getting at the difference between Hughes's storm and Conrad's in *Typhoon*. Conrad's typhoon is surely sublime, whereas Hughes's is beautiful; Conrad's storm demands admiration and respect, but Hughes's evokes a positive pleasure. This, no doubt, is a way of saying that *Typhoon* is a romantic novel — for the romantic artist typically strains after the sublime — and *In Hazard* a classical novel. But it is also a way of saying that the two books are so different in conception that it is superfluous to evaluate them with reference to one another: one is not evaluating instances of the same thing. To prefer one to the other is not to prefer a superior example of one kind of art to an inferior example, but one kind of art to another kind.

III

While Hughes is interested in the hurricane as a phenomenon *per se*, he is still more interested in its value as a catalyst. How will the individual members of *Archimedes*'s crew respond to the challenge it represents? Will they surmount it or crumple beneath it? Given the presence of Chinese on board his ship, as well as English, Welsh and Scots, it was no doubt inevitable that Hughes would seize the opportunity to explore the differences between the sensibilities of Westerners and Orientals. (Conrad, in *Typhoon*, shows no interest in the *Nan-Shan*'s Chinese, who remain so many cattle.) Most importantly, Hughes chooses to trace the spiritual biographies of the young men Dick Watchett and Ao Ling, who are both twenty years old. Apropos of this contrast, he offers us the following proposition:

> The powerful innate forces in us, the few prime movers common to us all, are essentially plastic and chameleon-like. The shape and colour which they come to present at the mind's surface bear little seeming relation to the root: appear characteristic rather of the medium through which they have struggled to the light.
> Where men's environment, their education, differ fundamentally, flowers from the same hidden root will *seem* to bear no kinship: will differ 'fundamentally' too. (p.179)

The specific point of comparison which Hughes offers us has to do with the relationship between adolescent children and their parents, and particularly sons and fathers. Typically, he says, the Anglo-Saxon adolescent revolts against his father, while the Chinese obeys his. Hughes's investigation goes well beyond these particular terms, however, as he elucidates the stages through which the changing religious sensibilities of Dick and Ling pass.

Dick is "perhaps actually more devout than the average" boy (p.138). He finds that, when he wants something, God is nearly always ready to answer his prayers: but he never makes requests he knows to be unfulfillable (for a premature bicycle, for instance). He is, it seems (like Hughes himself), fatherless: when he visualizes God, he cannot get "beyond a fleeting vision of black whiskers and tight knickerbockers" (p.139) — the outfit his grandfather wore for cycling excursions: "for God and Grandad had too much in common". By the time he is fifteen, this dependable, anthropomorphic child's God has been replaced by something altogether less personal: "a vague, limitless holiness" (p.144) who cannot be asked for small material benefits. The only proper thing to pray to this God for is

Grace. When, fearful of drowning after pouring oil for ten hours, he asks to be saved from off the sea, he finds himself caught between his child's conception of prayer and his post-Confirmation sense of it, and has suddenly to revise his request to: "only save me from drowning if that be already Thy will"! Now that he has mediated between what his boyhood sense of God and his youthful sense of God require, he feels "a most distinct and stabbing promise, of the kind he remembered so well, that he should be saved alive kindly" (p.149). That this is a regression of a kind there can be little doubt: yet it enables Dick to persevere with his task: not everything which goes into the making of a hero is heroic.

Dick's devoutness, his reluctance in his mid-teens to let go of his childhood God, contrasts sharply with the religious development of Ao Ling. Ling is in all ways a rebel. In his childhood he tastes famine and privation; his father sells his sister at the age of ten to buy food. One of his crucial experiences is observing the ease with which a rich man's door-keeper repulses a mob: he simply pushes the nearest man, and the whole crowd collapses like a house of cards (Hughes himself had witnessed such an incident in the famine-ridden Valley of the Sous in 1930). His reaction is to go alone to the shrine of the country gods and destroy them. His superstitious fear that they will rebuke him seems to be groundless: they are powerless to stop him. Yet, as he returns home:

> There was a rustling in the dry bamboo-clump. As he passed, in the dusk, something bounded out behind them. It was the god, the fractures showing as fiery seams in his flesh, his green face terrible with anger. Little Ling stumbled screaming into the kitchen, and fell flat on the floor. (pp.187-8)

Hughes demonstrates, in an almost Wordsworthian manner, that the child cannot break the taboos of his culture with impunity: Ling's imagination punishes him by reinventing the very supernatural authority from which he desires to emancipate himself.

Ling runs away from home when he is twelve, travelling widely and getting work where he can. In 1927 he deserts from the Kuomintang flag to the Red Army — a further act of revolt which leads to his 'conversion' to a new religion — Marxism.

> He absorbed the Marxian doctrine like a thirsty animal drinking. It refreshed every corner of his soul. For it freed him from his three great fears: fear of his father, fear of the supernatural, fear of the rich. (p.200)

Or so he thinks. But Hughes will show, in Ling, the inability of politico-religious doctrine to exorcise psychological demons. His presentation of

Ling is plainly a Freudian one: Ling's rejection of all conventional forms of authority is an extension of his rejection of the father. The passage which comes nearest to accounting for Ling's hatred of his father is the following — one of his earliest memories:

> The whole family were straddling the thatched roof of their cottage. The yellow flood-water swirled around them, and the mud walls beneath them were melting away. I suppose their peril was pretty acute. Ling was lying in his mother's arms. He must have been very young: for presently she gave him suck.
>
> However, hardly had the milk begun to come when suddenly his father tore him from her breast, and tossed him, howling furiously, into the rescue-boat which had just drawn near. (p.192)

The first paragraph reads flatly, its understatedness accentuated by the narrator's laid-back "I suppose . . .". The father's separation of his son from the mother then seems all the more gratuitously violent, emphasized as it is by the energetically alliterating verbs "tore" and "tossed". Here again we see the necessitarian character of Freud's psychology: in taking on the form of a continuous struggle against the father, Ling's short but eventful life is anything but 'freely' lived. From the Freudian point of view, Wordsworth's great truth "The child is father of the man" is a statement about psychic determinism. Ling's arrest and imprisonment at the behest of Captain Edwardes constitutes, then, what threatens to be the final victory of the father. Ling thinks of Edwardes as "this God-the-Father of a Captain" (p.206), and although his surreal dream towards the book's end is resistant to analysis, we can, I think, discern in the weird dream-figure of the Captain elements of Ling's "three great fears". The figure is supernatural in origin, rich in appearance — wearing "a pair of Chinese trousers from which flashed dazzling rays of gold light" (p.270) — and appears as a sadistic father-figure: cruelly *tearing* the golden scales off the majestic sea-dragon, the Captain wrings from it the despairing sobs of Ling's "own infantile voice, weeping to him out of the far years of the past". In dream, the self-protective carapace which Ling has built up is stripped away. "The Unconscious", Freud wrote, "is the infantile mental life":[10] the child in us never dies. It is interesting to note that Ling, unlike Dick, remains unperturbed by the storm. He cannot believe that the furnace-fires, blowing back, have power to harm him. Dick must pray before he feels reassured; but Ling's confidence that his Marxism will protect him is boundless. It is only when, in his dream, Captain Edwardes masters both the dragons of the sea (which have a fifth foot — an umbilicus of a sort? — growing from their navels) and the Ling-dragon, we see that Ling's sense of invulnerability is broachable: not by the visible and tremendous powers of nature, but by the ineradicable power of man the father, a power that his psyche cannot annul.

In Hughes's propositional metaphor, Dick and Ling are "flowers from the same hidden root": in saying that they "will *seem* to bear no kinship: will differ 'fundamentally' too", the italics and inverted commas hint at ambiguity. To see how Hughes elicits a kinship-in-difference, we can trace the rhythmic evolutions of perhaps the most teasing eidolon in the novel. At a wild party in Norfolk, Virginia, the girl — Sukie — who has attached herself to Dick Watchett, gets drunk and throws off her clothes.

> For a few seconds she stood there, her body stark naked. Dick had never seen anything like it before. Then she fell unconscious on the floor.
> . . . She had been lovely in her clothes, but she was far more lovely like this, fallen in a posture as supple as a pool. (p.17)

He rolls her in a hearthrug and returns, shaking, to his ship, where he lies awake for hours imagining her. When he falls asleep, "her naked body" flickers in his dreams. Presently, however, he awakens to find himself "staring, through the texture of his dream, into large, anxious, luminous eyes, only an inch from his own; eyes that were not Sukie's" (p. 18). It is Mr. Buxton's pet lemur Thomas — "hopping away on his unnaturally elongated feet, nervously folding and unfolding his ears." Soon *Archimedes* is on her way to Colon, and Sukie's image begins to fade in Dick's mind. Now he meets the dancing dolphins:

> At first Sukie had blazed in Dick's mind, lighting every part of it: but now already, after two days, she had contracted and receded like the opening by which you have entered a tunnel: turned more unearthly bright than the broad day, but very distant and small and clear. Yet now, as he watched the dolphins, for a moment light seemed to come back over his whole mind, gently flooding all its dark places, and then fading in a mood of pleasurable sadness. (p.23)

Dick's sensations and feelings are conveyed obliquely and imagistically here: the image of the tunnel is visual, precise, familiar; that of the return of light to his mind is imprecise (an example, perhaps, of the weaker, intermediate idea-image) yet luminous and tender. We have to wait a couple of paragraphs for Hughes to tell us why the dolphins should have this effect on Dick. That night he sees another beautiful sight: "But it did not move him as the naked dolphins had done" (p. 24). *Naked* is the focal, energized word in this sentence, a disyllable which Hughes, with a poet's sense of placement, causes to cash in on the parade of flat monosyllables that precede it. It is a blunt word which pricks the romantic bubble of tender sentiment that was Dick's brightened mood. The dolphins' nakedness is not the only quality, however, which enforces their association with Sukie: when she passed out, it was to fall "in a posture as supple as a pool". The dolphins — "powerful mermaid"" at their water-play — possess the same sensuous liquidity with which Sukie had thrilled Dick.

Lissome Sukie is at least as important as God in bringing Dick safely through his long stint of oil-pouring. Sleeplessness and increasing weariness lead to a mental state at once vividly active and surreally dislocated. Dick creates an image of Sukie that he moves at will about the latrine (which at one point metamorphoses into a ferny cave), and continually talks to. But her image has a life of its own:

> 'You see,' he said when he met her again, about a hundred yards further down the cave, 'pouring oil out of this drum is my job.'
> 'Sure,' said Sukie: and leaning forward she stared close into his eyes, laying her beautiful cool eyes almost to touch his briny, swollen lids.
> 'Oh, sure!' she said again: and turning, hopped away on her unnaturally elongated feet, nervously folding and unfolding her ears. (p.132)

Sukie has become Sukie/Thomas: her eyes come as near as Thomas's did, and the last couple of clauses differ only by a change of pronoun from their earlier appearance. But Dick's prolonged exposure to danger, which matures him, has a price. Even as, towards the novel's end, he imagines "a chastened, adoring Sukie — fawning round his heroic person" (p.267), he realises that he has outgrown her, and he casts her image aside. Of this, Hughes writes in 'Fear and *In Hazard*':

> you *cannot* acquire the power of enduring, with sangfroid, continual danger of death without losing, at the other end of the scale, your finer sensitiveness.[11]

Although Hughes may not have faced danger of the order faced by Dick, this insight sprang from personal experience. After his Balkan adventure he had found his "finer perceptions, both in intellectual and in human relationships" so "badly damaged" that it took him months to recover.[12]

Perhaps the strangest component in the rhythmic series which grows out of Dick's encounter with Sukie follows in the wake of his bungled arrest of Ao Ling. When he comes to pick up the unconscious Chinaman:

> He was astonished at the softness, now, of the limp body in his arms: the smoothness of the skin: and his shame grew. Ao Ling hanging limp like that in his arms was almost as light as Sukie had been. (p.211)

The line separating the sensuous from the sexual is often a narrow one: Ling's wrist seems to Dick "limp as a girl's" (p.210). Both of Dick's encounters compel him to experience the 'Other', and to experience the Other in the body. But just as his prolonged exposure to danger damages his sensitivity in so far as his attitude towards Sukie is concerned, so it does with regard to Ling. His immediate feeling upon knocking out the Chinaman is shame, and he fantasizes about freeing him when they reach Belize: perhaps Ling will be eternally grateful to him, and save his life in turn "in some desperate fracas in Central China" (p.257). But not long afterwards he experiences a reversal of feeling:

> As for that Chinaman, how odd that he had been so concerned about him! Let him die. There are plenty of Chinamen in the world: one less makes no odds. (p.267)

That Dick's new strength is purchased at the cost of a new callousness is nowhere better shown than here: he has lost that sensitivity to the 'Other' which his encounter with Sukie bred in him. Momentarily he grasped the living humanness of Ling — but only to throw it away again as something of little worth. Yet it is now, at the novel's end, that Hughes shows us one way in which his two young men are kin: Ling, handcuffed on the hospital bed, begins to dream:

> He was surprised to find a Fukienese girl on the cot beside him. He raised himself on one elbow, to embrace her: but the fine hair on her face and hands warned him that she was but a fox in human shape. (p.269)

Ling, we must assume, is sexually experienced where Dick is not; but the congruence between his fox-girl and Dick's lemur-girl (the chime between "Fukienese" and "Sukie" can hardly be fortuitous) suggests the common rootedness of male erotic dreams. No sympathy may exist between their conscious minds, but in the deep unconscious we come upon eidola that link them with tantalizing threads.

IV

The experiences of Ao Ling and Dick Watchett point up the power which the archetypes of childhood exert over minds that are no longer the minds of children. Ling's dream reveals the compulsion that the father still exercises over his imagination; Dick's prayer shows the appeal that a child's God still holds for him in a time of stress. Between them there is of course this difference: that Dick's archetype is a source of comfort, Ling's only of pain. Yet neither has freed himself of regressive urgings which the rationalism of the growing man would wish to exorcize.

The author of *In Hazard* is no less fascinated by the limits of human freedom than the author of *A High Wind in Jamaica*. Both novels turn on the issue of survival. *A High Wind*, in focussing upon Emily and the pirates, had in some sense set the one against the other. In *In Hazard* there is no such division of interest — if *Archimedes* survives, her crew is likely to survive: personal good and social good amount to the same thing: to work for one's own survival is to work for the survival of all. What the novel seems to show, however, in revealing "the ceaseless professional heroism of all but one of those"[13] who man the ship, are the limits of human will and self-determination in so far as bravery and its contrary, cowardice, are concerned.

It is often assumed that these qualities are subject to the will, to acts of volition. The coward is what he is because he has failed to master himself: had he only shown sufficient will, he could have overcome his shortcomings. The hero, conversely, is one who has risen to the challenge consciously and effortfully. Heroism is will in action, cowardice the failure of will. Now it is a part of Hughes's achievement in *In Hazard* to show up the limitedness of such assumptions. The virtuous conduct of the First Mate, Mr. Buxton, illustrates the degree of truth which they contain; but the behaviour of Captain Edwardes and Mr. Rabb, the Supernumerary officer, represent extremes of response which cannot be explained in terms of the success or failure of will.

Let us first consider Mr. Buxton. When ordered by the Captain to attempt to secure Number 2 hatch, he moves gently and efficiently to do so. It is only when he arrives at the hatch-coaming that he realizes both the impossibility of fulfilling the order and the mortal peril in which, unthinkingly, he has placed himself. The first sea to break over the rail must carry him away. But he is saved from this fate by the hatch-tarpaulin, which leaps up and knocks him down, flattening him to the deck so that the wave passes harmlessly over him. When, subsequently, he sees the necessity of leading a group of the boys to Number 6 hatch, where something can be done, he is unable to move with his earlier alacrity:

> Mr. Buxton felt a curious unwillingness in his feet. All the top of him leant forward, but his feet seemed to creep backwards under him, like small rabbits looking for their holes.
> This is not so bad as the fore-deck, he said to himself; not half so bad. Safe as houses. 'Come on!' he yelled, and flung himself forward. (p. 57)

Momentarily he is weakened by his full consciousness of danger: but an effort of will in the form of a self-persuasion overcomes the reluctance. That is on the Wednesday. On the Friday he wakes from a ten-minute snatch of sleep in the wheelhouse to find a wave towering above him, and panics. He rushes out, cuts off his trouser-legs at the knee in order to swim better, and dons a life-belt. These are the involuntary actions of a body shocked, for a time, out of touch with intelligence: it is only when his intelligence has been brought spontaneously back into play by the wave which drops down the funnel-hole, that he realizes his own predicament and, by "paying attention to that most important thing of all, not losing his head" (p.120) — that is, by a willed exercise of self-discipline — recovers his equilibrium.

The behaviour of Mr. Rabb shows what can happen when the conscious mind goes into abeyance and remains there. It is interesting, however, that his initial failure to obey orders and assist with the covering of Number 6 hatch is a considered and even "wise" response. He has had enough experience of fear to know how it can disable a man:

> Obviously, now, the thing to do was to take no grave risks until he had got used to the situation, and his fear had melted away of itself — as it surely would, in a short while.
>
> He therefore decided to make his way to the bridge. That was a proper place, after all, for an officer to be in an emergency.
>
> But perhaps he might stop for a rest somewhere, on the way. (p. 63)

His response mixes logic and self-deception. Unlike Mr. Buxton, who moves without thinking to obey the Captain's command, Mr. Rabb thinks before doing so — and thinking gives fear the opportunity to master him. Once it has the upper hand —

> He was not really conscious any more. His actions were automatic as a sleepwalker's, with the unswerving tenacity of purpose of pure instinct — like a shark snapping. (p. 90)

Mr. Buxton's momentary panic is of the same order, unconscious and instinctual; but whereas his intelligence is caught (by sleep) with its trousers down, Mr. Rabb actively rationalizes himself into limbo: his mind connives at its own switching-off. Captain Edwardes can only get Rabb to leave the bridge by convincing him that the next sea to hit it will carry it away. Rabb comes to on deck and is, for a brief period, 'rational' again. When Buxton orders him to Number 2 hatch, his anger blazes up:

> Rabb was truly furious. Here! He had been working all the day, and night, superhumanly, and always chivvied by the mate! However, he turned to go: and really meant to go forward, only on the way those stinking black clouds began coming up again over his brain — fear had got him again. So he thought he would take a short rest first, and climbed down a companion; and found himself among the Chinese.

Like blind puppies huddling together from the cold. Rabb paused for a moment near them: his fear was reinforced by their communion of fear, and he began burrowing under them as if to disappear altogether from view. (pp. 96-7)

By the end of the book his sense of being persecuted has crystallized into the conviction that Captain and First Mate have tried to kill him. His perceptions are distorted, of course, but though he is perhaps a little mad, the distortion is not that great. In losing the sense of being a member of a community working for the survival of its members, he has transformed himself into a solitary individual. This renders him unfit for further sea-going, for the imperatives of his profession have to do with the mutual interests of a group; and Captain Edwardes has no alternative but to put in a report that will finish his career. The involuntary nature of Rabb's submission to fear is given in that phrase "and really meant to go forward": but to have an intention and to carry it out are two different things. When Captain Edwardes at the end of the book reflects upon Rabb, it is with sympathy and not with contempt:

The man was an efficient and popular officer; a clean-living man. He had broken down in the storm, that was true. But that was bad luck. A man has no right to have to face such a storm as that. (p.262)

"Bad luck" is a phenomenon that exists beyond will. Rabb is broken by a combination of circumstances — outwardly, a given predicament, and inwardly, given psychic conditions — over which he can exert no control. His experience again illustrates the limits of human freedom — of what it means for a man to be condemned to be himself — neither more, nor less.

But if the storm effects a kind of psychic contraction in Mr. Rabb, it effects a kind of psychic expansion in Captain Edwardes. Unlike most men, who are weakened by danger, Edwardes is strengthened by it; he is one of those "whose minds and bodies can only work at their highest pitch under its stimulus" (p.163). When the storm reaches a height that compels him to recognise that it is "no longer an issue between himself and his Owner, but . . . an issue between himself and his Maker" (p. 82), Edwardes feels himself "full of power, like a prophet" (p. 80); he is possessed by "a gigantic exhilaration" (p. 82). The part played by will in this expansion is minimal: the prophet is not great by virtue of will, but by virtue of innate potencies. Again, the Captain is "like an artist in a bout of inspiration" (p. 82) — and inspiration lies beyond the operation of volition: it is a mystical form of instinctuality. One may say, I suppose, that his possession of such powers (or better perhaps, *by* such powers) is a matter of luck: it is the Captain's good fortune to become, in the storm, a huge man, while it is Rabb's bad luck to be broken by it. Neither *chooses* to be the man he is, neither wills it.

The common language of vulgar thought would describe Captain Edwardes as a 'hero' and Mr. Rabb as a 'coward'. In depicting the involuntary nature of these extremes, Richard Hughes suggests again the extent to which men's behaviour is shaped by forces beyond their control, and the extent to which his understanding of the human psyche is deterministic in character.

V

Freud saw the basic aim of psychoanalysis as being to render conscious in a person what previously had been unconscious. For the patient, incapacitated by repression, "everything pathogenic in the unconscious must be transferred into consciousness"[14] in order that a cure may be effected. I have already described how Hughes himself came to understand the symbolic significance of his hurricane: his discovery was a making conscious of the unconscious. He seems to have regarded the extreme phenomenon as possessing the power of a psychic catalyst: it can force to the surface of a man's mind truths about himself that before have lain dormant.

Such a recognition comes within the tale to Mr.Buxton in the aftermath of the storm; and it seems to me that his recognition is as important for *In Hazard* as is Emily's discovery of her identity in *A High Wind in Jamaica*. The two events are handled in ways so remarkably similar as to suggest that Hughes intended a reader to connect them. Compare the following passages:

> And then an event did occur, to Emily, of considerable importance. She suddenly realised who she was. (*HW* p.134)
>
> Mr. Buxton, sucking his apple on the bridge, suddenly realised for the first time why he had gone to sea. . . (*IH* p.169)

Both Buxton and Emily muse on their discoveries, which are presented in a continuous and orderly form. Now compare:

> It must not be supposed that she argued it all out in this ordered, but rather long-winded fashion. Each consideration came to her in a momentary flash, quite innocent of words. . . (*HW* p.137)
>
> All this is too simple: but it is the gist of the conclusions Mr. Buxton now came to. The gist only, for being so hungry he thought in jerks, flashes of insight which were not connected up as I am putting them here. (*IH* pp.169-70)

". . . a momentary flash . . ."; ". . . flashes of insight . . .": Emily's and Buxton's discoveries are alike intuitive and discontinuous. While the similarities between the two processes are striking, however, the substance of what the two characters realize remains very different — so different, indeed, that they may be said to be contraries. Emily's discovery that she is she (or, more accurately, that she is I) causes her also to intuit those 'imperatives of identity' which later prompt her to kill the Dutch Captain. In discovering why he went to sea — "It was because he liked Virtue: and was not the Economic Man" (p.169) — Buxton discovers why he is willing to risk that very "parcel of flesh" which Emily's discovery requires at all costs the preservation of. Here is the crucial passage:

> the working of a ship calls for certain qualities — virtues, if you like — which do not seem to be appropriate today to the relations of employers and employed on shore. The shore-labourer's liability is limited: the seaman's is unlimited. The seaman may be called on to give the utmost that he is able, even to laying down his life. That is not an imposition on him, a piece of chicanery on the part of his employers: it is inherent in the profession he practises. A necessary draw-back? — Oddly enough, it even seems to be the reason why certain men, such as Mr. Buxton, embrace that profession in the first place. (pp.170-71)

Asking himself why a man should be drawn to the practice of virtue, the narrator says: "I can only suppose that Virtue (using the word in its Roman rather than its Victorian sense) is a natural instinct with some men: they really cannot be happy unless they can give it an outlet." *Natural instinct* is the very same force that caused Emily to conceal her raw identity: the preservation of the ego, of the self, became her fundamental concern. *In Hazard*, then, articulates a counter-truth that is also fundamental: the need to risk the self is also an innate need. Buxton's 'positive' instinct balances Emily's 'negative' one. Going to sea is an act of altruism. Hughes's analysis suggests, however, that Buxton's profession can only be said to be freely 'chosen' within the limits that constrain human choice. 'Natural instinct', on the one hand, drove Buxton to seek a profession that would allow him to practise Virtue; social circumstances, on the other, restricted his field of choice, for, as the narrator says, "Sea-going is almost the only profession open to the poor man" (p.170). Only if he'd been a different man could Mr. Buxton have chosen other than he did.

Hughes's imagination has softened in *In Hazard*. In *A High Wind* his pirates take a calculated risk in disburdening themselves of the children, and their altruism is cruelly mocked by circumstances. (There is no good deed which does not have its appropriate punishment.) One might distinguish the world of *A High Wind* from that of *In Hazard* by saying that the former is ruled by Nemesis, the latter by Providence. Both Nemesis and Providence are constructions, no doubt, of the human mind, attempts to turn a neutral universe into an anthropocentric one. When this is said, however, Hughes's imagination, which is fully alive to the infinite human need to impose structures of understanding on experience, has grown more tolerant.

Peter Thomas, in writing that *Archimedes* "remains afloat as much by accident as by endeavour",[15] points up nicely the fact that the ironies of natural chance may work in favour of human survival. Within the novel, it is the Captain and the First Mate who most clearly see that "their worst disasters" conspire to save them (p.164). Buxton offers us these insights:

> suppose their pumps had been working from the first? It was the free water at the bottom of the ship that would have been first pumped out. And with nothing to counteract the weight above, she might easily have turned right over. (p.162)
> Suppose the funnel had not gone, when it did? Suppose those guys had held, to more than their theoretic strength? A sailing-ship has been laid on her beam-ends with nothing aloft but her bare poles before now. The resistance of that enormous funnel would have been even greater, in proportion. If the funnel had not gone, and eased her, might not the ship have turned over? (p.164)

Buxton himself is saved by a chance irony — the tarpaulin which, in clubbing him to the deck, prevents the next sea from washing him overboard. Towards the end of the book we discover that the tidal wave raised by the hurricane has engulfed a town, killing its two thousand inhabitants. But, as Captain Edwardes sees, that same wave saved *Archimedes* by lifting her over banks which in normal sea-conditions would have wrecked her. This, he thinks, together with the fact that he has not lost a single man, is a sure sign that "the Lord our God is very merciful!" (p.244). This exclamation comes just four pages before Mr. MacDonald falls overboard and drowns, and might be described as tempting Fate. Are the gods just, do they make of our pleasant vices instruments to plague us, or do they tease us for their sport — cruelly? Although *In Hazard*, like *Lear*, leaves the question open (why posit gods at all?), it is, despite Mr. MacDonald, far from being a negative book. If a novel, like a poem, can express a stage in its author's psychic autobiography, then *In Hazard* indicates the ways in which Richard Hughes's mind had grown since creating the sardonic ego-centred world of *A High Wind in Jamaica*.

Chapter Nine: Theory (2)

I

In December 1938, some four and a half months after the publication of *In Hazard*, Richard Hughes devoted one of his occasional columns in *Time and Tide* to the discussion of certain theoretical literary issues[1]. He began by condemning "that particular form of escapism where the born . . . poet endeavours to escape from his destiny by way of politics". Since the orthodoxy of the period would say that it is the uncommitted poet who is the escapist, Hughes's stance in his article must count as one of his most controversial. But he denied that he was "preaching the doctrine of the Ivory Tower":

> The poet lives in the world: lives in even closer contact with it than the politician, because his whole body is one superlative sense-organ. For the poet, more than for anyone else, the visible world exists. He is not immune from the horror of things done or said or thought, he is less immune than the next man: but his peculiar remedy for them does not lie in action, it lies in passion. There is something of the redeemer-doctrine bound up in the nature of poetry. Looking at the thing in terms of psychological utility, one might say that the genesis of poetry is the resolution of conflict in the mind of the poet, and its justification is the resolution and sublimation of conflict in the mind of the reader. Only the *superhuman* intensity of the poet's capacity for passion makes this externalising of the resolution possible: no wonder, then, that he is tempted to escape from it into activity!

Hughes's article looks both forwards and backwards in time. On the one hand it is scarcely possible to read it and not be reminded of how he himself succumbed, in 1921, to the temptation to escape from "passion" into "action" — political action — and how, later, he regretted it. What he has to say about "the genesis of poetry" both picks up Robert Graves's 'Neurotic' theory of poetry, and connects with Hughes's use of the theory in explaining his fascination with *Phemius* and the hurricane. On the other hand, in advocating that the poet resist the "insidious temptation of propaganda", the piece anticipates the distinction made between the 'pure' novelist and the propagandist novelist in his article of 1948, 'The Writer's Duty'.

From these reflections on poetry, Hughes turns to the novel. Clearly, he is still out to provoke his reader:

> Novel-writing is plainly the most anachronistic form of mental activity, whether among the arts or sciences, that is still carried on today respectably (it has not yet been driven into the same corner as astrology and palmistry).

It is not 'in technique' that the novel is outmoded, but in its insistence that its business is with human lives and human affairs:

> It is a long time since science discarded the notion that Man is the beneficial purpose of the Universe: that the world he inhabits is its centre, and that everything in it was made for his enjoyment or for his salutary castigation. It is quite a time even since pictorial art discarded the notion that the human body was the only thing worth representing (if indeed such a theory was ever held, except by certain Academy painters). Yet it is still taken for granted that a novel must be 'about people'. Why? Why, if you recognise that a still-life or landscape by Cezanne may be of equal value with a portrait of his, is it still taken for granted that the universe of the novel alone must still be anthropocentric?

Why, then, he goes on to postulate,

> should not a school of novelists arise — say in twenty years' time — who not merely reduce Man to a position of equality with the other objects they evoke, but may even write novels containing no persons — human or otherwise — at all? If their evocations are as truthful and as vivid as ours: if the construction of the story is as satisfying in form: if above all the whole is of as absorbing interest as the novel of today, which of us — especially among those who concede these liberties as a matter of course to painting — could reasonably object?

That the author of *In Hazard* should entertain such thoughts should hardly surprise us. A number of the book's reviewers felt that Hughes's hurricane held a position of more than equality with *Archimedes*'s crewmen; and though one may think them guilty of misreading, one can see why they should feel this way. Marie Scott-James, in writing that Hughes's 'hero' is the wind, indicates how far along the road Hughes had come, for some readers, towards exemplifying his own theory.

At this point one may, perhaps, be forgiven for giving way to the temptation to speculate about the direction Hughes's fiction might have taken had not the Second World War occurred. Might he not have written an experimental novel treating of the life of objects which excluded or subordinated the life of human beings? — have continued to develop as an essentially poetic novelist?

But Hughes did not adopt the programme which his article of 1938 outlines: instead he took a deliberate step backwards towards the nineteenth-century novel. Opting for the novel of characters, the novel as instrument of social and historical analysis, the anthropocentric novel, he re-committed himself to that literary form which he had described as being "antiquated to the point of medievalism: totally discredited in every other region of thought". Some of his reasons for doing so I have already mentioned in the biographical section of this book. Before moving on to discuss others, it is pertinent to glance at the French *nouveaux romanciers*, whose novelistic programme Hughes anticipated with uncanny accuracy in 1938, and whose emergence in the second half of the 1950s he no less precisely prophesied.

In an essay first published in 1957, Alain Robbe-Grillet, the chief theorist of the *nouveau roman*, declares: "The novel that contains characters belongs well and truly to the past, it was peculiar to an age — that of the apogee of the individual":[2] the novel of characters was a bourgeois art-form, but the twentieth century has "abandoned the idea of the omnipotence of the individual". Citing *Nausea, The Outsider, Journey to the End of Night* and *The Castle*, Robbe-Grillet argues that "the creators of character, in the traditional sense, can now do nothing more than present us with puppets in whom they themselves no longer believe". Robbe-Grillet's programme addresses itself to emancipating objects from the tyranny of anthropomorphism:

> All around us, defying our pack of animistic or domesticating adjectives, things *are there*. Their surface is smooth, clear and intact, without false glamour, without transparency. The whole of our literature has not yet managed even to begin to penetrate them, to alter their slightest curve.

In speaking of purifying objects and liberating them from the tyranny of human meanings, Robbe-Grillet is close to the Hughes of 1938. The Frenchman later says:

> So that the first impact of objects and gestures should be that of their *presence*, and that this presence should then continue to dominate,

taking precedence over any explanatory theory which would attempt to imprison them in some system of reference, whether it be sentimental, sociological, Freudian, metaphysical, or any other.

But there is a problem here. One may well enquire as to what extent it is in fact possible to realise, in language, the unconditional otherness of objects. Even if we leave aside the Saussurean distinction between signifier and signified (between the word as material object and as meaning), we are still faced with the fact that language in action cannot be divorced from consciousness. Robbe-Grillet himself recognizes that objectivity in the sense of "a completely impersonal way of looking at things — is only too obviously a chimera". Furthermore, it remains the case that even a novelist attempting to free objects from human associations must subject them (if he is not to produce chaos) to some form of ordering. A camera panning steadily round a room is unselective, all-inclusive, in its perception of objects; but it is not free: in picturing *this* room, *this* series of objects, it acknowledges the principle of selectivity. Richard Hughes, in conceiving of a novel dealing with inanimate things, writes:

> The new novel would be an exact parallel of the old because it would be in the same relation to natural science that the novel of today is to history and biography. Where the novel of today tells us plausible things about what might, but has not, happened to people who might, but do not, exist, the new novel would tell us of things that might, but do not happen to objects and substances which might, but do not exist.

Like Robbe-Grillet, Hughes conceives of the overthrowing of what he calls "a false, anthropomorphic, anthropocentric universe" — even that "attenuated anthropomorphism" served up by "Sir James Jeans and the other devotees of 'The Great Mathematician'". But he too does not recognise the problem that I have defined: how, in practice, is the novelist to liberate objects from his own perceiving consciousness? He would, no doubt, were he alive today, be fascinated by the insistence of the physicist Fritjof Capra "that the human observer is not only necessary to observe the properties of an object, but is necessary even to define those properties".[3] Or, as Werner Heisenberg puts it, "What we observe is not nature itself, but nature exposed to our method of questioning".[4] Quantum theory denies the Cartesian partition between the I and the world: "the classical ideal of an objective description of nature is no longer valid".[5] What price, then, the detachment of language from the mind using it — in a novel or any other form of discourse?

Hughes does not, in fact, propose the writing of a new kind of novel without adding an important qualification: "If their evocations are as truthful and as vivid as ours" etcetera "which of us . . . could reasonably object?" To which theoretically one might answer: None of us, I suppose. But such a reply would be naive. Hughes himself was criticized for daring to raise a hurricane to the status of a 'character' in *In Hazard*. It is not, therefore, surprising, that M. Robbe-Grillet's novels should, as he himself puts it, not have "been greeted on their publication with unanimous warmth":[6]

> From the disapproving semi-silence into which the first (*The Erasers*) fell, to the violent mass rejection by the daily press of the second (*The Voyeur*), there was little progress, except for the number of books sold, which was appreciably greater.

Robbe-Grillet was convinced that he was writing for 'man in the street' but it would seem that the man in the street found — and still finds — him extremely difficult to read. What indeed is the common reader to make of a novel without recognizable characters and a recognizable story? Was it not inevitable that novels of the order postulated by Hughes and Robbe-Grillet would in general only prove palatable to those trained to recognize the conventionality of those novels against which the new novel sets its face? The new novel began with the disadvantage of having to create the audience which could appreciate it — and it is in fact characteristic of so-called post-modernist art (whether in painting, music or literature) that its practitioners have been obliged to supply the theoretical apparatuses by which their works might be understood.[7]

But whilst Hughes was undoubtedly capable of writing a novel of the kind he had imagined, there is no evidence to suggest that he seriously considered doing so. Once the idea of writing a novel "of my own times" had worked its way through to his conscious mind, it seems that he had no choice but to embark on it. He always argued that the true writer works under compulsion, writes because he must: and indeed should not put pen to paper unless he cannot do otherwise. *The Human Predicament* represents — it is there in the adjective — a commitment to the socio-historical novel of characters, of knowable individuals. Fundamental to this commitment is the following ethical perception: that the novel performs a function crucial to the health of a civilized society, a function that no other art-form can perform with equal cogency. Hughes's most succinct statement of his belief is contained in his Blashfield Address of 1969 to the American Academy of Arts and Letters.[8] In this Address, the fruit of long years of reflection, he may fairly be said to be saying the most important thing he knows: a truth which humanity ignores at its peril.

At the root of his argument lies a perception of the ultimate aloneness of human beings. Modern societies may continue to improve methods of communication, may create vast cellular constructions in which people live like bees in hives — yet these individuals (in a phrase opposed to Donne) "remain incommunicable islands":

> Even in married love we can't become *self*-conscious with the other partner's own 'I-ness': we are still each in solitary confinement, only tapping out loving messages on the dividing wall.

It is against this state of affairs that Hughes can affirm the importance of the novel:

> Only when reading novels (or watching plays and films, to the extent that these too are forms of fiction) do we repeatedly adopt someone else's 'I am' for our own, are let out of our solitary cells, think what the other man thinks even while he is thinking it, 'identify' with him and feel what he feels.

Hughes, of course, is not the only twentieth-century novelist to contrast the knowable people of novels with the unknowable people of life. Here is E.M. Forster:

> In daily life we never understand each other, neither complete clairvoyance nor complete confessional exists. We know each other approximately, by external signs, and these serve well enough as a basis for society and even for intimacy. But people in a novel can be understood completely by a reader, if the novelist wishes; their inner as well as their outer life can be exposed. And this is why they often seem more definite than characters in history, or even our own friends.[9]

The two novelists would seem to occupy the same strongpoint — or bunker. But Forster, in taking care to distinguish between Homo Sapiens and Homo Fictus — the one made of blood and bone, the other of black marks on a page — is at once more circumspect and less confident than Hughes, who does not feel it necessary to remind us that people in novels and people in the street are not the same: enough that reading gives us the illusion that this is so. Hughes's trust in the novel would seem to be absolute.

If he does not trouble to make Forster's discrimination, however, he makes others. The most significant of these is between those who can *assert* that all human beings are persons (Churchmen and Humanists, for example, or historians and biographers), and the novelist, who brings us to experience them as such. Historian and biographer construct their subjects from external evidence: "Biography [is] the perspective drawing of an object, History a diagram of the interaction of such objects". Biographer and historian present their subjects to us for objective contemplation: the biographer or the historian may tell us what George Orwell or George III did, and what, on occasion, A or B said. But if, says Hughes, they depart from description and, by acts of imagination, think themselves into their subjects (as some do), they become, to that extent, novelists. Hughes is not out to denigrate historians and biographers, to set them up in theoretical opposition to novelists: the biographer, rather, is the novelist's "nearest cousin". But, as I shall go on to argue, Hughes's definition of history is a narrow one; and, in *The Human Predicament*, he himself writes as historian and biographer as well as novelist.

Having defined the specific virtue of the novel, he deplores the man who not only regards novel-reading as a waste of time, but thinks his dismissal of fiction proof of his serious-mindedness. Now arguments about the value of novels — or, to avoid what is a comparatively modern term, *prose fiction* — are as old as the genre, and it is typical of fiction to include debates about its own value within itself. In *The Tale of Genji*, the tenth-century Japanese novel which Hughes rated alongside *War and Peace* and *The Red and the Black* as an influence on his fictional practice, Murasaki Shikibu causes her hero, Prince Genji, to put both sides of the argument. Finding his adopted daughter, Lady Tamakatsura, absorbed in a romance, he expresses the traditional Confucian contempt for *monogatari*:

> I sometimes think that young ladies exist for no other purpose than to provide purveyors of the absurd and improbable with a market for their wares. I am sure that the book you are so intent upon is full of the wildest nonsense. Yet knowing this all the time, you are completely captivated by its extravagances and follow them with the utmost excitement . . .[10]

He quickly relents, however, and begins to speak approvingly of them:

> There is, it seems, an art of so fitting each part of the narrative into the next that, though all is mere invention, the reader is persuaded that such things might easily have happened and is as deeply moved as though they were actually going on around him. We may know with one part of our minds that every incident has been invented for the express purpose of impressing us; but (if the plot is constructed with the requisite skill) we may all the while in another part of our minds be burning with indignation at the wrongs endured by some wholly imaginary princess.

Comparing history with fiction, Genji finds reason for valuing most highly the latter:

> For history-books such as the Chronicles of Japan show us only one small corner of life; whereas these diaries and romances which I see

piled around you contain, I am sure, the most minute information
about all sorts of people's private affairs . . .

Warming still further to the task of defending the novel, Genji produces his
own theory as to why the novel came into being in the first place. The
novelist's experience has moved him

> to an emotion so passionate that he can no longer keep it shut up in his
> heart. Again and again something in his own life or in that around him
> will seem to the writer so important that he cannot bear to let it pass
> into oblivion. There must never come a time, he feels, when men do not
> know about it.

One could hardly hope to find so accurate an account of how Richard
Hughes was moved to begin *The Human Predicament* as this theory set out in
a novel written a millenium before!

Hughes goes much further than Murasaki in his defence of the novel,
however. Is not the despiser of novels "confessing an unwillingness to face
the essential nature of his fellow-men and himself?" He suggests that the
novel has, in history, contributed morally to the advancement of
civilization. He does not believe it purely coincidental that penal reform
and the abolition of the slave trade, for example, occurred in a century
during which novels came to be more widely read than any other kind of
book: these social reforms, he asserts, were "indubitable fruits of a new . . .
recognition that criminals and even Negroes were not Things but Persons".
Naturally he cannot *prove* that the mass reading of novels has had the effect
of expanding human consciousness and awakening human conscience:
certain kinds of propositions are susceptible neither of proof nor disproof:
and this is one of them. Hughes is arguing partially by intuition: the
acceptance of his proposition by a reader depends upon its power to
provoke in him or her spontaneous agreement — or the reciprocal
confirmation of intuition. Hughes does not, however, leave the argument
there: there yet remains to be teased out a political implication, and it is a
challenging one. The rejection of the novel, for him, masks something still
more dire than escapism — it masks solipsism. The solipsist is one who
cannot recognize other people as persons, as living egos, like himself: he
sees them rather as "machines mass-produced on the genetic assembly-
line", "things to be regarded . . .as mere obstacles or raw materials or
tools" — to be cleared out of the way, or utilized. A "mankind", he says, "in
which such solipsists gained the upper hand would be a mankind headed
for destruction". But of course this is what has happened in recent history:

It was the vast failure to learn that lesson that others are as much persons as oneself which built the gas-ovens. The archetypal non-reader of Fiction was Hitler.

At this point literary theory, political philosophy and psychological analysis come together: for one of Hughes's purposes in *The Human Predicament* is to show Hitler, the totalitarian, as a solipsist for whom others are "mere obstacles or raw materials or tools". Hughes is not, of course, saying that the Nazis murdered six million Jews because they (the Nazis) didn't read enough novels; but he *is* saying that novel-reading fosters an order of humanist awareness which contrasts sharply with the reductivism characteristic of Nazism and other comparable political (or for that matter politico-religious) movements.

The Blashfield Address brings me back to Hughes's distinction in his essay of 1948, 'The Writer's Duty', between the 'pure' novelist and the propagandist novelist. Can the distinction be maintained? Can the author of *The Human Predicament* claim to be a 'pure' writer? Two related issues need to be aired here: the meaning of the terms 'propagandist' and 'political', and the question of *intention*. The intention of the propagandist novelist, says Hughes, is "to move people in a particular political direction":[11] he wishes, that is, to *persuade*. Hughes, conversely, may be said to want to *present*: if, he says, he introduced political ideas into a novel, they would be a means and not an end. The end would be "the story I had to tell". Now in this book I have been at pains to argue that Hughes is far more than a mere story-teller — that he is a novelist of ideas. As soon as *ideas* are perceived to exist in a work of fiction, I would suggest, assent and dissent are automatically brought into play. Those readers who argued passionately about Hughes's portrayal of children in *A High Wind* were not content to think that they were merely reading a story. Hughes might, of course, argue that he had not intended to *persuade* his readers that children were like this; but that was not how it seemed to certain readers, and they, surely, were right to perceive that something important was at stake in the book. This brings me to the two problematical terms, 'propagandist' and 'political'. In his splendid essay on Dickens, George Orwell writes:

> every writer, especially every novelist, *has* a 'message', whether he admits it or not, and the minutest details of his work are influenced by it. All art is propaganda. Neither Dickens nor the majority of Victorian novelists would have thought of denying this.[12]

If this broad sense of the term 'propaganda' is accepted, it seems impossible to deny that *The Human Predicament* is a work of propaganda. The novel authoritatively proposes a theory of the relation of the human individual to the wider world, so that assent and dissent are immediately brought into play. Furthermore, as I shall argue in the next chapter, it seeks to confront the reader with the question 'Are people persons?' in such a way as to compel the answer 'Yes'. Hughes himself may have thought of the term 'political' in a pretty precise sense as relating to the ideologies behind particular parties or systems of government. Such a definition would nowadays satisfy few people; and I myself feel that Hughes's theorizing about personality is inescapably political. Hughes may have wished to hold on to his sense that he was a 'pure' writer: but, as the Blashfield Address — which is openly propagandist — shows, matters had gone too far for that purity to be maintained (if, indeed, it had ever been a 'pure' purity). *The Human Predicament* is not, fundamentally, a different kind of novel to Koestler's *Darkness at Noon* — or, for that matter, *Nineteen Eighty-Four*. Hughes might have kept clear of 'politics' in a limited sense, but that his was a political sensibility in the broadest sense seems to me undeniable. How, situated in history as he was, could he have been otherwise? And how, being a novelist, could he have refused that sensibility free play in a fiction of his own times?

II

One need only set 'The Writer's Duty' and the Blashfield Address against the ill-starred University poem 'The Heathen's Song' to see how far Hughes travelled as a religious man. It is the distance between paganism and Christianity. As a very young man, Hughes valued Beauty above Truth. Beauty is a constant: it may be touched and savoured: it endures, like Keats's urn. Truth is a much more elusive thing: grasp at it, it tends to slip through your fingers: it is relative, protean. In his unsent letter to Amabel Williams-Ellis, Hughes wrote:

> . . .truth is to my mind an island: i.e. if you will walk about on it looking for it, you are all right as long as you argue in circles (though even then you will obviously get no further) but if you proceed logically in a straight line — whatever direction you take — you are bound sooner or later to fall off into the sea.

This is Hughes the dandy, flexing a wit that delights in *reductio ad absurdum*. But the published title of the Blashfield Address in Britain — 'Fiction as Truth' — is determined, even aggressive (attack being the best form of defence, according to the proverb). This is the manifesto of a writer whose commitment roots itself in moral perceptions which emerge from a deeply religious sensibility.

Hughes's early Introduction to his verse had, for the purposes of discussing the nature and origins of poetry, defined Man as a Neurotic Animal, a Communicative Animal, and a Pattern-Making Animal. To these a number of his post-war writings imply the addition of a fourth: Man as a Religious Animal. Distinguishing in 'The Writer's Duty' between the politician and the writer, he suggests that whilst the politician's power must always be imposed on some who are unwilling to accept it, every reader accepts the power of the writer "of his own free will". The writer's power is a copy of the power that God wields: one may sense God's power, but choose to ignore it. The duty of the 'pure' writer, then, is not to offer solutions to problems, "new answers to old riddles":

> Rather it lies in the framing of new riddles, posing new questions. In that too he works in imitation of his Maker. Whose every word to man is — not an answer, but a question.[13]

Comparisons of the writer's work to the work of God, of creator to Creator, are of course deeply rooted in the Christian tradition. Milton in *Areopagitica* writes:

> Who kills a man kills a reasonable creature, God's image; but he who destroys a good book, kills reason itself, kills the image of God, as it were in the eye.[14]

Among the Romantics, who made great play with the comparison, Coleridge held his "primary imagination . . . the living power and prime agent of all human perception", to be "a repetition in the finite mind of the eternal act of creation in the infinite I AM"; and his "secondary imagination", by whose power all artists create, to be identical with the first "in its kind of agency, and differing only in degree, and in the mode of its operation".[15] Caroline Glyn, who talked with Hughes about his writing, told Michael Bakewell that Hughes "did see fiction as incarnational, you know . . . he did see himself as carrying a certain work of God". The Blashfield Address, I think, suggests a specific importance for the novelist working "in imitation of his Maker": as God, in creating the world, has brought persons into being, so the novelist, through mimetic creation, brings us to experience persons from within as Others possessed of the same order of individual being as ourselves.

It is the ability which constitutes the novelist's "truth". There is no more contradiction between Hughes's notion that fiction is truth and his notion that truth is an island than there is in Milton's discussion of truth in *Areopagitica*. Milton presents us there with a myth: Truth came into the world as "a perfect shape most glorious to look on" — but afterwards was hewed by "a wicked race of deceivers" into a thousand pieces, and scattered to the four winds, so that it is beyond men to reassemble Truth's original form.[16] But he also says that Truth is protean,

> and perhaps tunes her voice according to the time, as Micaiah did before Ahab, until she be adjured into her own likeness. Yet it is not impossible that she may have more shapes than one. What else is all that rank of things indifferent, wherein Truth may be on this side or on the other, without being unlike herself?[17]

Truth is multifarious, and wears a different face in different times and cultures — and this is also a truth which the novelist seeks to express.

The version of the Blashfield Address which Hughes delivered at Coleg Harlech to the English-language section of The Welsh Academy on 1st September 1973 suggests that his mind had darkened to some degree in the four years since the talk was delivered in its original form. "Today," he suggested, "even the novelists themselves seem to have lost faith in themselves." To contemplate the novelist who spoke of himself as an entertainer merely and, condescendingly, as a purveyor of "'comfort for the spinster and the secretary, a temporary refuge for the reader in an imagined world'", thoroughly depressed him. Later still, in a letter to me of 23rd January 1976, he referred to "Robbe-Grillet's heresy". The theological metaphor radiates irony. To one who now saw the novelist's responsibility as being to recall to us what we truly are, *persons*, the practice of such novelists as Robbe-Grillet and Claude Simon (who, as I write, has been awarded the Nobel Prize for Literature) could only seem a turning away from the true religion. For, in characteristic novels such as *Jealousy* and *Triptych*, these novelists render human behaviour in an objective (if not always, in the case of Robbe-Grillet, external) and dispassionate manner. Human figures (they have ceased of course to be *characters*) are given equality of status with things, and human actions and speech as much or as little significance as a row of trees on a plantation or the play of neon lights on a wet roadway. Yet the *nouveau romanciers*, in breaking with the anthropocentric tradition of "the most anachronistic form of mental activity", had done no more than address themselves to a programme similar to that which Hughes himself had enthusiastically outlined in 1938 — at the mid-point, precisely, of his life-time.

Chapter Ten: *The Fox in the Attic* and *The Wooden Shepherdess*

I

In the Note which precedes the text of *The Fox in the Attic*, Hughes states that *The Human Predicament* is conceived as a long historical novel . . . a novel designed as a continuous whole . . . The decision to publish it volume by volume was taken because he was such a slow writer. The unfinished status of a work of art must create problems for the critic, and where the form and scope of the work remains uncertain, those problems are not lessened. In his Note Hughes leaves open the question as to whether the *Predicament* was to be a trilogy or a quartet (and indeed, late in his life, he told his secretary, Lucy McEntee, that he couldn't see the job being done in less than *five* volumes). The tripartite division of both *Fox* and *Shepherdess* suggests, however, that practical considerations dictated the necessity of volume-by-volume planning. The only sensible policy with regard to the discussion of *Fox* and *Shepherdess* seems to be to think of them as equivalent components of a notional whole of uncertain size: a whole whose thematic life is unitary, whose meaning would be cumulative, and whose overall form manifests itself in the life of its parts. In this chapter, then, I use the term 'novel' of the unfinished whole, the term 'volume' to denote *Fox* and *Shepherdess*, and the term 'Book' to denote each volume's largest parts: as did Hughes himself.

Hughes's pre-war novels might be described as 'unicellular': each pursues a single, integrated Event (*integrated* because it is constituted of many smaller connected events from conception to completion). *The Human Predicament*, however, is a multicellular organism, designed to stimulate the mind's "polyphonic faculty of connecting". The term Hughes used when discussing his later technique with Caroline Glyn — "multiple contrast" — suggests how juxtaposition becomes one of the chief weapons in his armoury. By counterpointing discrete, diverse and often dissonant fragments of human experience, Hughes hoped to provoke questions and recognitions in a reader's mind. A simple instance is the ironic contrast between atheistic Augustine and religious Mitzi in Chapters 6 and 7 of Book Three of *Fox*. Augustine is convinced that her blindness must turn Mitzi against God; but in reality it has precisely the opposite result — of bringing her to Him. A more complex instance of "multiple contrast" is offered in *Shepherdess* by the variety of perspectives bearing upon sex. Gilbert's semi-necrophilous conjunctions with his paralysed sleeping wife, Augustine's obscure desire for and guilt towards the adolescent Ree, Norah and the girls' uncontrollable rollings upon the slaughterhouse child Brian, Hitler's incest with Geli Raubal: none of these image 'normal' sexual behaviour. Yet the question they are liable to throw up is: What *does* constitute sexual 'normality'? Is there such a thing? Hughes's brief chapters, therefore, might be compared to the many facets of a large jewel: as you turn the jewel slowly under a steady source of light, different facets reflect it glitteringly and teasingly up at you.

But those brief chapters also build into sequences, and *Fox* and *Shepherdess* have their larger movements. The presence in them of a number of common concerns and motifs suggests that Hughes was seeking to establish some degree of organic patterning in these volumes. Both, obviously, feature a running contrast between life in Britain and life in Germany during the Twenties and Thirties. Both, again obviously, treat of violent and climactic historical events: the Munich Putsch in *Fox* and the Night of the Long Knives in *Shepherdess*: the one a reverse for Hitler, the other a triumph. (Hughes, we see, has lost none of his interest in the violent act: the Night of the Long Knives, indeed, is the most violent of all his scenes of violence, with all restraint and humanity thrown to the winds.) Other features common to both novels derive from the way Hughes uses his central character Augustine: and these I shall discuss at a later point in this chapter.

The major formal difference between *Fox* and *Shepherdess* has to do with the handling of time: with, specifically, the accommodation of 'fictional time' to 'historical time'. In restricting the events narrated in *Fox* to a few weeks of 1923, Hughes achieves a solid and highly satisfying accommodation between the two. Beginning *Shepherdess*, and faced with the problem of how to continue — how, that is, to retain narrative continuity and yet get significantly on in time towards 1945 — he fell between two stools. Book One of *Shepherdess*, opening in July 1924 in America, has a solidity comparable to that of *Fox*. Conscious, however, that he had scarcely made any inroads into the time-span which he had set himself to cover, Hughes in the subsequent Books resorted to a strategy which weakened the volume. What this strategy amounts to is a gradual acceleration — the squeezing of more and more objective historical time into fewer and fewer pages. Books Two and Three move us on at increasing speed: 'The Meistersingers' from winter 1923 (it goes back in time to pick up Mitzi) to April 1926, and 'Stille Nacht' from June 1926 to June 1934. Midway through Book Three, a piece of sleight-of-hand dissolves away six years in three chapters, and we slip from 1928 to 1934. Hughes's need to move his novel on has two results: a rapid switching of scenes tends to deprive the characters' lives of the firmness and depth of suggestibility which earlier Books had possessed; and Hughes feels obliged to supply linking passages which fill us in on what historically was taking place in Britain, Germany and America. Hughes's accessible, even chatty style cannot conceal the fact that these passages are essentially documentary, informational. Consider, for example:

> Everyone rallied behind the honest and even Quixotic Baldwin, the man they believed to detest all crunches (indeed last July's derided appeaser) now brought face-to-face with things which have *had* to come to the crunch. Baldwin was stressing the Constitutional point that yielding to outside pressure like this must sound the death-knell of parliamentary rule; and even Thomas (the railwaymen's leader) had answered that once the Constitution was challenged "then God help Britain unless the Government won!" — and had stumbled out of the House of Commons in tears. (*WS* p.234)

This passage is half-presented as thoughts going through the mind of Gilbert Wadamy: but only half-so — for it would seem quite artifical if presented wholly so. At such points, in fact, Hughes has ceased to write as a novelist and begun to write as a historian — a point I shall come back to later. The speeding up of fictional and historical time, far from proving exhilarating, causes *Shepherdess* to sag. It is impossible so to telescope historical events and leave anything for the mind to grasp of a truly novelistic richness — for unelaborated facts are not what the novel-reading imagination is attuned to going to work on. Book Three recovers — notably in Chapter 23 when Hughes returns to his characteristically indirect method of presentation of history (with imagery and obliquity of suggestion once more coming into their own) — but the problem of finding a satisfactory accommodation between fictional and historical time remained to be faced again in Volume Three.[1]

In his earlier novels, he had adopted the ploy of first-person narration. His narrators are historicized personas, imaginative projections of himself into the nineteenth century (*High Wind*) and the recent past (*In Hazard*).

But from *Fox* and *Shepherdess* embodied narrator has altogether disappeared, to be replaced by an impersonalized voice which, assuming the authority of a traditional omniscient narrator, comments as and when it wishes upon characters and events, and at one crucial stage advances a theoretical statement about the relation of the individual ego to its world which underpins the entire undertaking. The authoritative cast of the stance taken by Hughes is indicated by the pronominal form he favours — not the first person singular, but the first person plural: 'we', 'us', 'our':

> That primitive truth about selfhood we battle against at our peril. (*FA* p.101)
> But suppose that in the name of emergent Reason the very we-they line itself within us had been deliberately so blurred and denied. . .(*FA* p.103)

This first person plural draws the reader back into historical time, implicating him or her in its events and motions. The narrative voice assumes an authority for its conceptions and perceptions which is absolute. At such moments, it is as if Hughes were speaking with the impersonal voice of history itself.

II

Fundamental to Hughes's conception of the human predicament is an analysis of the relationship of self to others: of each human consciousness to humanity in general. He proposes that modern Western civilization, "in the name of emergent Reason" (*FA* p.102), has developed two paradigms for the understanding of this relationship: that of the Cartesian cogito, which restricts the 'I' to an "adamantine pinpoint"; and that of Humanism, which seeks to extend self outwards infinitely, dissolving 'I' into 'we'. Nineteenth-century Liberalism has reinforced the first of these paradigms by calling "on man to renounce even his natural tendency to love his neighbour" (p.105) in accordance with the economic doctrine of Laissez-faire. Although these paradigms may appear to be exclusive, Hughes's analysis suggests that they will in fact constitute the alternate responses of a single, lost identity when Liberalism and Humanism combine as Liberal Humanism. Unable to love universally, as it is bid (for love can properly only be felt for individuals), the ego withdraws, frustrated, into itself; from where it may again sally out for another attempt: and so the cycle of frustration continues. Life at either extremity threatens psychic sickness. Withdrawal into the Cartesian 'I' threatens solipsism:

For the absolute solipsist — the self contained wholly within the ring-fence of his own minimal innermost 'I' and for whom 'we' and 'my' are words quite without meaning — the asylum doors gape. (p.102)

— For true selfhood is never wholly curtailed within the individual ego: the self spills over "into penumbral regions" which enable it to gain a "footing in the perceived" (p.101). Alternately, extension into the 'we' of Liberal Humanism, by undermining this footing, threatens to destabilize the self which, says Hughes, achieves its "emotional balance" by defending itself in relation to certain qualities and in opposition to others:

It is the we-they and meum-alienum divisions which draw the sane man's true ultimate boundary on either side of which lie quantities of opposite sign, regions of opposite emotional charge: an electric fence (as it were) of enormous potential. (p.102)

The position of this fence is subject to continual shifts, as personal, local and national boundaries and allegiances alter over historical time, and old oppositions ("such as Christian and Paynim") give way to new (such as "Papist and Protestant"), and "these in turn to distinctions of colour and race, local habitation, social class, opposite political systems . . ." (p.103).

Hughes's analysis, we see, is a twentieth century restatement of Blake: it is by contraries that we live, and whosoever seeks to destroy the contraries seeks to destroy human life. Hughes's thinking is anti-utopian: the self cannot 'belong' unless there exists something to which it does not belong: belonging implies limits. People define themselves not simply by what they are, but by what they are not. It would seem, then, that the human predicament is by definition intransigent, insoluble. If psychic health cannot be maintained without the existence of 'we-they' boundaries, then friction, antagonism, war, must remain permanent fixtures on humanity's agenda. Nations may develop ever more sophisticated means of communicating with one another, but the factionalization of human interests is ineradicable.

If we set these theoretical chapters of *Fox* against the Blashfield Address, the tensions in Hughes's mind during the last two decades of his life are clearly revealed. In the Address he speaks approvingly of the nineteenth century as an age of progress, when in the Western world necessary human reforms came about in the context of a general recognition that people were 'persons' and not 'things'. Yet this advance can hardly be divorced from the phenomenon of Liberal and Christian Humanism which he criticizes in *Fox*. And novel-writing, surely, which he praises for its contribution to human enlightenment, is symptom as well as cause of that historical development. The Address comes at the end of the Sixties, *Fox* at the beginning: and it might be argued that the change of emphasis in the later text is evidence of a softening of attitude in Hughes towards the liberal tradition. I am more inclined to think, however, that Hughes's attitude towards Liberal Humanism remained ambitious and unresolved. As a historical development it is morally beneficial but psychologically unsound. When we recall, from Hughes's early work, the datum that 'good' and 'evil' may be the same, we perceive the consistency of his imaginative mind. To discern that the moral world is a teasing and intractable realm — as did Lowrie in *The Sisters' Tragedy* and Minnie in *A Comedy of Good and Evil* — is to discover one of the fundamental difficulties of the human predicament.

Hughes pursues his analysis of identity and belonging with reference both to the experience of nations and individuals. In *Fox* his general comments concern Britain and Germany; in *Shepherdess* he considers America. In England in 1914, he suggests, "there was something of an emotional void" (*FA* p.106). But Germany's invasion of Belgium immediately revitalized the 'meum-alienum' polarity. With right and wrong now sharply defined, the emotions of love and hate could once again powerfully centre themselves — the one on one's comrades, the other on the enemy. After the war there was a retreat from both: the retreat from hatred (a wholly natural response to the horror of the trenches) necessitated an equivalent retreat from love, so that the recently-found axis was soon undermined. Turning to post-war Germany, Hughes describes the situation as one of nightmare, as rampant inflation ate away at the foundations of society and left people "desperately incommunicado like men rendered voiceless by an intervening vacuum" (*FA* p.119). The "inexplicable suffering" this caused could not indefinitely remain objectless: in a situation which cried out for scapegoats, no shortage of identifications of a tormenting 'they' were forthcoming:

> Jews, Communists, Capitalists, Catholics, Cabbalists — even their own elected government, the 'November Criminals'. Millions of horsepower of hatred had been generated, more hatred than the real situation could consume: inevitably it conjured its own Enemy out of thin air. (p.120)

But then, of course, the law of contraries must give birth also to a fictive 'we': the need to love as well as hate created

> its myths of Soil and Race, its Heroes, its kaleidoscope of Brotherhoods each grappling its own members with hoops of steel. (p.121)

Desperate problems, desperate remedies. To recognize a 'meum-alienum' polarity is a fundamental human need, but its cost to a nation in crisis can be incalculable. Rather than present it as a piece of authorial omniscience, Hughes puts an explanation of the situation in post-war America into the mouth of one of his characters, Ree's cousin Russell. This indicates, perhaps, that it is more tentative than his analysis of Britian and Germany. Russell suggests that after the war America "found herself left with a wealth of hatred minted for war still nowhere near spent, yet suddenly robbed of its object" (*WS* p. 76); blaming the world for its pains but withdrawing ("just like a turtle with bellyache") into its isolationist shell, America deprived herself of an external identity upon which to vent her frustrations. In order to work off her excessive war-emotion, then, she had no option but to divide against herself, and to invent for this purpose an artifical issue. Prohibition. Augustine suggests that "the whole Prohibition behaviour-pattern" might be regarded as a form of "Play Therapy" (p.77): but equally it might be seen as a symptom of national schizophrenia.

The closeness of abstract idea to living issue is illustrated particularly clearly in Chapters 16 to 22 of Book One of *Fox*. First we are treated to a theoretical discussion in the Mellton drawing-room between Augustine, Jeremy and Mary. All possess Liberal consciences and instincts, but, in a period of considerable social change, disagree about the responsibilities of the old ruling class. Augustine, by living in retreat for a number of years, has neglected his duties as a member of the Anglo-Welsh squirearchy. He is willing to let the old social divisions wither away before the modern spirit of egalitarianism. His conception of humankind is of a procession of independent and self-sufficient consciousnesses similar to his own. For Jeremy, the torch of liberty which Augustine pretends to uphold is merely the torch of anarchy. The quiet revolution to which Augustine's conduct assents is rather a dissolution. Jeremy declares that humanity cannot cope with an excess of freedom, and flees from it into revolutions which produce tyranny. This to Augustine is nonsense: men do not retreat from freedom, tyrants wrest it from them. For her part, Mary feels that Augustine has contracted out of mankind, and that "governing" is a simple fact of life, observable every day in ordinary human relationships. The argument climaxes around an old metaphor:

> The imperative mood is the very warp on which that sacred pattern of humanity is woven: tamper with those strong Imperative threads and the whole web must ravel . . .
>   'No!' cried Augustine giving the table such a thump the glasses rang (*Heavens! How much of all this nonsense could she have been saying out loud?*) 'Your web can't ravel, because . . . Emperor's New Clothes! There IS NO web There's no thread, even, joining man to man — nothing!' (p. 68)

The Cartesian 'I' opposes the Humanist 'we' in brother and sister, with Augustine, for the time being, getting the last and loudest word. But noise does not make problems melt away. The question of where one draws the we-they boundary, of how far one allows self to extend its penumbra, is dramatized in the disagreement of Mary and Gilbert over what is to be done about Nellie and Gwilym Hopkins. Mary wants to offer Nellie one of the Mellton cottages. Gilbert demurs. It isn't that he doesn't want to do something for Nellie, but that his immediate responsibilities are to his own servants and employees — and the cottage is required for some of them.

> If you don't draw the line somewhere (Gilbert argued), you soon cease being able to do your duty by your own people, the people to whom it is *owed*. One's duty to mankind at large isn't in that same way a personal, man-to-man relationship: it's a collective duty, and one's service to Liberalism rather are its proper discharge — not random little drop-in-a-bucket acts of kindness. (p. 86)

The phrase "draw the line" here clearly relates the particular issue to the metaphor proposed in the general theory. Beyond his immediate responsibility to his dependents, Gilbert recognizes only a political responsibility. Not so Mary, who wishes to draw the boundary-line of personal responsibility at a much greater distance. There is a real issue of principle here, and one not easy to resolve. In the event, the problem is solved in a manner that requires neither Mary nor Gilbert to compromise their positions. Hughes never openly suggests in *Fox* or *Shepherdess* that the point at which an individual draws the 'we-they' line may have anything to do with his or her sex: but it is surely notable in this case. Gilbert's stance is taken on the basis of a logic that is not only, perhaps, masculine, but paternal. Mary's stance grounds itself in *feeling*, in a sympathy which does not automatically subject itself to the revisions and adjustments of rational argument. The drawing-room argument bears also upon Augustine's experience at Flemton. We see here just how strong a solvent of traditional social ties is Augustine's reclusiveness. The Flemton gossipers can feed upon the fact that Augustine brought in dead Rachel's body from the sea-marsh precisely because he is now unrespected and suspected by the townsfolk. When his property is attacked, we see that his irresponsibility has invited this. It is only after this has happened that he recalls Jeremy's ironic references to "Flemton's tricoteuses" (pp. 65, 92). It is interesting to consider that both Mary's and Augustine's problems (Mary's with Gilbert, Augustine's with the tricoteuses) may be traced to the same source: the death of little Rachel on the sea-marsh. Book One of *Fox*, then, seems to demonstrate pretty conclusively the existence of the "web" which

Augustine so passionately denies. It will reach out to involve even one who refuses to acknowledge its existence.

Through the brothers Wolff and Lothar Scheidemann, Hughes explores the contrary powers that a redefinition of the 'meum-alienum' boundary may release. In Wolff — whose name is precise: he sleeps in a pile of furs, sharing his attic with a fox — we see a nature for which all emotion must be extreme. Since the 'awakening' of his political conscience in his youth, Wolff has been a political assassin. Although he is, as it were, a killer by Pavlovian response, his murderousness is 'pure', altruistic: he kills on behalf of an ideal, a political principle. The war has now pushed him over the threshold into madness: unable, on account of his belief in Germany's transcendental destiny, to accept the truth of her defeat, he exists in a state of psychic deadlock, cut off from reality:

> in the course of his self-immolation on the altar of 'Germany' Wolff's over-altruist self had by now so atrophied it could no longer contain this his Disaster: yet of its nature that disaster allowed no normal outlet — neither into God nor man. Final escape could only be into the absolute unreality of death; but in the meantime Wolff had turned, as to Death's twin and surrogate-on-earth, to Romantic Love: sole comparable realm, with Death's, of the Unreal. (*FA* p.283)

The object of his extravagant love is Mitzi. When he persuades himself that she is in love with, of all things, an *Englishman*, his extreme love activates his conscience and calls up an extreme hatred: the lovers must be killed. Creeping through the house to smother Mitzi, he is a mixture of Othello and Tarquin. But when, en route, he changes his mind and decides to kill her with a knife, his fantasy-murder becomes a *liebestod*, a love-death romantic and perverse. The semi-erotic terms in which he imagines killing her, ending with "the knife pumping in the wound, the withdrawal and the hot blood welling to his elbow" (p.285), suggest that the murder-act will possess for him the force of a sexual consummation. But Otto is in Mitzi's room, and Wolff withdraws. So lost to himself has he become that his conscious mind (preoccupied as it is with revenge) remains unaware of the directions that his unconscious mind is giving to his body. His death provokes one of the strangest and most powerful passages in Hughes's fiction:

> Mitzi's hair . . . blood, running in its fine gold, running down till it crimsoned the snow.
> Mitzi's blood, spouting — floods of it — lakes of it, warm and exquisite! — *Seas* of it . . .
> Look! The sun himself dangled a rope of glutinous blood from his

globe — emulous, wanting to join those seas like a waterspout.

On a fountain of blood like a bobbing ball on a water-jet Wolff's soaring soul was mounting to heaven — high, high into the interminable blue ... but then something bit it! Bat-winged and black, something sunk teeth in it, tore it.

The abominable attack was so sudden — no time to recall Wolff's soul to his body, it was caught out there bare: spirit to spirit in hideous unholy communion. *Despair!* Down he was rocketing falling twisting ... oh agony agony! Blackness, everywhere black: noise ... pain, everywhere pain — *unbelievable* pain!

'I ABHOR THINGS STRANGLED ...'

From his temples the sweat spurted, and his teeth met through his tongue. (p.302)

Wolff's death is a return to the mother (we may recall that death is "Mother Death" for Mr. Williams in *A Comedy of Good and Evil*). The sun attached to the sea by "a rope of glutinous blood" is not only the noose with which he hangs himself, but an imagistic version of the child attached to the mother by the umbilicus. But even as Wolff imagines a triumphant return to the blood-warm seas of the womb, something "Bat-winged and black" bites the cord, severing it, and sends him plunging hurtfully into absence. It is worth pointing out that the passage echoes one from *In Hazard*, where Ao Ling experiences a strange dream:

Round them the sea roared and heaved: but out of it rose a single tree. Its leaves were of white jade. Its trunk was about as thick round as a man could clasp; and up the middle ran a transparent tube of pale yellow. The foliage was dense, and tinkled when a leaf fell. But now it was lightning-riven: and caught in the cleft was a blue-faced bat-winged duke, hollering in agony with his enormous monkey-mouth and hammering incessantly on the drums which were hung about him. (pp.270-71)

Here again the sea suggests the amniotic lake, and the tree rising from it the umbilicus. The appearance of the rare and curious epithet "bat-winged" in both passages is a tantalising detail. The "bat-winged duke" is an attendant demon, perhaps (in accordance with Freud's dictum that "Parents appear in dreams as *emperor* and *empress*, *king* and *queen* or other exalted personages"[2]) a father-figure: but his grotesqueness is half-comic, and has in it nothing of the ferocity generated by the *Fox* passage. There the schizoid Wolff acts as his own nemesis: so that, perhaps, we should see the entity that attacks his soul as his own crushed ego — returning at the last to deny his soul its wished-for communion.

It has been a part of Hughes's thesis to suggest that the internal 'enemies' conjured up in the Germany of the Twenties and Thirties are unreal; so too then must be the 'friends'. Through Lothar, Wolff's younger brother by two years, Hughes portrays both the adhesive power and the fictive nature of the love released by the forces that he has described. His treatment of Lothar is often close to satire: as where, for example, he writes that the gymnasium's "sweet strawberry-smell of fresh male sweat" causes Lothar to "snort . . . like a horse left out to spring grass" (*FA* pp.123-24). Nevertheless, we are not allowed to overlook the sinister implications behind the cult of the body pursued by such Brotherhoods as his. Lothar is learning judo for a reason: so that, when the circumstances arise, he will be able to break an opponent's arm or leg. For him we see that violence, developing its own aesthetic, has usurped the place normally held by art or sex:

> At grips with some older and angrier and stronger but helplessly-fumbling human body he had then been astonished to find how deeply his aesthetic emotions could be stirred by his own impeccable performance. The aesthetic satisfaction of that culminating moment could be almost epileptically intense . . . (p125)

The violent act grants him entry into passages of narcissistic self-contemplation. But it is for Lothar that Hughes reserves the wickedest irony in the novel. Moving to Kammstadt, he becomes a member of the local Nazi cell and later a recruit to Ludwig Kettner's S.A. squad. Politics is his religion, and Hitler — all-seeing and all-knowing — his God. When in June 1934 Gruppenfuhrer Kettner cannot go to Wiessee because of a broken leg, Lothar dons Standartenfuhrer badges of rank and goes in his place — only to find himself arrested and ferried to Stadelheim Prison. It is here that we discover the cost of his blind, uncritical reverence for Hitler. Hitler, he thinks, must correct the mistake that has occurred: like a God of Love, he must intervene to save his faithful son. But even as he imagines Hitler's arrival to rescue him, Sepp Dietrich gives his firing-squad the signal, and Lothar dies alongside his fellow S.A. members, "with a look of intense surprise on his face" (*WS* p.368). He thus pays the price of his life for giving to a man what only gods should receive: for men are mortal, fallible, careless — even treacherous, as the event demonstrates. Blindly to love is as dangerous as blindly to hate.

The two characters in whom Hughes embodies the major running contrast in the novel are Mitzi von Kessen and Adolf Hitler. Hitler is Hughes's "absolute solipsist" whose identity has withdrawn "wholly within the ring-fence of his own minimal innermost 'I' " (*FA* p.102). To regain his "footing in the perceived" he must turn to "pathological dreaming" (p.104). For such a being the pronouns 'we' and 'my' are without meaning, and the "asylum doors gape" for him — or, perhaps, in the additional terms of the parallel passage in the Blashfield Address, "the doors of hell"[3]. To Hitler other people are not 'persons' but 'things', not individuals to be respected but instruments to be utilized. Hitler is Hughes's "archetypal non-reader of Fiction". Hitler's career shows "that a mankind in which such solipsists gained the upper hand would be a mankind headed for destruction".[4]

An investigation into the phenomenon of Hitler's solipsism not only uncovers one of Hughes's profoundest intuitions about selfhood, but illustrates the thematic continuity of his artistic enterprise. Hughes's understanding of Hitler is clearly indebted to his understanding of the child-mind. Hitler, to put it crudely, has failed to grow up: his ego is comparable to that of a child as yet unaware of the existence outside himself of other persons of equivalent reality, and of wants and needs as imperative as his own. We recall that Emily, newly aware of the uniqueness of her selfhood, toyed with the idea that she herself might be God — a fantasy counterbalanced by her sense of her innate wickedness (a version, seemingly, of original sin). Only further experience — and the killing the Dutch Captain — resolved this dialectic. Hitler's ego is one that has failed to mature: in him a child's amorality exists alongside the intelligence of a physically-mature man. The childhood dialectic between (to borrow useful, if pat, Freudian terms) 'ego' and 'super-ego' has not in Hitler resulted in the triumph of super-ego, nor has it remained (as in the mature adult) unresolved. Ego, rather, has carried all before it. Hitler's "fixed conviction that he was the universe's unique sentient centre, the sole authentic incarnate Will it contained or ever had contained" (*FA* p.266), is equivalent to the sense that one is God.

Hitler's childishness (I use the word without pejorative inference) is suggested by Hughes with consummate art. When taken from the Hanfstaengl's house at Uffing in the wake of the Putsch he's described as "trailing Putzi's prized English rug by one corner like a child who has been playing Indians" (*FA* p.272). Taking advantage of the rapport Hitler in actuality established with little Egon Hanfstaengl, Hughes creates an ironic link between the two. The closeness of 'Egon' and 'ego' was surely an historical windfall for Hughes (a gift of Clio herself). Even before Hitler has made a personal appearance in the novel, an unidentified character incorrectly names him Egon, and has to be corrected (p.193). Much later, little Egon is driven into a frenzy by one of his adored Uncle Dolf's uncontrolled tirades:

> the little boy dived head-first in a sofa and lay there blindly slashing — berserk, completely cuckoo. From the tree a tilting candle dripped hot wax on the face of the china doll in the crib. (*WS* p.172)

— an emblem richly suggestive of the cruel power which Hitler and his Party will in the future yield. The word "cuckoo" will be caught up later when, on the Night of the Long Knives, Hitler is described as a "cuckoo-chick" who "soon sees all the legitimate nestlings tumbled out" of the nest he occupies (p.323).

Hughes inevitably interprets Hitler's sexual peculiarities as a product of his solipsism:

> how could that monistic 'I' of Hitler's ever without forfeit succumb to the entire act of sex, the whole essence of which is recognition of one 'Other'? (*FA* p.266)

Hitler's relationship with his niece, Geli Raubal, is "quasi-incest":

> This sexy young niece was blood of his blood, so could perhaps in his solipsist mind be envisaged as merely a female organ budding on 'him' — as forming with him a single hermaphrodite 'Hitler', a two-sexed entity able to couple within itself like the garden snail. .. (*WS* p.320)

The "perhaps" here is less a recognition of the improbability of this psychological explanation than an acknowledgement of the strangeness of Hitler's sexual demands — which seem to have gone far beyond the simplicities of copulation. Geli had at length to shoot herself to escape him.

It is natural to connect Hitler with Wolff Scheidemann: their rhyming forenames immediately signal an affinity. Psychically they are similar in that in each of them the penumbra of the self has melted away, leaving neither capable of full relationship with other individuals. Instead, in reaching outwards for a meaning capable of validating their lives, each finds it in Germany — though with a crucial difference. Having identified himself with a triumphant Reich, Wolff lapses, with Germany in chaos, into chaos himself. Hitler begins where Wolff ends: *his* dedication to the resuscitation of the Reich means that 'personal' fulfilment and racial fulfilment amount to the same thing. Germany's destiny is Hitler's, and Hitler's Germany's. (So, when Germany falls in 1945, must he.) It is when he is in hiding at Uffing, and the pain from his dislocated shoulder causes him to hallucinate, that Hughes brings him to his nearest point of approach to the young assassin. "Tossing desperately on his attic bed", Hitler imagines himself to be drowning: perhaps, after all, he *did* leap into the Danube from the bridge at Linz in his youth, so that it is the Danube he can now hear singing in his ears (Hughes himself, we recall, had heard the Danube singing in *his* youth as he and his friends rowed down it in 1924[5]):

In the green watery light surrounding him a dead face was floating towards him upturned: a dead face with his own slightly-bulging eyes in it unclosed: his dead Mother's face as he had last seen it with unclosed eyes white on the white pillow. Dead, and white, and vacant even of its love for him.

, But now that face was multiplied — it was all around him in the water. So his Mother *was* this water, these waters drowning him!

At that he ceased to struggle. He drew up his knees to his chin in the primal attitude and lay there, letting himself drown.

So Hitler slept at last. (*FA* p.268)

Hitler's hallucination involves imagined suicide; Wolff commits actual suicide. Hitler's drowning into sleep is a metaphorical death, and dying for him, as for Wolff, takes the shape of an assumption into the Mother, into the waters of the amnion. The ultimate retreat for the solipsist, then, is a retreat into the womb, a realm where identity as *separateness* is unknown, and the embryo floats in a unified and secure physical continuum. But where Wolff's 'dream' is savagely shattered, Hitler's brings him easeful release. Both passages are recognizable as Hughesian eidola, and, like Ao Ling's dream, demonstrate Hughes's increasing tendency to stage the eidolon within the consciousness of one of his characters: to make it a complex mental event. Over against the figures of Hitler and Wolff, Hughes sets that of Mitzi von Kessen. The following passage, which appears in one of the theoretical chapters at the end of Book One of *Fox*, is clearly anticipatory:

Perhaps in the neighbourhood of death or under the shadow of heaven man, in a dissolution as potent as the splitting atom his analogue, *can* experience love only ... or, in the shadow of madness and hell, conceivably hate only. (p.103)

In the novel as we have it, these opposite but complementary "dissolutions" occur in Mitzi and Wolff respectively — though it seems not unreasonable to conjecture that Hughes planned to portray a third dissolution: in Hitler as, in his bunker in a beseiged Berlin, he faced the choice of capture or suicide. Like Wolff, Mitzi experiences a psychic crisis when pre-existing accommodations between self and world are disrupted. In Wolff's case it is Germany's defeat in 1918 which precipitates the crisis; in Mitzi's it is the onset of blindness. But where Wolff's crisis propels him into a desperate unreality, Mitzi's propels her into a new reality. Both, one may say, experience the death of ego; but where in Wolff this death means the loss of everything, in Mitzi it means the finding of everything. Mitzi is saved from despair by the realization that her sight was a gift from God: all she is and has is His. The barrier that separates her from Him is the barrier of self-love:

she must, in the words of Thomas-à-Kempis, "go wholly out of herself, and retain nothing of self-love", in order to find Him.

> Now, when she probed to her own very innermost pinpoint 'I am', it was like looking into a tiny familiar room through a window and finding herself instead looking out — upon landscapes of infinite width: no longer her little 'I am' inside there at all, but only His great 'I AM'.
> The times when a separate 'Mitzi' still seemed to exist were no more than a lingering nightmare she hoped to be rid of for ever as soon as she woke up after His likeness, a nun: no longer her little 'I will' there ever again, but only His WORD. (*WS* p.117)

We may set Mitzi's ideal — to destroy will in herself — diametrically against Hitler's: for Hitler is Will Incarnate — the incarnation, that is, of a sort of Hegelian spiritual principle: the will of Germany itself. If in Mitzi's early days at Carmel there's a danger in her intense awareness of God's presence, it takes the form of a sublimity buttressed by extreme introspection. The experienced nuns are aware of this danger, and seek to defuse it by involving her in the common life of the convent. She must develop a sense of community, a shared humility.

Mitzi is a worshipper, Hitler an object of worship. Mitzi is a seeker after fulfilment and salvation, Hitler an instrument of fulfilment and salvation for others. The Labour Camp Commandant that Jeremy's party meet at Ulm in June 1934 declares that Hitler is

> what a Christian would call a 'saint' — there's no other word for the manifest spiritual power working through him; and yet he's as simple and unassuming to meet as you and me. And gentle: all children love him at sight.... What Hitler has done for us is to wake us out of the nightmare we've lived in for sixteen years. He has started us Germans hoping again, when we'd almost forgotten how to hope. (*WS* pp.337-38)

Precisely what this Saviour amounts to, Hughes portrays clearly in the Night of the Long Knives: he has come not to bring peace, but a sword, and, as we have seen in the case of Lothar Scheidemann, it is a sword that will fall on believers as well as unbelievers. Mitzi must seek, like all mystics, within herself for God; Hitler has, it seems, discovered his own godhead: yet there the similarity ends, for the God within Mitzi dwarfs her, reduces her to utter insignificance, while the God within Hitler is not to be distinguished from Ego itself. The God of Love that Mitzi finds at the onset of her blindness does not remain constant: the advent she experiences at the very end of *Shepherdess* is "so stark" that she can "barely endure" it. God strips her soul "naked" and examines it with a minuteness that is savage in its intensity:

No man can see his own soul clearly and live: he must hood his eyes which look inwards as if against a dazzling by light when the light is too much — though this is a dazzling by darkness, his soul is too dark to bear looking at. Yet God can look: as the eagle can stare at the brightness of the sun, so God stared at even the blackness within without blinking; and under the burning eye of that burning relentless Love she was molten metal heaved in a crucible under its scum . . . (pp.387-88)

God's love, as Hopkins knew, manifests itself at different times in tenderness and ferocity; God is eagle and dove, tiger and lamb. The scrutiny to which He subjects Mitzi's soul is, I feel, a preliminary to the testing which her faith will experience in a world where "the devil as a roaring lion walketh about, seeking whom he may devour" (p.386). For although the Carmelite order is a 'closed' one, it exists in the world, and its insulation is not absolute. Hughes, it seems, offers a contrast between the way of the Carmelites as religious order and the way of the Nazis as political party and quasi-religious order. The nun seeks to purge herself of sin through devotion to her community and through the spiritul means of prayer and contemplation; Hitler's party seeks to purge Germany of what it takes to be corruptive elements through the material means of pogrom and firing-squad. Both movements throw up their 'saints'. Against the Ulm Commandment's belief that Hitler is one such, we may set the Reverend Mother of Carmel's remembrance, when faced by Mitzi's candidature, that another girl had, a bare generation before, experienced difficulties in gaining admission; and yet had now, as St. Therese of Lisieux, attained canonization. Can Mitzi be another St. Therese?

The dialectical importance to the novel of Hitler and Mitzi is indicated by the titles of the completed volumes — *The Fox in the Attic*, *The Wooden Shepherdess*. Foxes are introduced immediately but casually in the first: "here in a sodden tangle of brambles the scent of a fox hung, too heavy today to rise or dissipate" (p. 13). The fox may not be visibly present, but its scent is persistent: somewhere in the vicinity, it will come when called. In the event, that call will come not in Wales but Bavaria: "curled on the sofa in an attitude of sleep but with his bright eyes wide open, lay a fox" (p.141). Are foxes so easily domesticated, tamed? We should beware of the deceptiveness of this fox's attitude. When one night Reineke howls for no apparent reason (the mating season is three months away), we may well wonder what has disturbed him, Now attics fill with foxes: not only Reineke, but Hitler and Wolff — the last of whom sleeps in furs. Both men are hunted animals, both are holed up, trapped: yet one will live to hunt again in his own right. There are foxes on both sides of the political divide in the Bavaria of 1923. Von Kahr, one of the Munich 'triumvirs' whom the Putsch is designed to unseat, is twice referred to as "the old fox" (pp.205, 213). Seemingly trapped, he turns the table on the revolutionaries by a ruse that lands them with useless rifles. But Hitler will catch up with him, and even old scores: for von Kahr's body will be found in July 1934 in a swamp near Dachau — pick-axed to death. In ten years, Hitler's foxy cunning has turned into the savagery of the wolf.

The 'wooden shepherdess' is a church in Connecticut: "tiny and old ... nearly disused ... half buried in trees ... naive and lovely ... deserted" (p.34), and with a bell that can't be tolled. The church is an emblem (like the ruined temple in the opening chapter of *Fox*?) of a religion fallen into desuetude, a power on which the twentieth century seems to have turned its back, as upon an irrelevance. To connect the church with Mitzi is an easy matter. Rightly, a shepherdess should have a flock, but the flock has deserted her: Mitzi, driven into increasing isolation by her blindness, retreats from the world. In comparison with the symbol of the fox, that of the shepherdess is "significantly reticent"[6]: and the fact that there are more references to foxes in *The Wooden Shepherdess* than shepherdesses[7] suggests the fox's dominance of the second novel, as of the first. On the face of it, no interpenetration would appear possible between these symbols: yet one of the strangest moments in the novel suggests otherwise. Waking into an utterly lightless world, Mitzi blunders about and burns her hand on the stove before it occurs to her that making noises might help her to tell what kind of a room or what part of a room she is, at any time, in. So she zig-zags about her bedroom "uttering little staccato fox-like cries", and attempting to interpret their reverberations. Her "feral yapping" wakens her brother Franz:

> For a moment he thought it really was their little fox as before; but he soon realised this was no natural fox. Indeed it was a most queer, uncanny sound: moreover it was coming from the room next to his: from Mitzi's room. Something was in there with Mitzi.
>
> A were-fox? — He shivered, and his skin prickled with goose-flesh. (*FA* p.237)

The shepherdess may become a fox, then — and even, for a brief moment, turn a self-possessed brother into the fox's traditional prey, a goose! We are not told whether Mitzi's experiment is useful to her: but whilst it may be attractive to conclude, from Franz's reaction, that the 'impersonation' was misguided, I suspect that such a conclusion is a little too facile. Richard Hughes's world has always been one in which contraries can turn into one another: and what, after all, was Ao Ling's Fukienese dream-girl "but a fox in human shape"?

III

The analysis I have just offered of Mitzi, Wolff and Hitler (and, to a lesser extent, Mary and Gilbert Wadamy) may suggest that *The Human Predicament* is a schematic novel: the behaviour of its characters illustrate a thesis. This is a conclusion which it is difficult to resist. It may, of course, have been the behaviour of the characters which suggested the thesis, rather than the thesis which suggested the behaviour of the (unhistorical) characters: yet it is difficult to imagine that Hughes's thesis did not, once it had clarified itself in his mind (and then got itself into the novel), act as a form of conscious 'input' into his creativity. If I am right in thinking this, then the 'free' derivation of event from the unconscious which Hughes always maintained was his way of working could not have been as 'free' in *The Human Predicament* as in the pre-war novels. Certainly there are ideas in *A High Wind* and *In Hazard*; but those ideas are implicit or, where they are not, seem to arise spontaneously from the circumstances described. In *The Human Predicament* one cannot but become aware of the framework of ideas which Hughes proffers, and *Fox* and *Shepherdess* seem to me to lose something in imaginative spontaneity as a result. They are the work of an older man and, perhaps, a wiser man: but once a man has worked out consciously his ideas about the world of humankind, there is no guarantee that he will be a better writer for it: and indeed (as Coleridge found) he may be a worse. When this has been said, however, it is possible to exaggerate the degree of schematism in *The Human Predicament*: it is doubtful whether a reader, following the contours of "the novel behind his eyes", experiences the framework in anything like the organized fashion an analytical account of it may suggest. Hughes's characters are never ciphers, abstractions clothed in the flesh of words; as people they are richly imagined and embedded in the contingencies of daily life (except where — as with Wolff — 'daily life' is quite removed from the commonplaceness of a common life). Even Hitler — who, as a historical figure, does not immediately receive the same intimacy of treatment as the purely fictive characters — springs to life: a process of gradual metamorphosis will take him from semi-comic Chaplinesque posturer to fully-fledged machiavel. But before we return to Hitler, we must look at Hughes's reluctant 'hero', Augustine Penry-Herbert.

In the previous chapter we saw that Hughes's thinking about 'personhood' involved a crucial discrimination. In *life*, even in married love, a person can never become "self-conscious with the other partner's own 'I-ness'"[8], can never perceive "what Sartre calls the 'Other'" — to know, that is, the consciousness of another in a manner as immediate and irreducible as one knows oneself (when 'knowing' means 'experiencing', not 'understanding'). Only when reading novels (or perhaps when watching plays and films) do we "adopt someone else's 'I am' for our own". Although Hughes invokes Sartre here, his conception of the origin of self-consciousness is Cartesian rather than Sartrean. For Emily, personal identity is a self-derived fact; emerging gratuitously in a situation when she is separate from others, it is an intuition which immediately establishes itself as an absolute. For Sartre, bodily self-consciousness arises out of one's sense of one's body as it appears to *others*. One commentator summarizes Sartre's position as follows:

> I am an object for my own consciousness only through my having become conscious of others' consciousness of me. Others cannot then be *merely* objects for my consciousness or I would not become an object for myself. The structure of self-consciousness, then, is logically social, but since I finally am an object for myself only through the provenance of others' perception of me, what I am (as an object) depends upon others and not upon myself. And this is why they are hell: my identity, even for myself, depends finally upon them.[9]

Emily's emergent consciousness of her body is certainly of an "object" in something like this sense — it is of "this particular rather pleasing little casket of flesh": but self-consciousness for her is a *personal* rather than a "social" fact. As we have already seen, Augustine Penry-Herbert's notion of humankind is Cartesian: humankind consists for him of a procession of independent and self-sufficient consciousnesses. His identity, we must then presume, is, to his way of thinking, autonomous, self-defining and self-sustaining.

What I called Hughes's "crucial discrimination" at the beginning of the last paragraph begs, I believe, an important question. It is: On what grounds should a reader incline to accept the testimony of novels that human beings are persons? The answer, surely, is that the testimony of novels accords with the reader's extra-novelistic observation and experience. The novel confirms a judgment the reader has made, although it may deepen that judgment immensely. *The Human Predicament*, I think, is less doctrinaire than the theory advanced in the Blashfield Address. Specifically, it allows for the selfhood of an individual to spill over so that a footing is gained in the perceived. The nature of that overspill (in Hughes's words), or the degree to which a person's self-consciousness is determined by others (for Sartre), or the fact that we *judge* others to be persons though we cannot *know* them to be so (in my formulation): these are three ways of getting at a matter which Hughes in his novel explores through his central character. Augustine functions as a species of antenna, a consciousness thrust out into a number of more or less alien environments. He is an experimental 'self' exposed to the probing actions of the 'Other' — or, indeed, to many Others.

For the purpose of this experiment, Hughes takes great pains to establish Augustine's recalcitrance. His literary ancestry includes the 'naive' hero, and the 'superfluous man' of Russian literature. The naive hero is compelled to test comparatively simple and dogmatic preconceptions against a complex unstructured reality. One of the most typical forms taken by this testing is the Sentimental Education. Augustine's encounters with the Other will often, then, take the shape of encounters with girls: with Mitzi (in *Fox*), with Ree, Janis, Sadie and Joan (in *Shepherdess*) and with Norah (in volume three). The superfluous man, as John Bayley defines him, is "the hero whose intelligence and aspiration can find nothing to work on and through in the objective social world".[10] He emerges when a particular kind of sensibility (which in Russian novels often owes a good deal to Hamlet and the Byronic hero) finds its progressive impulses cramped and frustrated by the prevailing social system (in Russian novels by that perpetuated by Tsardom). Although Augustine is neither a Hamlet nor a Byronic hero, he is neither insensitive nor unintelligent. His kind of superfluity is defined by his social circumstances, his theoretical persuasions, and his existential purposelessness.

When *Fox* opens, he is living a completely withdrawn life in the family mansion in south west Wales. Born, like Hughes himself, in 1900, he has grown up in the belief that he will die in the trenches of Europe; so that, when the War abruptly ends, he inherits a wholly unlooked-for life-expectancy. He never, in the space of the two completed volumes, exhausts the legacy of unpreparedness for life which 1918 bequeathes him. His purposelessness is only aggravated by the fact that, as a member of the Anglo-Welsh squirearchy, he is rich: inherited wealth relieves him of the burden of earning a living. The recipient of an Oxford education (again like Hughes), he has acquired an ideological freight — Liberal, atheistical, post-Freudian, modern — which amounts to a theory of what life ought to be like: but he has a very limited practical experience of people and affairs. Perhaps his fundamental intellectual error is his belief — shared by his friend Jeremy — that an "age of illimitable human progress and fulfilment" is now dawning, an age in which "the very words 'God' and 'gilt' must atrophy and ultimately drop off the language" (p. 73). For Augustine, the new politics and the new psychology go hand in hand as instruments of liberation. In a moment of luminous insight he perceives that theirs was the first generation in the whole cave-to-cathedral history of the human race completely to disbelieve in sin. Actions nowadays weren't thought of as 'right' or 'wrong' any more: they were merely judged social or anti-social, personal fulfilment or frustration ... (p. 73)

But, as Jeremy argues, "that lands us with two dichotomies instead of one ... and sometimes they clash". Augustine does not see that there is no fixed entity called 'society', that what might be deemed 'social' in one culture, one country, one class, even one locality, may not be deemed 'social' in another. Nor does he recognise that 'personal' and 'social' may not cohere — that duty and desire can clash with painful results. We shall see that, far from being emancipated from the burden of sin and guilt and the tyranny of 'right' and 'wrong', he is inescapably a child of his time — a sensibility shaped by a particular culture and class. His experience will demonstrate — to us if not always to him — that 'absolute freedom' of the kind he believes himself to embody only constitutes another form of bondage, and that his personality is not a self-defining and self-sustaining phenomenon.

The formal structures of *Fox* and *Shepherdess*, in so far as 'structure' derives from the motion and interaction of characters, are very alike. Both enact a movement out of singularity into multiplicity, out of solitariness into relationship. At the beginning of both volumes Augustine exists in withdrawal: first at Newton Llanthony, and then in the Connecticut woods — where he has for a second time lapsed into a "limboish mark-time life" (p. 45). In each case an encounter with a girl-child — the first dead, the second very much alive — compels him to reappraise his attitude to the world of others, and to venture out from within the ring-fence of his own ego. The formal movement of each separate volume may be likened to an ever-widening spiral; with Augustine's first human contact, the arm of the spiral breaks into motion, circling out to touch lives at greater and greater distances as the central awareness formulates attitudes to remoter and remoter happenings. To some extent the reader's relation to events is like Augustine's: for the reader too begins in lonely isolation, growing into knowledge as Augustine does — but soon outpacing him. Augustine and the reader (for is not Augustine the reader's 'surrogate' inside the novel?) are first persons brought to consider the implications of 'we' and 'they'.

The opening of *Fox* is particularly charged with significance. Hughes's imagination appears here to surprise itself in the act of parturition. Augustine, his burden, and his male companion (who, after this first chapter, disappears so completely that he might never have existed) emerge from a drenched and silent sea-marsh. Consider:

Beyond the bamboos their path tunnelled under a seemingly

endless ancient growth of rhododendrons and they had to duck, for though the huge congested limbs of this dark thicket had once been propped on crutches to give the path full headroom many of these were now rotten and had collapsed. At the very centre of this grove the tunnel passed by a small stone temple; but here too the brute force of vegetation was at work, for the clearing had closed in, the weather-pocked marble faun lay face down in the tangle of ivy which had fallen with him, the little shrine itself now wore its cupola awry. Thus it was not till the two men had travelled the whole length of this dark and dripping tunnel and finally reached the further border of all this abandoned woodland that they really came right out again at last under the open whitish sky. (pp. 14-15)

From a sea-marsh ... through a rhododendron tunnel ... and out under the sky... The symbology is perfectly clear — and yet, I believe completely unconscious on the writer's part: for Hughes told me that he had not recognized the full suggestibility of the passage until he read an essay I sent him in 1975.[11] Augustine must emerge into Hughes's consciousness before he can emerge into *self*-consciousness.

It is both ironic and instructive that Augustine should be recalled to life by an experience of death. The corpse over his shoulder is a "dead mite of alien world"; but no sooner does he introduce it into his house than he has a strange experience:

these guns and rods of his, and even the furniture, the kettle and the loaf had suddenly become living tentacles of 'him'. It was as if he and this long-loved gunroom were now one living continuous flesh. It was as if for the first time being 'he' was no longer cooped up entirely within his own skin: he had expanded, and these four walls had become now his final envelope. Only outside these walls did the hostile, alien 'world' begin. (p. 17)

Augustine perceives that the self is not confined within the body, within the individual; it can expand to include a room, a house: and why stop there? At the same time, the experience suggests him to be something of a crustacean: has he not made his home in a shell, a secure retreat from all that is other? Much later in the volume, Wolff's experience in the Lorienburg attics will echo this early event:

In a whole year spent here he had grown into a unity with the very timbers of these attics... Look! Like the bones in Ezekiel already these beams were covering themselves with flesh, with skin — and it was *his* flesh and skin they were growing... He would breathe into these dry beams soon, and then these attics would live... (pp.300-301)

Augustine's and Wolff's experiences are antithetical but complementary: Augustine's expansion of self signals an emergence from the womb, while Wolff's contraction of self signals a re-entry into it. Augustine's experience is a prelude to further life, Wolff's a prelude to suicide.

It is only after this experience that Augustine disburdens himself of the dead child. This too is suggestive:

> When at last (in a remote and half-darkened formal place of elegance, a room he never used) Augustine did lift the morsel off his shoulder, he found that it had stiffened. This had ceased to be 'child' at all: it was total cadaver now. It had taken into its soft contours the exact mould of the shoulder over which it had been doubled and it had set like that — into a matrix of *him*. If (which God forbid) he had put it on again it would have fitted. (p. 18)

Putting off this "matrix" of himself, we may say, Augustine is putting off his dead self — the persona of reclusive squire — prior to venturing out into the world in search of experience.

It is an article of faith to him that his own generation is so unlike all previous ones that they constitute "different species" (p. 23) — a phrase that will immediately recall the space between children and pirates in *A High Wind*.

> The kind of Time called 'History' ended at the Battle of Waterloo: after that, Time had gone into a long dark tunnel or chrysalis called the Victorian Age. It had come out into daylight again at the Present Day, but as something quite different: it was as impossible to imagine oneself both a Victorian or born in 'History' as ... as born a puma. (p. 23)

'Time', Augustine feels, has detached itself from 'History' and been reborn as something else. He cannot define it; but if, as he seems to feel, 'History' is fixed, dead, remote, then his own age may be taken to be fluid, living, immediate. The "tunnel", of course, Augustine himself has traversed. The dilapidated shrine and ivy-entangled "weather-pocked marble faun" in retrospect may be seen as emblematic of those forms of religion which Augustine believes his generation to have cut itself free of with the help of Freud. The inhabitants of even the recent past strike him as "grotesques" —

> outsides only: hollow bundles of behaviourist gestures, of stylised reactions to stimuli like Pavlov's dogs. (p. 24)

Or, I am tempted to add, Dickensian caricatures. Such figures as Uncle Arthur and Uncle William, and Dr. Brinley, the Flemton coroner, are not "persons" to Augustine (that is, people like himself). 'History', then, is (or rather *was*) the collaborative creation of a host of such puppet-like unrealities. From such an absurd and artificial process, Augustine believes himself emancipated: his own life, it seems, cannot belong to History. The novel will 'correct' Augustine on the two issues interrelated here. First we shall see that one of these "grotesques" — Dr. Brinley — is just as much a person as Augustine is: for Hughes, entering his mind, will show him to us from the inside as precisely what Augustine denies — an "inside". Second, we shall see that Augustine's belief that his life can be lived independently of something called 'History', unaffected by a flow of historical events, is quite false.

History is actual and all-inclusive, and we are all living it — willy-nilly. Augustine will be able to hold on to his misconceptions only because of his intellectual complacency and thick-skinned insularity. Only at the end of *Fox* will enough of the reality of Germany, both as a place of 'otherness' and a country consciously living its history, impinge upon his consciousness to compel him into flight.

Augustine's easy assumption of superiority to politicians and politics is very much a product of his Oxford 'education'.

> At Oxford (that intense white incandescence of young minds) everyone had been agreed that only inferior people feel an itch for power, or even consent to have it thrust upon them... To Augustine, even honest statemen and politicians seemed at best a kind of low-grade communal servant — like sewer-cleaners, doing a beastly job decent men are thankful not to have to do themselves. (pp. 69-70)

The parenthesis is half-sympathetic, half-ironic. Augustine's distaste for politics, however, is soon revealed as the mere tip of an iceberg of ignorance. His incomprehension of the reality of economic life in Germany is total. He cannot even begin to imagine the social consequences of inflation. His response to the "incredible noughts" on the banknotes he receives in exchange for a ten-shilling note is to think "What a joke!"; his realization that he's just become a billionaire makes "his head swim a little" (p.132).

At the dinner-table of his aristocratic relation, Baron Walter von Kessen, a staunch Bavarian monarchist, he is comically but instructively out of his depth. He's vaguely aware that 'Germany' is a fairly new concept (it is only forty-eight years old), and that Bavaria until quite recently was a sovereign country, but these are facts that possess no vital significance for him. Unable to comprehend that what's at stake at this critical moment in time is Bavaria's ideological identity, he's oblivious to the animated conversation of the male von Kessens. Interpreting their jokes and allusions from an English viewpoint, he perpetrates one *faux pas* after another — saved only, as it happens, by the fact that his relations understand him as little as he understands them. An enquiry about the British Labour Party prompts Walter to relate his part in the events of five years before. Then, a Centre Party deputy to the Bavarian parliament, he had been in Munich when revolution unseated the Wittelsbach king. It's not enough to say that Walter recounts events here — he *relives* them passionately and dramatically. His hatred for the Socialist leader Eisner is plain. History, we see, is a living force for Walter: he is a political animal. He speaks of the past with an intensity which makes it present. In the spacious dining-room of this ancient baronial castle it is Augustine's convictions and habitual ways of feeling that are out of key. It is he who, in thinking that he can exist insulated from history, is refusing to inhabit the present.

In bed that same night, Augustine once more links for us the issues of history and personality: he

> began to wonder about people like Walter. Were they actually the way they talked — *unreal* creatures, truly belonging to that queer fictive state of collective being they seemed to think was 'Life' but which he thought of as 'History'? Or were they what they looked — real people, at bottom just as human and separate as Englishmen are? (pp.154-5)

According to the lights of his preconceptions, he ought to see Walter as a grotesque like his uncles. But experience has shifted his perception, though not as yet decisively. The whole episode furnishes a good example of how Hughes moves the reader, by way of Augustine, towards the recognition that people are "persons". That Augustine should equate the unreal with the 'fictive' is the novelist's joke: Augustine is at once fictive and historical, unreal and real.

In the event, he shelves the problem: perhaps he'll be nearer an answer when he gets to know Mitzi better — "For Women ... are surely, surely always the same, the whole world over..." But it would be truer to say that it is Augustine who is the same the whole world over: for he resolutely refuses to see (though he has eyes, and she is blind) Mitzi as she truly is. He sees rather, what he wishes to see, through the rose-tinted glasses of a romantic sensibility. It is only when he finds that she has gone into a convent that he wakes up to the fact that she had no interest in him — and, by way of that awakening, to the realization that something in Germany frightens him. His experience on the shore of the frozen Danube is a kind of epiphany — or, to use Hughes's own term, it is an eidolon:

> Even now the river was not everywhere frozen: here and there where the current was strongest there were still patches of dark grey water that steamed in the sun, so that the solitary swan indefatigably swimming

there was half-hidden in vapour. But elsewhere the Danube seemed to be frozen solid in heaps. It was wild, yet utterly still. Huge blocks of ice had jostled each other and climbed on top of each other like elephants rutting and then got frozen in towering lumps: or had swirled over and over before coagulating till they were curled like a Chinese sea. None of them had remained in the place where first it had frozen: each block was complete in itself but now out of place — like a jig-saw puzzle glued in a heap helter-skelter so that now it could never be solved.

It was all such a muddle! Although it was utterly still it expressed such terrific force it was frightening: the force that had made it — thrusting floes weighing hundreds of tons high into the air, and the force it would release when it thawed. When that ice melted at last it would go thundering down the river grinding to bits everything in its path. No bridge could possibly stand up to it. The longer you looked at its stillness, the greater your feeling of panic .... Augustine *hated* Germany: all he wanted now was to get away as quick as he could. (p.351)

The description conveys with muscular immediacy the tremendous power imprisoned in post-war Germany. It suggests a country balked and frustrated, a people politically and spiritually disorganized. Beneath the perverse and petrified shapes of ice, the current of tradition still flows, but is visible only intermittently. The lone swan, emblem of grace and purity (and for Shelley and Yeats of the free soul), seems in danger of being swallowed up in the vapour which the sun causes to rise up from the water and the ice. The problems symbolically embodied in this enormous confusion of ice are unsolvable, but nothing is more certain than an eventual release of pent-up force. No bridge will be able to withstand it. Bridges are emblems of communication and connection. Hughes's sudden introduction of the second person — "The longer you looked at its stillness, the greater your feeling of panic ..." — puts the reader in Augustine's place. Augustine himself doesn't stop to analyse his experience: it remains for him an intuition. In seeking to say what it is an intuition *of*, I shall settle for the term *otherness*: something beyond understanding, something mysterious and irreducible, yet something *there* — and set over against oneself. What Augustine apprehends in the Danube is at once personal, the sudden incursion into his introverted sensibility of something that is external and formidable, and general, a symbolic encapsulation of the condition of a country and a culture. He has, perhaps, sensed the future in the instant: for the contained and brutal power that has touched his mind will invade Europe and much of the world. The 'Other' which Augustine experiences here, then, might be said to be the raw essence or spirit of history — an immaterial power whose inherence in these chaotic banks of ice is momentary. But his flight from it could not have been more headlong had he understood what it meant.

These happenings enable us to make certain statements about Augustine. Once launched upon a certain course, he will allow the current of events to carry him along with it: but, typically, he recoils before arriving at a true terminus. His actions, characteristically, are *re*actions. He advances towards certain recognitions, but does not ponder experience deeply enough to compel it to throw up general truths or precepts which then form a basis for future sallyings-forth. If wisdom is a ladder which may be mounted rung by rung, it is a ladder which he never seems to make an effort to climb. He lives neither by passion nor reason, but only by vague shades of these: his encounters never throw up moments of self-discovery which change him for himself ineradicably. Indeed, there appears to be no reason why he should ever be significantly different from what he is to begin with (Hughes says that his sea-voyage alters him, but it is not an alteration that I feel expresses itself in terms of personality.) It is easy to see why some readers of *The Wooden Shepherdess* should have expressed their disappointment with Augustine, at his failure significantly to grow. And yet, although I feel that Hughes, as the novel itself grew, may have felt tied by the function he had allotted Augustine, I also feel that it would be wrong to require of Augustine (and I mean Augustine, not Hughes) what the character cannot deliver. His whole nature is predicated upon the fact of unpreparedness; and if his character refuses to come into clear and unambiguous focus for us, that may be *our* fault for expecting a rounded nineteenth-century sensibility to be laid out for us in a novel which, bespeaking the nineteenth-century in a number of ways, is still a modern novel. For is not that very quality of unfocusedness — as if Augustine, despite his dogmas about life, remains, finally, a mystery to himself in his refusal to take himself seriously — peculiarly modern? Is not Augustine's very refusal to work himself out in his mind, his readiness to live life hamfistedly and almost provisionally, is not this a quality which subjectively we experience in ourselves? Do we not, for example, refuse to answer questions which have clarified themselves in our minds — as if, in answering them, we might discover truths about ourselves or the world which we would rather not know?

It would be an understatement to say that Augustine knows himself imperfectly. His experiences in Connecticut in *The Wooden Shepherdess* show just how flimsy is his notion of himself as a free, self-determined and self-determining individual. The theme of the Book is announced symbolically by the watersnake that flashes "in the dwindled summer cascade ̦scarcely tinkling into the one pool deep enough to swim in". The sexual attitudes of the Pack assault whatever shreds of romanticism are left in Augustine's sensibility after his experience with Mitzi. His response is almost one of culture-shock. From the start he is "more than a little dumbfounded" (p. 50) that American teenagers should be allowed out, unchaperoned, after dark. "The British upper-class culture Augustine himself had been reared in had tended to 'sex its pubescents in half'" — with consequent repressions for the boys. What the Pack has done is to extend the 'penumbra' of selfhood in a way quite new to this Englishman. To them, 'we' are teenagers, 'they' all others. It is a dividing-line which cuts across ties of family and class such as those Augustine pays allegiance to. The Pack practises freedoms of which he might be assumed, in theory, to approve; but, face to face with such emancipations as girls drinking, he finds those freedoms difficult to accept. "It was shocking ..." (p.52). The drinking-party on the roof of his shack challenges his belief that the words 'right' and 'wrong' no longer have meaning for him. "The fact is he didn't know yet what to think: was this Progress or Decadence?" His misunderstanding with Janis demonstrates conclusively not only that he is very much a moral being, but that his values are culturally relative. Encouraged by her passionate behaviour to think she means to have intercourse with him, he is shocked when she draws back "at the very last moment of all" (p. 75). (She for her part is equally shocked that he should attempt to overstep "the rules of the game" — rules which allow every satisfaction but that to be got from copulation itself.)

> Augustine had always been led to suppose that a girl, on the rare and almost incredible times that she starts, most certainly wouldn't have started a thing that she didn't intend to go through with; and then for the man to draw back is the grossest of insults... (p. 74)

Janis's *mores* in this instance are utilitarian: she has no wish to be an unmarried mother. Augustine's, in comparison, are much more purely ethical.

His hypothetical persuasion that *sin* has ceased to be, for his generation, a meaningful word; that *guilt*'s days of currency are numbered; and that "Conscience is an *operable* cancer" (*FA* p. 73), is shown to be hopelessly optimistic by his involvement with Ree. When he rejects her offer of her child's body on the night of his recovery of the bootleg whisky from the sunken Bearcat, he feels "ashamed in ... strangely conflicting ways" (p.108). He is ashamed of himself for having brought her — a child — to the point of offering herself to him, ashamed of causing her pain by rejecting her, ashamed of the desire he has stifled in himself. His conflict of emotion may even imply that he is conscious of lacking the will to translate his theoretical amorality into deeds. He finds himself placed in a kind of moral Catch-22 in which he is an all-ways loser.

> This load on his heart, this leaden lump at the very corre of his being seemed mighty close to what people like Mitzi must mean by 'sin'!
>   But there couldn't be '*sin*' if there wasn't a God to offend — which there wasn't, of course ... And so, was it Freud whom Augustine in fact had offended against? Or the God Who Didn't Exist? Or would some wholly impartial observer, perhaps, have deemed him in Dutch with both? (p.113)

He finds himself experiencing a feeling (the sense of having sinned) which, intellectually, he denies existence to. Once, he had condemned the Russians for making a god of Marx: but is he not here near to making one of Freud? Has he not failed his 'liberator', defeated by what looks suspiciously like a moral absolute ("*A-child-is-a-child-is-a-child*") despite his nagging doubts ("*or*, IS *it?*" — p.112)? It seems characteristic of him that his final surrender of his virginity to Sadie should prompt no reflection, while his refusal to give it up to Ree haunts him. It is the error of the not done which remains to trouble his mind.

It is in the last-quoted extract that Augustine comes as near to fulfulling Sartre's apprehension that identity is social, and dependent upon others, as he ever comes. Ree's behaviour towards him compels him to become an object for his own contemplation: he perceives himself, for the first time, to be a sinner. He signally fails, however, to reach out beyond himself to her, to speculate about *her* nature: to imagine how she might perceive him, and what she might feel towards him. "Hell", then, for him might well be said to be "other people": for though Ree doesn't cause him to see himself through her eyes (as Sartre's conception would seem to require), she certainly causes him to see himself in a way quite novel to him — and thoroughly disquieting. If we were to make the assumption that Hughes offers Augustine to us as a *pattern* of man — or modern man — then we would have, I think, little option but to conclude that his view of people's capacities imaginatively to reach out towards others is unduly pessimistic. I do not feel, however, that we need to make this assumption. Augustine's limitations are strategic: his reluctance to see others as *persons* only demonstrates to the reader the more insistently that that is what they are.

His adventures in Germany and America show the 'Other' to have two faces for him — the racial and the sexual — though these may be intertwined. The 'Other' comes into being for him in so far as it breaks in to tease Ego and to demand that Ego question its complacent assumptions about itself and the further world. That the 'penumbra' of the self has a bodily dimension we see in his dream of Ree, where his apprehension of the Other recalls Dick Watchett in *In Hazard*. Through Augustine, this imperfectly self-conscious antenna, Hughes demonstrates that personality is ineluctably historical.

IV

Augustine, of course, is a specifically English antenna, and in him Hughes embodies something of the myopia and insularity of the upper-class English in the inter-war years. In *Shepherdess* his friend Ludo will confront him with a striking home truth:

> 'You're capable only of seeing the world through your own English eyes, so all you see is a mirror reflecting your own English faces and can't conceive that what makes Germans tick is other than what makes you tick yourselves.' (p.260)

— another challenge to the complacencies of Ego. Hughes's contrast of life in interbellum England and Germany presents us, then, with calculated extremes of style and substance: life at Mellton, with its hierarchical orderliness and its domesicity, seems to go on outside History. (Wantage the butler is conscious of a slow process of change that is devaluing Service, but Mellton remains a complacent household.) Life in Germany is by contrast dynamic, radically insecure: History's pulse is everywhere to be felt. The creation of such a contrast necessitated a degree of selectivity from Hughes — certain emphases, certain exclusions. In neither *Fox* nor *Shepherdess* does he get to grips with English politics and politicians as he does in Bavaria. The brief entry of Sir John Simon in *Fox* seems to promise that Simon will be brought into close-up: but this never happens, and the thread is not pursued. Even the General Strike seems, from Hughes's treatment of it in *Shepherdess*, less a piece of serious history than a game played out between opposing teams. Set over against the insular Englishness of all this, of course, are the machinations of Adolf Hitler, a world-historical individual; and we are treated to detailed accounts of two of the violent events he is partly responsible for: the Munich Putsch and the Night of the Long Knives. The effect of this deliberate imbalance is to suggest that Britain exists 'outside' the stream of history-making, while Germany exists in it: and not only are the Germans making history for themselves, they are making it for Europe and the world.

The human predicament has a historical dimension: the most significant single factor in half a century of world history is German nationalism. It is with this, then, that Hughes as a historical novelist is centrally concerned: it will be the spirit of Germany as it finds expression in National Socialism that the Allies must fight in 1939. In the meantime, Hughes sends out his English probes to experience the historical 'Other': in *Fox* Augustine, in *Shepherdess* a party of English people (including Augustine and Jeremy), and in the early chapters of volume three a pair of upper-class English girls — who, Unity Mitford-like, meet Hitler in the flesh at Berchtesgaden.

When in the Blashfield Address Hughes comes to compare Fiction, Biography and History, it is in terms of their treatment of the human individual that he distinguishes between them:

> no form of Non-fiction can do for us what Fiction does. Not even Biography, Fiction's nearest cousin. One speaks of a biography's 'subject' though it is rather as an object that he is shown; constructed from external evidence much as the detective constructs his criminal (or your analyst you). The biographer cannot *become* him without breaking out openly into Fiction — as some of them do... History is an even remoter abstraction: Biography, the perspective drawing of an object, History a diagram of the interaction of such objects.[12]

Now it seems to me that *The Human Predicament*, as that hybrid form a 'historical novel', includes all these types of writing inside itself. Hughes approaches his material now in the guise of Historian, now in the guise of Biographer, and now (though most frequently) as Fiction-writer. He is at his weakest when (as I have said) he loses touch with particularity and settles for something that is neither good 'diagrammatic' writing nor good fiction. That 'diagrammatic' writing may be vital and interesting, however, the theoretical chapters which close Book One of *Fox* show: for what role has Hughes adopted here but that of historian of the psyche? Hughes's analysis implies that the historian, the biographer and the fiction-writer produce distinct kinds of discourse; but in the hands of the historical novelist the three may become intimates, interweaving and reinforcing one another. Nor is it always easy to tell where one ends and another begins: History tends to melt into Biography, and Biography into Fiction. Hughes's dedication to accuracy means that 'the fictive' must itself be shaped and penetrated by the historical.

His treatment of Hitler encompasses all three kinds of writing; so, in order to examine the mode of the historical novelist in some detail, let us turn back to the Fuhrer.

I have already, in discussing Hitler's sexuality, quoted a couple of short passages in which Hughes writes with the 'diagrammatic' objectivity of the historian. Here is a slightly longer extract:

> Incest (or quasi-incest at least) seems perhaps the obvious
> theoretical answer in cases of psychological blockage which stem from
> an overweening solipsism, like Hitler's. This sexy young niece was
> blood of his blood, so could perhaps in his solipsist mind be envisaged
> as merely a female organ budding on 'him' — as forming with him a
> single hermaphrodite 'Hitler', a two-sexed entity able to couple within
> itself like the garden snail ... (*WS* p.320)

This is the historian as psychologist. Hughes uses his position of authority
as omniscient narrator to float a theory, an abstract and general structure of
understanding, just as if he was an expert in abnormal psychology.

Here is a passage in which he offers us a 'perspective drawing' of Hitler:

> 'The formula is much the same everywhere these days,' said a rather
> squat actor-type, rising and moving down centre: 'First: a portentous
> message that he'll be a bit late — detained on most important business.
> Then, about midnight — when he's quite sure that his entrance will be
> the last — he marches in, bows so low to his hostess that his sock-
> suspenders show and presents her with a wilting bouquet of red roses.
> Then he refuses the proffered chair, turns his back on her and stations
> himself at the buffet. If anybody speaks to him he fills his mouth with
> cream puffs and grunts. If they dare to speak a second time he only fills
> his mouth with cream puffs. It isn't that just in the company of his
> betters he can't converse himself — he *aims* to be a kind of social upas,
> to kill conversation anywhere within reach of his shadow. Soon the
> whole room is silent. That's what he's waiting for: he stuffs the cream
> puff half-eaten into his pocket and begins to orate. Usually it's against
> the Jews: sometimes it's the Bolshevik Menace: sometimes it's the
> November Criminals — no matter, it's always the same kind of speech,
> quiet and winning and reasonable at first but before long in a voice that
> makes the spoons dance on the plates. He goes on for half an hour — an
> hour, maybe: then he breaks off suddenly, smacks his sticky lips on his
> hostess's hand again, and ... and out into the night, what's left of it.' (*FA*
> p.199)

The passage is vivid but objective. It is in fact a 'version' of an original
description of Hitler given by a fellow-guest at a party in 1923, and quoted
by Konrad Heiden in *Hitler, a Biography* (London 1936). Hughes told me he
had never read this book: he was, however, familiar with Alan Bullock's
Hitler: a Study in Tyranny in which Heiden's biography is quoted:

> Hitler had sent word to his hostess that he had to attend an important
> meeting and would not arrive until late: I think it was about eleven
> o'clock. He came, none the less, in a very decent blue suit and with an

extravagantly large bouquet of roses, which he presented to his hostess as he kissed her hand. While he was being introduced, he wore the expression of a public prosecutor at an execution. I remember being struck by his voice when he thanked the lady of the house for tea and cakes, of which incidentally, he ate an amazing quantity. It was a remarkably emotional voice, and yet it made no impression of conviviality or intimacy but rather of harshness. However, he said hardly anything but sat there in silence for about an hour; apparently he was tired. Not until the hostess was so incautious as to let fall a remark about the Jews, whom she defended in a jesting tone, did he begin to speak and then he spoke without ceasing. After a while he thrust back his chair and stood up, still speaking, or rather yelling, in such a powerful penetrating voice as I have never heard from anyone else. In the next room a child woke up and began to cry. After he had for more than half an hour delivered a quite witty but very one-sided oration on the Jews, he suddenly broke off, went up to his hostess, begged to be excused and kissed her hand as he took his leave. The rest of the company, who apparently had not pleased him, were only vouchsafed a curt bow from the doorway.[13]

It is a fascinating exercise to compare the two passages. Hughes preserves, one after another, the significant details of his source: the message, the late arrival, the bouquet of roses, the cakes, the long silence, the anti-semitic oration, and the kissing of the hostess's hand as Hitler takes his leave. The only alteration of fact concerns the proffered chair, which in the original is accepted. The only significant omissions are the crying of the child and the description of Hitler's expression while being introduced — this last an omission I'm unable to account for, since it adds to the eccentricity of his behaviour. The significant additions are almost all visual, aimed at increasing the vividness of the description: so, Hitler's sock-suspenders show when he bows, his roses are "wilting", the cakes become particularized as "cream puffs" (the last of which he stuffs into his pocket prior to launching into words), his voice makes "the spoons dance on the plates", and the kiss lavished on his hostess's hand is delivered by childishly "sticky lips". None of these does violence to the original or weakens the historicity of the actor-types's monologue.

Heiden's account must have cried out to be appropriated, for it is rich with visual effects that any novelist would have been proud to have invented. What it needed, however, is equally obvious — 'translation' into colloquial English, into the manner of speaking of a specific person. (The two passages are much of a length.) Hughes gives the description to a "squat actor-type" who knows just how to deliver it in order to make the most of it. For him it can justifiably take the form of a *speech*, becoming direct, present-tense, dramatic, rich with gesture and emphasis (consider, for instance, the wealth of conjunctions, which point the listener's (the reader's) attention to a new fact or action, a development in the situation). No one, as Dr. Reinhold is made to remark afterwards (the comment is originally Heiden's), who encounters Hitler is likely to forget him.

Hitler in both passages is an eccentric. In Heiden's account his eccentricity carries an ominous force, possesses sinister overtones. The novel transforms this tone, the actor-type bringing a humorous quality into his narrative that serves to disarm behaviour that might otherwise give serious cause for alarm, colours it as the antics of a social misfit. To this end there are a number of significant adjustments in style and tone: the blunt description of Hitler yelling in a powerful penetrating voice is transformed into metaphor, the comic hyperbole of spoons dancing on plates; the detail of the child being wakened is omitted (this too particular a detail in what the actor-type presents as a typical occurrence); the violent single-mindedness of Hitler's verbal onslaught on the Jews is softened by being buffered by droll references to the cream puffs and the sticky lips they create; and the measured sternness of his leave-taking in the original is given a throwaway abruptness in: "and out into the night, what's left of it".

At the same time, however, there are indications in the actor-type's speech that there is more to this buffoonery than might strike the idle ear. A final difference between the two versions is that whilst Hughes provides clues to the solution of the riddle of Hitler's behaviour within the anecdote itself, Heiden provides a separate commentary after the story. The actor-type goes no little way towards making sense of his eccentric: he states that Hitler actually *aims* to poison conversation, so that when the room is silent he can take over the whole party. Behind the posturing lies a formula for self-advertisement, a strategy for self-advancement. In his biography, Heiden spells out what the novelist leaves his reader to infer:

> He was a social climber who had no desire to be agreeable but had the courage to attract attention. For this purpose there were three golden rules, which he was not the first to discover: make a point of arriving late, then you are noticed; take no part in the conversation, thereby making yourself at most agreeable but not otherwise attracting notice; then, suddenly, start gabbing like a maniac, so that everyone is reduced to silence, for thereby you force people to pay attention to you; then go away before the company breaks up, so that those who are left behind can talk about you, which deepens the impression. (pp.104-105)

Heiden's characterization of Hitler as a "social climber" is a sobering estimation; nevertheless his analysis reveals the strategic calculation behind the apparently crazy conduct. The strange becomes the logical. It isn't surprising that the account should give the thoughtful Dr. Reinhold pause; it might well give Hughes's reader pause, too.

Hughes's version is clearly the work of a novelist, but a novelist handling his subject with the objectivity of a biographer.

Only in one chapter does Hughes allow himself the full liberty of the novelist in depicting Hitler — that is, of getting inside Hitler's mind and showing him to be a person. The chapter in question is the climax of Hughes's gradual approach, and is carefully set in context. After the failure of the *putsch* of 1923, Hitler escapes to the home of his friend Putzi Hanfstaengl at Uffing. There, exhausted and in considerable pain from a dislocated shoulder, he lies sleepless in the attic of the house:

[1] ... suddenly the bells started ringing: the Sunday bells of Uffing, beating on his ears with their frightful jarring tintinnabulation. Whereon somebody must have started pulling a clapper in Hitler's own head too, for his own head started chiming with the bells of Uffing. His head was rocking with the weight of its own terrible tolling.

[2] Flinging back the blanket Hitler gazed desperately round. His trusty whip stood just out of reach, but how he longed to hear again instead of those clanging bells the whirr of its clean singing thong of rhinoceros-hide — the whirring, and the *crack*! If he had given those three traitors a taste of it instead of letting them through his fingers he'd have been in Berlin by now — yes, in BERLIN!

[3] ' *Woe to the bloody city! It is all full of lies and robbery ... the noise of a whip* ...' (To think that this very hour he should have been riding triumphant through Berlin!) ' *...the noise of a whip, and the noise of the rattling of the wheels, and of the prancing horses, and of the jumping chariots ...*' (In Berlin, scourging the money lenders from the temple! A city in flames!) ' *There is a multitude of the slain, and a great number of carcases; there is none end of their corpses, they stumble upon their corpses...*'

[4] Scourging the hollow barons ... scourging the puking communists ... scourging the Lesbians and the nancy-boys with that rhinoceros-thong!

[5] But that barrel — it was changing shape: now tall now short, now fat now lean ... erect, and swelling ... and out of the swelling barrel a remembered figure was rising — smooth, and gross, and swaying and nodding like a tree. It was a man's figure from his own penurious teen-age in Vienna: it was that smooth-faced beast at the Hotel Kummer, bribing the bright-eyed hard-up boy with cream puffs, promising him all the pastries he could eat and daring to make passes at *him*, at Adolfus Hitler!

[6] Then under the hammering of the bells the figure collapsed — suddenly as it had risen.

[7]   Scourging the whores, the Jews ... scourging the little flash jew-girls till they screamed...

[8]   Now the dark corners of the room were filling with soft naked legs: those young Viennese harlots sitting half-naked in the lighted windows all along the Spittelberggasse (between the dark windows where 'it' was already being done). For once upon a time the young Hitler used to go there, to the Spittelberggasse: to ... just to look at them. To harden his will; for except by such tests as these how can a lad with the hair new on him be assured that his will is strong? The boy would stare, and walk on a few yards; then come back as 'strong' as ever — back to the most attractive and most nearly naked and stare her out again, pop-eyed.

[9]   He called it "the Flame of Life", that holy flame of sex in the centre of a man; and he knew that all his whole life *his* 'Flame' had to be kept burning without fuel for at the first real touch of human, female fuel it must turn smoky, fill his whole Vessel with soot. This was Destiny's revealed dictate: if ever Hitler did 'it' the unique Power would go out of him, like Samson and his hair. No, at most if the adult male flesh itched intolerably it might be deviously relieved.

[10]   After all, how could that monistic 'I' of Hitler's ever without forfeit succumb to the entire act of sex, the whole essence of which is recognition of one *Other'? Without damage I mean to his fixed conviction that he was the universe's unique sentient centre, the sole authentic incarnate Will it contained or ever had contained?* (*FA* pp.264-66)

I have given a lengthy extract here, because in this passage it is possible to see Fiction-writer melting into Biographer, and Biographer into Historian. The extract begins with the objective prose of a third-person narrator. Then, deftly, Hughes shifts from the objective realm of the chiming bells to the subjective realm — Hitler's head chiming *with* the bells. With the verb "longed" in paragraph 2 we discover Hitler's feelings: the prose now poises itself between pure 'stream-of-consciousness' and pure objective reportage: the distinction between author and subject is collapsed, and author enters into subject — or subject into author. Thus, in "If he had given those three traitors a taste of it instead of letting them through his fingers he'd have been in Berlin by now — yes, in BERLIN!" the idea appears to issue simultaneously from novelist and character. This ambiguous position is maintained up to the end of the parenthesis in paragraph 8; at which point the novelist suddenly recovers his distance from his subject (the withdrawal is signalled by the clearly objective "For once upon a time"). The remainder of paragraph 8, and the whole of paragraph 9, might have been written by a biographer. This is Hughes's 'perspective drawing' again. With paragraph 10 he withdraws — and we withdraw — still further, to the distance of the diagrammatist: whose hegemony is signalled in the appearance of the authorial 'I' as omniscience surveys the field.

The act of imagination which produces the earlier paragraphs in the extract is much more radical than that required to produce the account of Hitler at the party. Here, in fact we see the historical novelist operating at full stretch, for the imagination which produces the Uffing passage is at once fictive and historical: Hitler ceases to be an 'outside', he becomes a person.

But what is the 'historical imagination', and how does it relate to the fictive imagination? Comparing the products of novelist and historian in *The Idea of History* (1946), the philosopher of history R.G. Collingwood concludes that "As works of imagination [they] do not differ" except in so far as "the historian's picture is meant to be true" (p. 246). "Truth" for Collingwood requires the observance of three rules of method which the novelist is free to ignore: the localization of his picture in space and time, the observance of self-consistency, and "relation to something called evidence". Now it seems to me that *The Human Predicament* observes the first and second of these rules throughout, and the third when dealing with material appropriate to the historian: the acts and speech, that is, of persons who actually lived. But Hughes goes beyond these parameters in portraying Hitler in the chapter I have quoted from: he makes us privy to Hitler's stream of consciousness. This would seem to make his method unhistorical. But let us persevere with Collingwood. Collingwood discriminates between what he calls the "inside" and "outside" of an event; by the latter he means "everything belonging to it which can be described in terms of bodies and their movements"; by the former "that in it which can only be described in terms of *thought*" (my italics). The historian's work may, for him,

> begin by discovering the outside of an event, but it can never end there; he must always remember that the event was an action, and that his main task is *to think himself into this action, to discern the thought of its agent.* (p. 213; again my italics)

This suggests a very different notion of history from that supplied by Hughes in his Blashfield Address. Collingwood would not be satisfied with history that is merely diagrammatic and external. How, then, does the historian come to discern the thought of the historical agent? Precisely, says Collingwood, through the historical imagination. This, using Kantian language, he terms *a priori*, signifying that "it is in no way arbitrary or merely fanciful" (p.240). He further denies the "prejudice" which holds that what is imaginary must be fictitious or unreal: "The imaginary, simply as such, is neither unreal nor real" (p.241). The historian's task, then, can never consist merely in assembling a patchwork picture of his subject from sources and authorities ("scissors and paste history"). These sources and authorities are not automatically "evidence", since evidence for Collingwood is also subject to verification and approval by the historical imagination. "Everything is evidence which the historian can use as evidence... The whole perceptible world ... is potentially and in principle evidence to the historian" (pp.246-47). The historian's end must be the creation of "a web of imaginative construction" verified and justified alone by his own critical intelligence.

I suggest, then, that what Richard Hughes gives us in his portrayal of Hitler at Uffing is "a web of imaginative construction" which represents the fictive and historical imaginations at a point of harmonious rapprochement. To bear out the truth of this, it is necessary to demonstrate that the substance of Hitler's thoughts self-consistently concurs with "something called evidence" — that it is not merely arbitrary and fanciful.

The key to the unity of the early paragraphs is the whip. Hitler's disturbed mind focusses on images of revenge, and the whip is the weapon with which he imagines himself carrying it out. This whip existed, a gift to Hitler early in his political career from Elisabeth Büchner, the landlady of his favourite guest-house in Berchtesgaden. It provides Hughes with a ready-made symbol, expressive of Hitler's sadism and repressed sexuality. In *Hitler: the Missing Years*, Hanfstaengl describes Elisabeth as "a towering Brünnhilde type with a flashing gold tooth", and goes on sardonically to comment that Adolf

> had developed for her one of his unproductive, declamatory passions. He used to play the romantic revolutionary for her benefit, stamping round and cracking his rhinoceros-hide whip. (pp. 82-3)

The intimate relationship between the racial, sexual and political in Hitler's consciousness is brought out through the scourging, which is to fall indiscriminately upon the barons, the communists and the false triumvirate (Lossow, Kahr and Seisser); lesbians, homosexuals and whores; and Jews. As chastiser of the wicked, Hitler identifies himself with Christ. *Folie de grandeur* indeed! — but no more than an imaginative application of the "evidence". Dietrich Eckart, editor of *Völkischer Beobachter*, once confided to Hanfstaengl while sharing a room with him at the Büchners, that

> something has gone completely wrong with Adolf ... Last week he was striding up and down in the courtyard here with that damned whip of

his and shouting, 'I must enter Berlin like Christ in the Temple of Jerusalem and scourge out the moneylenders', and more nonsense of that sort. I tell you, if he lets this Messiah complex run away with him he will ruin us all. (p. 83)

What Eckart reports as an objective fact about Hitler is transformed in Hughes's text into a subjective psychological truth.

The whip also provides the cue for the passages in italics. Here Hughes takes his largest imaginative liberty with Hitler. According to Hanfstaengl, Hitler had "learnt a lot" from the Bible, atheist though he was by the time Hanfstaengl came to know him.[14] In a letter to me of January 1976, Hughes wrote:

I have always been a bit uncomfortable about the legitimacy of the Nahum quotation since it is most unlikely that Hitler was familiar with the Minor Prophets. But the passage had struck *me* so forcibly while writing the chapter that I used it as a kind of shorthand to illustrate his frame of mind.

It isn't difficult to see why Hughes found *Nahum* so relevant: the voice of Nahum in the passage quoted is also that of Jehovah, threatening the downfall of Nineveh in the seventh century before Christ (see *Nahum* 3: 1-3 in the Authorized Version). But there is a painful historical irony here: a "great patriot" and a "passionate" nationalist, Nahum was "the last of the great classical Hebrew poets".[15] Over two millenia later, Nahum's own race is to be "scourged" by this blasphemous self-styled "Messiah".

Hitler's hallucinations resurrect memories from his youth. Young Adolf's daring of the Spittelberggasse and his encounter with the homosexual at the Hotel Kummer are both described by his boyhood friend August Kubizek in *Young Hitler* (London 1954), the only intimate biography of this period of his life. Here is Kubizek's portrayal of their meeting with the homosexual:

One evening, at the corner of Mariahilferstrasse, a well-dressed, prosperous looking man spoke to us and asked us about ourselves. When he told him that we were students ... he invited us to supper at the Hotel Kummer. He allowed us to order anything we pleased and for once Adolf could eat as many tarts and pastries as he could manage. Meanwhile, he told us that he was a manufacturer from Vöcklabruck and did not like anything to do with women, as they were only gold diggers. I was especially interested in what he said about the Chamber music which appealed to him. We thanked him, he came out of the restaurant with us, and we went home.

There Adolf asked me if I liked the man. "Very much," I replied. "A very cultured man, with pronounced artistic leanings."

"And what else?" continued Adolf with an enigmatic expression on his face.

"What else should there be?" I asked, surprised.

"As apparently you don't understand, Gustl, what it's all about, look at this little card!"

"Which card?"

For, in fact, this man had slipped Adolf a card without my noticing it, on which he had scribbled an invitation to visit him at the Hotel Kummer.

"He's a homosexual," explained Adolf in a matter-of-fact manner. I was startled. I had never even heard the word, much less had I any conception of what it actually meant. So Adolf explained this phenomenon to me. Naturally, this, too, had long been one of his problems and, as an abnormal practice, he wished to see it fought against relentlessly, and he himself scrupulously avoided all personal contact with such men. The visiting card of the famous manufacturer from Vöcklabruck disappeared into our stove. (p.175)

In the novel this incident undergoes a radical transformation, demonstrating clearly the difference between, as Hughes defines them, Fiction and Biography. Kubizek is content to present his friend's response objectively: Adolf is self-possessed and unperturbed; he takes the encounter in his stride. Hughes, reconstituting the event as hallucination, makes the figure lurid and epicene, a tempter both repellent and attractive: "gross" and bestial, he is also "smooth", "smooth-faced". Hughes, perhaps, noted the ambiguity in Kubizek's statement that homosexuality had long been one of Adolf's "problems". The fiction-writer seeks to probe behind the surface which the biographer finds it not within his brief to penetrate.

For a while it looks as though Hughes is going to treat the Spittelberggasse incident in a similar way. With the second sentence of paragraph 8, however, there comes the withdrawal I have mentioned — the return to an objectivist view of Hitler. In discussing "the Flame of Life" Hughes continues to draw on Kubizek. Kubizek admits that he often had to struggle in order to grasp the meaning of his friend's "bombastic formulae", but defines this particular entity as "the symbol of sacred love which is awakened between man and woman who have kept themselves pure in body and soul and are worthy of a union which would produce healthy children for the nation" (p.172). Hitler's obsessive chastity reveals itself as one of the foundation-stones supporting Hughes's broad interpretation of him as a solipsist.

In his review of *The Fox in the Attic*, Stephen Spender wrote that "Mr. Hughes 'creates' the characters of Hitler and some of his colleagues as though they were fictitious in the way that his unhistoric characters are".[16] His inverted commas and qualificatory "as though" keep the right options open. Hughes's inner Hitler is, in Collingwood's terms, a product of the *a priori* imagination, a creation at once fictional and historical: *historical* because Hughes, having soaked himself in the "evidence", has thought himself into an historical action and discerned the thought of an historical agent; *fictional* because the thought of that agent consists of more than reflection on the significant public event (the Putsch) which has brought him where he is, and takes the form of an hallucination fed by memory and informed by fear and desire.

In satisfying Collingwood's three rules, Hughes's portrayal of Hitler would seem to merit the ascription of "truth". Collingwood's account of the historical imagination, of course, is not one to which all academic historians would subscribe. Absolute truth is a chimera, and all historical discourse is limited by the subjectivity of the historian. So, at least, I imagine a counter-statement might run. The argument belongs to the philosophical realm. Certainly historians have applauded the historicity of *The Human Predicament* as regards its portrayal of Hitler: Joachim Fest (in a private letter of which I have seen a copy) and Alan Bullock, who, in a footnote on p.113 of *Hitler: a Study in Tyranny,* refers his reader "for a graphic reconstruction of the whole episode" of the Putsch to *The Fox in the Attic.* Hughes's Hitler is as convincing and authentic a version of Hitler as we are likely to get from a historical novelist.

V

The Wooden Shepherdess was the last new book that Hughes completed. It is therefore interesting to remark the pronounced element of recapitulation that it contains. This recapitulation extends back not only to *The Fox in the Attic* (as one would expect) but to *In Hazard* and *A High Wind in Jamaica.* We ought, I suppose, to spot the metaphorical link between the frozen Danube at the end of *Fox* —

> When that ice melted at last it would go thundering down the river grinding to bits everything in its path (p.351)

— and the Connecticut stream at the beginning of *Shepherdess:*

> spring's melting snows must send a torrent down this wide gully of hot white stones... (p. 3)

but reminiscences of the pre-war novels are so marked as to demand notation.

In general, the eidolon is less in evidence in Hughes's long novel than in his earlier ones — as if his conscious concern with the history of his own times had dictated the curbing of his poetic and sensuous talents. When the monkey who fights himself (having no one else to fight) reappears from *A High Wind* (see above, p.140). it is not only a very different context, but in a decidedly reduced condition. Ree's cousin Russell, we recall, explains Prohibition as a result of America's post-war isolationism: deprived of an external object on which to vent her frustrated war-emotions, she has divided against herself:

> 'Just like a lonesome old monkey reduced to fighting front legs against back, his hind feet doing their best to scratch out his eyes and his teeth sunk deep in his own private parts...' (p. 77)

The image implies a sort of schizophrenia, as it had in the earlier book. But where, in *A High Wind*, the eidolon was allowed to expand, to float free of a controlling context, it is in *Shepherdess* placed and constrained. The very fact that it is *speech* enjoins upon it the curb of a comparative naturalism.

The other recapitulations all relate in some way to Augustine, and may be considered under two heads: Augustine the rum-runner, and Augustine and girls.

Pressed into service as a sailor on the rum-runner which unintentionally carried him off from St. Malo, Augustine behaves in ways that recall the children on board first *Clorinda* and then the pirate-schooner. Compare the following pairs of passages:

> [1a] Soon, running up the ratlines and prancing on the yard (as if it were a mere table-top) had no further thrill for John or Emily either. (*HW* p. 64)
> [1b] ...monkeying [!] up the ratlines to spend a misty hour aloft on watch at the masthead... (*WS* p. 45)
> [2a]The flying-jib, too, which was usually down, made an admirable cocoon for hide-and-seek: one took a firm grip of the hanks and robands, and swathed oneself in the canvas. Once, suspecting Edward was hidden there, instead of going out on the jib-boom to look, the other children cast off the down-haul and then all together gave a great tug at the halyard which nearly pitched him into the sea. (*HW* p.152)
> [2b]It was better by far at sea, where even down in the tropics was better than this: in the belly perhaps of a close-hauled mainsail, half-standing and half-reclining, cooled by the steady downflow of air with your back in the curve of the canvas and feet on the boom ... Once, though, for a lark the skipper had put her about and he'd only just woken in time not

to get catapulted into the ocean! (*WS* p. 42)

The ship, for Augustine is a place of work; for the children a place of play: yet these passages affirm the continuity between the delights of the child and the pleasures of the man. Both have escaped the constraints of an earlier world. Augustine's sea-going changes him:

> Coarsened — or made just a little more 'realistic', if that is the word you prefer. It was much as happens in war: for just as a boy when his voice breaks now sings bass but loses his top-notes, so must the need for adjustment to action and danger — the downward shift of his whole emotional gamut to take it — leave him calloused a bit at the finer, more sensitive end of his thinking and feeling. (p. 10)

This, of course, recalls Dick Watchett after the hurricane:

> A man cannot stretch the gamut of his emotions, he can only shift it. If you reach out at one end, to cover the emotion of death, till you can cope with that comfortably, you can't expect to keep a delicate sensitiveness at the other end too. Just as there are baritones, tenors, trebles: but no one can sing the whole length of the piano. It was as if Dick's voice had broken now. He had some fine manly notes. But the old top-notes were gone. (*IH* p. 268)

Surrounded by the Pack, and haunted by Ree, Augustine at one point is "seized with a terrible longing for ships and for adult masculine company" (p. 45). It is not merely because he is leading a "limboish mark-time life" in Connecticut, but because the girl's attentions have drawn him into a complex region of feeling; the rum-runner was by contrast a place of comradely simplicity. Dick Watchett, after his deeper testing, entirely casts aside the memory of Sukie: she is, after all, a young girl, while he is "now a man. A sailor, a hard case" (p. 266). Affirming the known simplicity, he rejects the more delicate, unexplored and unresolved realm of experience.

Dick Watchett's encounter with Sukie feeds into Augustine's experience of girls at two points in *Shepherdess*. First consider his contracting experience of Mitzi:

> The passage of months and oceans had shrunk her image to something small and bright and picture-like: something seen as if looking back through a tunnel, or down the wrong end of a telescope. (pp. 5-6)

This echoes:

> At first Sukie had blazed in Dick's mind, lighting every part of it: but now already, after two days, she had contracted and receded like the

opening by which you have entered a tunnel: turned more unearthly
bright than the broad day, but very distant and small and clear. (p. 23)

Both girls' images shrink during sea-voyages, as their respective
rememberers travel away from them in space and time. But Augustine is
going to America (where Dick met Sukie), and there it will be the teenage
Ree who most affects him. It is in the brash new world of America that girls
will be found who break the constraints that prevail in Europe. In *In Hazard*
we saw how Dick's mind, hallucinating after many sleepless hours, melted
Thomas the lemur into Sukie to produce a strange lemur-girl; and how Ao
Ling's Fukienese girl became, in a troubled dream, "a fox in human shape".
When in Chapter 12 of Book One of *Shepherdess* Augustine dreams, his
dream is complex indeed:

> Sleeping, he dreamed of that fateful day back in Wales, the day he came
> home from the Marsh to his empty echoing house with a drowned
> child doubled over his shoulder, and found to his horror on lifting it
> down it had stiffened bent double. But there things changed: for he
> knew in this dream (without knowing the reason) that this time he
> couldn't just leave the tiny waterlogged body all night as it was in its
> sopping clothes on the sofa — he'd got to undress it, like putting a live
> child to bed. Yet as soon as he started to do so, he found that instead of
> bare skin underneath this child was downy all over with delicate fur;
> and a fur attractively soft to the touch, like a mole's... When he pulled
> her last vest over her head — leaving all the downy body uncovered
> except for the socks — he saw that the wide-open eyes in the small dead
> face were alive and were eagerly watching him take her clothes: nor
> were these even the pair of eyes which belonged, they were Ree's...
> (pp. 52-3)

The image of the furred animal-girl is such an insistent one in Hughes's
novels that it is difficult to resist the thought that it must have been an image
which the writer had himself experienced in dream-form. Literally,
Augustine strips dead innocence bare and finds live experience lying there
in all her provocative, yet forbidden, sensuousness: his dream confronts
him with the unacknowledged desires of his unconscious in a quite
unambiguous way. But a still deeper level of self-borrowing remains to be
teased out. Rachel/Ree is neither a lemur-girl nor a fox-girl, but a *mole*-girl.
Why a mole? For an answer we must go back to a story published more than
fifty years before *The Wooden Shepherdess*. In 'The Cart', as Ursula Wortley
lies in bed on the night after her father has left home on a business trip, we
are told:

> Her eyes were bright and hard. She was seeing a mole, where it had lain

that day in the garden path, a dank streak on the shaded softness of its side, its four pink hands stiff to the air, and a faint smell from it.[17]

And when, later, hysterical with terror, she runs from the house: "Death, like a huge mole, ran at her side."[18] In associating Rachel/Ree with a mole, Hughes has dredged up an eidolon even more deeply-entrenched in his imagination than those of lemur or fox. The mole, it would seem, was for him a personal objective correlative signifying death.

In beginning this section, I referred to Hughes's references-back from *Shepherdess* to earlier writings as 'recapitulations'. 'Recoveries', or even 'recuperations', might be preferable terms, however. What are being recouped, in all cases but those relating to Augustine's sailing-experience, are idea-images, eidola. It seems to me that Book One of *Shepherdess* is the most integrated and memorable of the volume's three parts, and though the qualities of integration and memorability are not due to the presence of the images I have commented on (or in the first place to images at all), it is not, I think, coincidental that they are present there. Although I wouldn't wish them absent from the volume, their presence is perhaps an indication that Hughes's imagination, in harking back so noticeably, was no longer as fertile as it had been. Certainly there are fresh and vital things in the later Books, but there is also an increase in the amount of autobiographical material present: and I feel that though Augustine's Moroccan adventures are freshly-handled, they neither add anything essential to the novel's historico-psychological theme nor push Augustine towards some vital event that will serve to relieve his chronic indeterminacy. Is it too much to suggest that so marked an element of recuperation, an imaginative looking-back within the larger movement forward, implies that Hughes inwardly recognized that he would not carry his serial novel significantly beyond *The Wooden Shepherdess* itself?

Afterword

As I stated at the beginning of the last chapter, Hughes never decided how many volumes of *The Human Predicament* there should be. The intentions of a writer who worked very much by intuition, and (almost notoriously) refused to pre-plan his books, must inevitably be mist-enshrouded. But something can be said, despite its provisionality.

First as regards form. Fundamental to the form of the novel is the accommodation achieved between historical time and fictional time. How is a balance to be struck, and maintained? Hughes was not, in retrospect, entirely happy with the transitional chapters he'd employed in *Shepherdess* as a means of filling in important historical background and transporting his action forward over intervals of years. He told me he was considering dropping this tactic, and focussing in each Book on a series of linked events confined to a limited period of time. He wanted to build up a sense of the density of history such as he'd achieved in the three Books of *Fox* and the first Book of *Shepherdess*. Between each Book, he thought, a time-gap would exist. What we have of Volume Three is consistent with such a strategy.

Now to the characters. Augustine's developing relationship with Norah in Volume Three points in the direction of marriage. Hughes's first attempt to start the volume (a single short abandoned chapter) presents us with an Augustine already wedded to "English Noll". Would the girl from Slaughterhouse Yard have succeeded in revitalizing the Penry-Herbert family line? Would the marriage have failed due to the huge gap — social, educational, temperamental — between the partners? It is impossible to say: but the latter appears the likelier outcome.

Hughes had in Volume Three already manoeuvred two of his most prominent characters into key institutions: Jeremy Dibden is a civil servant in the Admiralty (as was Hughes himself during the war), and Gilbert Wadamy is a junior Minister in Ramsay MacDonald's National government. Hughes's aim was clearly to secure vantage-points from which he could report from inside, first on Britain during the years of appeasement, and second on Britain during the war years themselves. The mutual irritation that Jeremy and Gilbert cause one another will be institutionalized when Gilbert becomes Jeremy's Minister in the wartime Coalition.

Augustine himself looks to have been destined to enter the Navy (fleeing Norah to go to war) so that Hughes could present certain events at sea through the eyes of an active participant. The research that Hughes had done while at the Admiralty on the *Graf Spee* (see above, pp. 71-71a) would doubtless have been pressed into use. He was also attracted to the exploits of the British cruiser *Cossack*. This ship was instrumental in rescuing 300 allied prisoners from the German tanker *Altmark* in Josing fjord on 16th February 1940, and it later played a significant part in the sinking of the battleship *Bismarck* in May 1941.

Augustine's destined wife hails from Coventry, and Coventry figured notably in Hughes's intended treatment of the home front during the war. His eldest son Robert had married a Coventry girl whose father, a member of the city fire-brigade, combated fires thoughout the two periods of blitz (November 1940, April 1941). He was away from home for days at a stretch, and his wife (many of whose experiences go into the making of Norah) couldn't know whether he was alive or dead. Norah's Dad and Mum in Slaughterhouse Yard look the likeliest characters (though Hughes never developed them in the writing he completed) to assume these roles. Also present in the Yard are Nellie and Sylvanus. Little Syl, it seems, was to grow up twisted and bitter, and, in playing "an important and bedevilled role", to provide a youthful 'double' for Hitler. Hughes's own experience of the blitz of Bath would doubtless have fuelled his account of the Coventry blitz.

But this subject in all probability, and the defeat of the *Graf Spee*, would have found their places in a fourth volume. Hughes at one point thought of ending the third volume with the fall of France — from which, one thinks, some treatment of the Dunkirk evacuation could hardly have been omitted. But his latest thoughts on ending the book revolved around the Spanish Civil War, which began in 1936 and ended early in 1939: Hughes's reasons for abandoning it included not only his realization that he couldn't simply present Augustine and Norah's marriage as a *fait accompli*, but must go back in time to account for it, but his realization that he couldn't exclude some consideration of the Civil War from a novel that aimed to encompass and explore the movement of Europe as a whole towards war.

The question: How would he have treated the Civil War? brings us to the Bavarian von Kessens, who figure prominently in the two completed volumes. It seems that Mitzi's younger brothers, the twins, figured significantly here. Hughes wanted to show the Civil War entirely from the fascist side, feeling that the republican loyalist viewpoint was already well known to British readers. He once described his intention as one of providing "a kind of descant" on a familiar theme. He had, after a (not surprisingly) lengthy search, located someone in London who had fought for Franco and was willing to talk about his war experiences. The von Kessen twins, "so-called volunteers", were to be fliers in the nationalist airforce.

It is difficult to read *The Wooden Shepherdess* without feeling that the crucial opposition is that between the blind nun Mitzi and the figure of Hitler himself. In a letter of 25th September 1959 to an agent, Richard Gregson — the only occasion, seemingly, on which Hughes committed to paper any connected thoughts on how his characters might develop — he wrote:

> Ironically, the only one of the whole von Kessen family destined to cut any figure in the world later on will be the discarded Mitzi. For as the years pass (it is not a rapid process, of course) she develops alongside the devotional powers of a St Teresa of Avila — and without ever becoming an intellectual — much of her prototype Teresa's practical capacities in handling the affairs of her convent and Order. Thus in the latter days the "Blind Abbess" becomes a symbolic and pretty important figure in the anti-Nazi world, occupying among the Romans rather the position Pastor Niemoller occupied among the Lutherans. Her passive resistance to the regime is rocklike, and she only survives concentration-camps because in the last resort Hitler dare not crown her a martyr; but she exasperates sympathisers (including ultimately the American forces) by a refusal equally rocklike ever to lift a finger against it *actively*.

This was written before Hughes completed *Fox*. Glances at other characters in the letter show that he later changed his mind about some of them: for example, he says that Otto von Kessen, Mitzi's uncle, "will be involved in the 'Generals' Plot' of July 1944 against Hitler"; but in the event Otto received shorter shrift — beaten to death with his own wooden leg at the end of *Shepherdess*. It nevertheless appears that Hughes's intentions regarding Mitzi remained pretty firm.

How would *The Human Predicament* have ended? There is good reason to believe that the final section of the last Book would have focussed on Hitler's final days in his Berlin bunker before cutting to Montgomery's acceptance of the German surrender on Lüneberg heath. It must be a source of abiding regret to Hughes's frustrated readers that he never set his imagination to work upon the last obscure, eventful hours of the senile Chancellor.

Notes

Chapter One

1. 'Eheu Fugaces', *Virginia Quarterly Review* Vol. 51 No. 2 (Spring 1975) p.260. This article was based on a broadcast, 'Childhood Days', given in 1950 over the Home Service.
2. *ibid.*
3. Autobiographical Introduction, *An Omnibus* (1931) p.viii.
4. 'Eheu Fugaces' p.262.
5. *ibid.*
6. *Confessio Juvenis* (1926) p.9.
7. *ibid.* p.10.
8. Part of a fragment quoted in my Introduction to *In the Lap of Atlas* (1979) p.7.
9. *The Eye of the Beholder* (1957) p.167.
10. Autobiographical Introduction p.xi.
11. Quoted by Penelope Hughes in *Richard Hughes: Author, Father* (1984) p.92.
12. Autobiographical Introduction p.xvii.
13. *ibid.* p.xii.
14. *ibid.*
15. *ibid.* pp.xv-xvi.
16. *Confessio Juvenis* pp.14-17.
17. 'I Live in Merioneth', *Homes and Gardens* (March 1962) p.92.
18. *Gipsy-Night* p.56; *Confessio Juvenis* p.52.
19. 'I Live in Merioneth', p.92.
20. Autobiographical Introduction p.xvii.
21. *Goodbye to All That* (Penguin 1960) pp.195-6.
22. Autobiographical Introduction p.xviii.
23. *ibid.* p.xix.
24. *Fiction as Truth*, Selected Literary Writings ed. Richard Poole (1983) p.133.
25. *ibid.* p.138.
26. *ibid.*
27. *ibid.* p.137.
28. Autobiographical Introduction p.xxii.
29. 'Poet with Frying Pan', *Sunday Telegraph* July 25, 1965 p.14.
30. Douglas Day, *Swifter than Reason* (1963) p.27.
31. 'Poet with Frying Pan'.
32. *On English Poetry* p.1.
33. Autobiographical Introduction p.xxii.
34. Gipsy-Night pp.21-23.
35. *Gipsy-Night* p.45; *Confessio Juvenis* p.40.
36. *Gipsy-Night* p.44; *Confessio Juvenis* p.36.

37. Autobiographical Introduction p. xix.
38. *Fiction as Truth* p.18.
39. June 17, 1921 p.124.
40. Autobiographical Introduction p.xxi.
41. 'A Life Sentence': Memories of Richard Hughes, *The Listener* May 10, 1979 p.658.
42. *Gipsy-Night* pp.49-51; *Confessio Juvenis* pp.49-51.
43. *Gipsy-Night* pp.57-8; *Confessio Juvenis* pp.65-6.
44. *Gipsy-Night* p.41; *Confessio Juvenis* p.27.
45. *Gipsy-Night* p.64.
46. Autobiographical Introduction p. xxii.
47. 'Diary of a Steerage Passenger': *A Moment of Time* (1926) p.233.

Chapter Two

1. Autobiographical Introduction p.xxvii.
2. *ibid.* p.xxviii.
3. 'In the Abbey Shadow' by Peter Thomas: *The Anglo-Welsh Review* Vol. 21 No. 47 (Summer 1972) p.89.
4. *Fiction as Truth* p.88.
5. *ibid.* p.33.
6. 'Will Radio Develop a Literature of its Own?' *World Review* (November 1946) p.35.
7. *Fiction as Truth* p.34.
8. *ibid.* p.35.
9. *ibid.*
10. 'Tolstoy in Wales': *Sunday Telegraph Magazine* 1971.
11. *Fiction as Truth* p.89.
12. *ibid.* pp.89-90.
13. Peter Firchow, *The Writer's Place* (1974) p.191.
14. Autobiographical Introduction p.xxx.
15. 'The Gentle Pirate', *The Listener* June 16, 1938 p.1268.
16. *Fiction as Truth* pp.89-90.
17. 'The Gentle Pirate' p.1269.
18. *ibid.*
19. *ibid.*
20. Charlotte Williams-Ellis in conversation with Penelope Hughes.
21. *Richard Hughes: Author, Father* p.11.
22. *Fiction as Truth* p.56.
23. See *Richard Hughes: Author, Father* pp.61-2.
24. Autobiographical Introduction p.xxxii.
25. *ibid.* pp.xxiv-xxv.
26. *ibid.* p.xxiv.
27. *ibid.*
28. *Fiction as Truth* p.39.
29. 'Richard Hughes, Artist and Adventurer': *Everyman* April 9, 1931 p.329.
30. 'Strange Christmases', *Harper's Bazaar* December 30, 1930 p.96.
31. *New York Evening Sun* September 26, 1929.
32. *Time and Tide* October 18, 1929.
33. *Time and Tide* October 25, 1929.
34. *Time and Tide* November 1, 1929.

Chapter Three

1. 'Nightingales and Daggers in Morocco': *Radio Times* October 17, 1930 p.161.
2. 'Nightingales and Daggers' p.180.

3. *ibid.*
4. But see my Introduction to *In the Lap of Atlas* for a discussion of the provenance of Hughes's Berber tales.
5 *Richard Hughes: Author, Father* pp.21-2.
6. This and the following extract: 'Last Words from Augustus', *Sunday Telegraph* November 5, 1961 p.20.
7. 'I Live in Merioneth' pp.93-94.
8. *Fiction as Truth* p.45.
9. *ibid.*
10. 'A Life Sentence' p.658.
11. 'Jamaica Today', *The Geographical Magazine* December 1939 p.105.
12. *Fiction as Truth* p.29.
13. *Richard Hughes: Author, Father* p.78.
14. See *The Eye of the Beholder* by Lance Sieveking pp.175-6.
15. Compare the letter home quoted by Penelope Hughes in *Richard Hughes: Author, Father* pp.51-2, to which the broadcast account looks indebted.
16. *Richard Hughes: Author, Father* p.79.

Chapter Four

1. 'A Life Sentence' p.659.
2. 'Polish Impressions', *The Spectator* September 17, 1948 p.358.
3. 'Politicians are Specialists', *Our Time* Vol.7 No.13 (October 1948) p.338.
4. See *Fiction as Truth* pp.59-63.
5. See *Richard Hughes: Author, Father* pp.72-3.
6. *Time and Tide* November 26, 1949 pp.1185-6.
7. See *Fiction as Truth* pp.107-117.
8. For R.S. Thomas, see 'R.S. Thomas talks to J.B. Lethbridge', *The Anglo-Welsh Review* No.74 (1983) pp.39-40.
9. In conversation with Michael Bakewell.
10. *Fiction as Truth* p.68.
11. *ibid.* p.65.
12. *ibid.* p.66.
13. *ibid.* p.69.
14. 'Notes on the Way', *Time and Tide* July 6, 1940 p.708.
15. 'Richard Hughes, Artist and Adventurer' p.328.
16. *The Writer's Place* p.187.
17. *Fiction as Truth* p.52.
18. *The Writer's Place* p.190.
19. *Richard Hughes: Author, Father* pp.132-33.
20. See above p.42.
21. See above pp.49-50.
22. June 28, 1969 pp.30-31.

Chapter Five

1. Retitled 'Dream' in *Gipsy-Night*.
2. *Gipsy-Night* p.44; *Confessio Juvenis* p.36.
3. *Gipsy-Night* p.17.
4. *ibid.* pp.21-22.
5. *Gipsy-Night* p.52; *Confessio Juvenis* p.24.
6. Introduction to *Georgian Poetry* (Penguin 1962) p.xiii.

7. *Gipsy-Night* p.21.
8. *ibid.* p.59. This poem is in *Confessio Juvenis* (p.54) retitled 'The Broken Wing'.
9. *Gipsy-Night* pp.49-51; *Confessio Juvenis* pp.49-51.
10. *Gipsy-Night* pp.39-40; *Confessio Juvenis* pp.32-33. Punctuation as in *CJ*.
11. *Venus and Adonis* lines 1033-36; "I stood tip-toe upon a little hill" lines 72-80.
12. *Gipsy-Night* p.15; *Confessio Juvenis* p.23, where t hyphenated.
13. *Gipsy-Night* pp.37-38.
14. *Gipsy-Night* pp.65-66; *Confessio Juvenis* p.67. Punctuation as in *CJ*.
15. 'Wales and the Welsh', *Review of Reviews* June 15, 1924. *My People*, says Hughes, "is a cold-blooded and wilful trading on English ignorance, prompted by personal dislike of his fellow-countrymen, and having at most only a local application to one or two valleys" (p.461).
16. *A Moment of Time* p.60.
17. He published only two poems in later years: in the March 1931 and July 1931 issues of *New Statesman and Nation*.
18. Amabel Williams-Ellis, *All Stracheys are Cousins* (1983) p.88.
19. For this latter, see especially Lance Sieveking, *The Eye of the Beholder* p.166.

Chapter Six

1. *Fiction as Truth* pp.17-18.
2. *ibid.* p.18.
3. See above pp.18-19
4. *Fiction as Truth* p.18
5. *ibid.* p.46-47.
6. *ibid.* p.19.
7. *ibid.* p.20.
8. Phoenix Edition (Chatto & Windus 1931) p.8.
9. *ibid.* p.16.
10. *Introduction to the English Novel* Volume One (1951) p.13.
11. *ibid.* p.15.
12. *ibid.* p.27.
13. *Fiction as Truth* p.20.
14. *ibid.* p.21.
15. *Literary Essays of Ezra Pound* ed. T.S.Eliot (1954) p.4.
16. 'A conversation with Richard Hughes' *The Listener* October 23, 1975 p.546.
17. *Confessio Juvenis* p.89.
18. *Plays* pp.123-24.
19. *ibid.* p.124.
20. See above p.111.
21. *Fiction as Truth* pp.131-32.
22. See *A Treatise of Human Nature* ed. L.A. Selby-Bigge (1888) pp.1, 8-9.
23. *A Treatise of Human Nature* pp.630-31.
24. Mary Warnock, *Imagination* (1976) p.133.
25. *The London Mercury* November 1929.
26. *The Sketch* August 3, 1938 p.230.
27. Translated J.H. Bernard (1892) pp.176-77.
28. *Not Without Glory* (1976) pp.26-27.
29. *Fiction as Truth* p.25.
30. In, respectively, *Tradition and Dream* (Penguin 1965) pp.81-84; Guide to Modern World Literature Vol.1 (Teach Yourself Books 1975) p.317.
31. *Newsletter of the English Centre of the International P.E.N.* (Summer 1968) No.8 p.24.

Chapter Seven

1. Princeton 1971 p.40.
2. See above pp.172-76.
3. *The Voyage of the Beagle* (Everyman 1936) pp.18 and 26 respectively.
4. This and the following extract: Sixth ed. (1892) p.278.
5. *Plays* p.182.
6.. 'A conversation with Richard Hughes' p.546.
7. See, for a stimulating account of the child in nineteenth and twentieth century literature, *The Image of Childhood* by Peter Coveney (Peregrine 1967).
8. Book V Chapter IV (Constance Garnett's translation).
9. Sixth edition p.142.
10. J.A.C. Brown, *Freud and the Post-Freudians* (Pelican 1961) p.28.
11. Kegan Paul 1942 p.23.
12. *The Origin of Species* Sixth ed. p.125.
13. Compare: "at the same time she knew, beyond all doubt, in her innermost being, that she was damned, that there never had been anyone as wicked as her since the world began." (p.157)
14. See *Freud and the Post-Freudians* p.3

Chapter Eight

1. *Fiction as Truth* p.43
2. *ibid.* p.44.
3. For he had begun to see it much earlier. See above p.83.
4. *Fiction as Truth* p.48.
5. *ibid.*
6. *ibid.* pp.97, 101.
7. *The Daily Telegraph*, July 15, 1938.
8. See above pp. 64-65.
9. See especially paragraph 23 in 'Analytic of the Sublime'.
10. *Introductory Lectures on Psychoanalysis* (2nd ed. 1933) p.178.
11. Truth p.44. Compare *In Hazard* p.268.
12. See above p.35.
13. 'Notes on the Way', *Time and Tide* July 6, 1940 p.708.
14. *Introductory Lectures on Psychoanalyis* p.239.
15. *Richard Hughes* (1973) p.66.

Chapter Nine

1. 'Notes on the Way' December 3, 1938 pp.1686-88.
2. *Snapshots/Towards a New Novel* (1965) p.60. Subsequent quotations come from pp.61, 53, 54, 52 respectively.
3. *The Tao of Physics* (Fontana 1976) p.144.
4. *Physics and Philosophy* (1963) p.96.
5. *The Tao of Physics* p.71.
6. *Snapshots* p.43.
7. See Christopher Butler, *After the Wake* (1980) pp.14-15.
8. This is printed as 'Fiction as Truth' in *Fiction as Truth* pp.70-74.
9. *Aspects of the Novel* (Pelican 1962) pp.54-55.
10. *The Tale of Genji*, translated in one volume by Arthur Waley (1938) p.500. Other extracts, p.501.
11. *Fiction as Truth* p.60.
12. *The Collected Essays, Journalism and Letters of George Orwell*, Vol.1 (Penguin 1970) pp.491-92.

13. *Fiction as Truth* p.63.
14. Milton, *Prose Writings* (Everyman 1958) pp.149-50.
15. *Biographia Literaria* (Everyman 1956) p.67.
16. *Prose Writings* p.175.
17. *ibid.* pp.181-82.

Chapter Ten

1. See the Afterword, below.
2. *Introductory Lectures on Psychoanalysis* p.128.
3. *Fiction as Truth* p.71.
4. *ibid.* p.74.
5. See above pp.34-35.
6. Peter Thomas, *Richard Hughes* p.85.
7. See pp.12, 66, 197.
8. This and the following quotations, *Fiction as Truth* p.71.
9. Arthur C. Danto, *Sartre* (Fontana 1975) p.120.
10. In *Tolstoy and the Novel* (1966) p.18.
11. See the extract quoted above in the Foreword.
12. *Fiction as Truth* pp.72-73.
13. Heiden pp.102-103. Bullock, revised ed. (Pelican 1962) p.81.
14. *Hitler: the Missing Years* p.21.
15. Robert H. Pfeiffer, *Introduction to the Old Testament* (1952) pp.596-97.
16. See 'The Miniature and the Deluge', *Encounter* XVII (1961) p.78.
17. *A Moment of Time* p.129 (see above pp.151-53).
18. *ibid.* p.133.

Bibliography

Section A restricts itself to English and American first editions. Section B, C and D add nine items to the bibliography included in *Fiction as Truth*. American publications are marked by an asterisk.

(A) Poetry

A.1   *Gipsy-Night and Other Poems:* Golden Cockerel Press 1922.
A.2   *Confessio Juvenis:* Chatto & Windus 1926.

Plays

A.3   *The Sisters' Tragedy:* Basil Blackwell 1922.
A.4   *The Sisters' Tragedy and Other Plays:* Heinemann 1924.
A.5 *   *A Rabbit and a Leg* (Collected Plays): A.A. Knopf 1924.

Miscellany

A.6 *   *An Omnibus:* Harper and Brothers 1931.

Novels

A.7 *   *The Innocent Voyage:* Harper and Brothers 1928.
A.8   *A High Wind in Jamaica:* Chatto & Windus 1929.
A.9   *In Hazard:* Chatto & Windus 1938.
A.10 *   *In Hazard:* Harper and Brothers 1938.
A.11   *The Fox in the Attic:* Chatto & Windus 1961.
A.12 *   *The Fox in the Attic:* Harper and Brothers 1962.
A.13   *The Wooden Shepherdess:* Chatto & Windus 1973.
A.14 *   *The Wooden Shepherdess:* Harper and Brothers 1973.

Stories

A.15   *A Moment of Time:* Chatto & Windus 1926.
A.16   *In the Lap of Atlas:* Chatto & Windus 1979.

Children's Stories

A.17   *The Spider's Palace:* Chatto & Windus 1931.
A.18   *Don't Blame Me:* Chatto & Windus 1940.
A.19 *   *Gertrude's Child:* Harlin Quist 1966.
A.20   *The Wonder-Dog* (Collected Children's Stories): Chatto & Windus 1977.

History

A.21   *The Administration of War Production* (with J.D. Scott): HM Stationery Office/ Longmans, Green and Co. 1955.

Selected Literary Writings

A.22   *Fiction as Truth:* Poetry Wales Press 1983.

(B.i) EDITING

B.1   *Poems by John Skelton*, with an Introduction: Heinemann 1924.

(B.ii) PREFACES (etc.)

B.2   *Soldiers' Pay* by William Faulkner: Chatto & Windus 1930.
B.3   *The Sound and the Fury* by William Faulkner: Chatto & Windus 1931.
B.4   *The Unexpected* by Frank Penn-Smith: Jonathan Cape 1933.
B.5   *Escape to the Sea* by Fred Rebell: John Murray 1939.
B.6   *The Venturesome Voyages of Captain Voss* by Captain John Voss: John Murray 1949.
B.7   *Headlong Down the Years* by Amabel and Clough Williams-Ellis: University of Liverpool Press 1951.
B.8   *Mosquitoes* by William Faulkner: Chatto & Windus 1964.
B.9   *The Magic Valley Travellers* ed. Peter Haining: Gollancz 1974.
B.10   *Welcome to Our District:* Official Guide of Deudraeth Rural District.
B.11   *Edward Wolfe, 1948* (Catalogue note to exhibition of paintings).
B.12   *A Note on the Artist:* Edward Wolfe Retrospective Exhibition catalogue, Arts Council 1967.

Abbreviations:

G — The Graphic; ES — Evening Standard; L — The Listener; NA — The Nation and Athenaeum; NSN — New Statesman and Nation; O — The Observer; RT — Radio Times; SRL — Saturday Review of Literature; SWG — Saturday Westminster Gazette; Sp — Spectator; STel — Sunday Telegraph; ST — Sunday Times; T&T — Time and Tide; TLS — Times Literary Supplement; VQR — Virginia Quarterly Review; WWG — Weekly Westminster Gazette; WR — World Review.

(C) ARTICLES

C.1   'What's Wrong with the Stage?': *ES* 5 June 1920.
C.2   'Diary of a Steerage Passenger': *SWG* 19 November 1921, pp.4-5.
C.3-   'A Diary in Eastern Europe': *WWG* 9, 16, 23, 30 September; 7, 21 October; 4
C.9   November 1922 (in seven parts).
C.10   'How Listening Plays are Done': *ES* 16 January 1924.
C.11   'The Cinema's New Rival': *Women's Pictorial* 29 February 1924.
C.12   'Wales and the Welsh': *Review of Reviews* 15 June 1924, pp.461-66.
C.13   'New Trends in the Theatre': *Forum* June 1925.
C.14   'Aspects of the Cinema': *The Outlook* 2 January 1926, p.8.
C.15 * 'Under the Nose, Under the Skin': *New York Herald Tribune, Books* pp.1, 6.
C.16   'Rum Runners I Have Known': *Daily Chronicle and Liverpool Mercury* 13 December 1929, p.8.
C.17   'Nightingales and Daggers in Morocco': *RT* 17 October 1930, pp.161, 180.

C.18 * 'Illogic and the Child': *SRL* 15 November 1930.

C.19 * 'Strange Christmases': *Harper's Bazaar* December 1930, pp.75, 96.

C.20 'The Relation of Nationalism to Literature': *Transactions of the Honourable Society of Cymmrodorion*, Session 1930-31, pp.107-28.

C.21 'My First Day in the Air': *Daily Express* 20 April 1931.

C.22 'Revolution in Tetuan': *G* 16 May 1931, p.264.

C.23 'Under the Nose and Under the Skin': *L* 10 June 1931, p.979.

C.24 'Time to Burn Boats': *Week-End Review* 10 October 1931, pp.424-25.

C.25 'All God's Chillun Got Wings': *NSN* 18 March 1933, pp.321-22.

C.26 'Cave Drawings: a New Theory': *NSN* 1 April 1933, pp.414-15.

C.27 'Northern Africa': *L* 19 April 1933, p.629.

C.28-
C.37 'Notes on the Way': *T&T* 19 September 1936, pp.1273-75; 26 September 1936, pp.1306-8; 16 October 1937, pp.1361-64; 23 October 1937, pp.1393-95; 30 October 1937, pp. 1428-29; 26 November 1938, pp.1638-39; 3 December 1938, pp.1686-88; 10 December 1938, pp.1778-80; 29 June 1940, p.684; 6 July 1940, p.708.

C.38 'The Gentle Pirate': *L* 16 June 1938, pp.1268-70.

C.39 'Tale-telling for Children': *G* 16 June 1938, pp.222-23.

C.40 'England's Green and Pleasant Sea': *The Star* 29 August 1938.

C.41 'Birth of a Hurricane': *L* 15 October 1938, pp.544-45.

C.42 'Jamaica Today': *The Geographical Magazine* December 1939, pp.105-14.

C.43 'Sailing': *The Saturday Book* 24 March 1946, pp.221-27.

C.44 'Will Radio Develop a Literature of its Own?': *WR* November 1946, pp.33-36.

C.45 * 'The Second Revolution: Literature and Radio': *VQR* XXIII, Winter 1947, pp.34-43.

C.46 'The Writer's Duty': *L* 22 July 1948, pp.131-32.

C.47 'Polish Impressions': *Sp* 17 September 1948, p.358.

C.48 'Star Tiger Down': *Sp* 8 October 1948, pp.457-58.

C.49 'Politicians are Specialists': *Our Time* Vol.17 No. 3, October 1948, p.338.

C.50 'Dry Land': *T&T* 26 November 1949, pp.1185-86.

C.51 'Make Parenthood Possible': *WR* December 1949, pp.48-52.

C.52 'Robert Louis Stevenson': *L* 16 November 1950, pp.533-34.

C.53 'Wales Through the Looking-glass': *L* 24 May 1951, pp.838-39.

C.54 'The Coronation in Wales': *T&T* June 1953.

C.55 'Albert Schweitzer': *Picture Post* 12 December 1953, pp.16-17.

C.56 'George Borrow: Victorian Rebel': *RT* 3 December 1954, p.4.

C.57 'The Birth of Radio Drama': *Atlantic Monthly* December 1957, pp.145-48.

C.58 'Augustus': *STel* 5 November 1961, p.20.

C.59 'I Live in Merioneth': *Homes and Gardens* March 1962 pp.92-95.

C.60 'Liturgical Language Today': *Province* Vol.XIII No. 4, 1962. (Subsequently published as a Church in Wales pamphlet.)

C.61 'Faulkner and Bennett': *Encounter* XXI, 3, September 1963, pp.59-61.

C.62 'Seven Mirrors for Parishes': *Six Lay Voices*, Church in Wales Publications 1964, pp.29-35.

C.63 'Poet with Frying-pan': *STel* 25 July 1965, p.14.

C.64 'African Authors — Read your Contracts!': *Nairobi Nation* 27 February 1967.

C.65 * 'Fiction as Truth': *Proceedings of the American Academy of Arts and Letters and Titute of Arts and Letters* Second Series No. 20, 1970, pp.16-22 ('The Blashfield Address').

C.66 'Not Things, but Persons': *Times Saturday Review* 21 March 1970, p.1.

C.67 'You Should have been Here Yesterday': *O* 17 January 1971, p.24.

C.68 * 'Eheu Fugaces': *VQR* LI, Spring 1975, pp.258-63.

(D) BOOK REVIEWS

D.1 *The Owl: The Topaz of Ethiopia* Vol. 1 No. 3 (1919) p.2.

D.2   *The Wisdom of Akhnaton* by A.E. Grantham, *Touch and Go* by D.H. Lawrence, *The Powers of the Air* by Sturge Moore: *SWG* 28 July 1920.

D.3   *Collected Poems* by Edward Thomas, *A Song of Life and Other Poems* by W.H. Davies, *Wayside Poems* by Gerald Bull: *SWG* 25 September 1920.

D.4   *Over the Brazier* by Robert Graves, *The Waggoner and Other Poems* by Edmund Blunden, *The Moon* by J.C. Squire: *SWG* 2 October 1920.

D.5   *A Village Sermon* by Herbert Asquith, *Poems* by Sir Cecil Spring-Rice: *SWG* 23 October 1920.

D.6   *Aria da Capo* by Edna St. Vincent Millay, *Otherworld: Cadences* by F.S. Flint, *The Romance of Youth* by E.E. Bradford, *Poems of Expression* by T.G.W. Henslow: *SWG* 30 October 1920.

D.7   *Outlines of Modern English Literature* by Harold Williams: SWG 6 November 1920.

D.8   *Absalom: A Tragedy* by Torahiko Khori, *The Poet in the Desert* by C.E. Scott Wood, *Songs of the Cattle Trail and Cow Camp* by John A. Lomax, *To-day and Yesterday* by William Dudley Foulke, *Hamewith* by Charles Murray: *SWG* 27 November 1920.

D.9   *The Collected Prose of James Elroy Flecker:* SWG 12 March 1921.

D.10   *Pengard Awake* by Ralph Straus: *SWG* 19 March 1921.

D.11   'Some Notes on W.E. Henley' (Review of 3-volume *Collected Works*): *SWG* 19 March 1921.

D.12   *The Gods of Mexico* by Lewis Spence: *Sp* 25 August 1923.

D.13   *The Eighth Wonder* by A.S.M. Hutchinson: *Sp* 22 September 1923.

D.14   *Three Plays* by Luigi Pirandello: *WWG* 29 December 1923.

D.15   *Come Hither* ed. Walter de la Mare: *Sp* 29 December 1923.

D.16   *Beasts, Birds and Flowers* by D.H. Lawrence: *NA* 5 January 1924.

D.17   *Essays on Poetry* by J.C. Squire: *WWG* 19 January 1924.

D.18   *The Story of My Heart* by Richard Jefferies: *WWG* 2 February 1924.

D.19   *The Fanatics* by Miles Malleson, *The Dance of Life* by Hermon Ould, *Outward Bound* by Sutton Vane, *Three Plays* by Anatoli Vasilievich Lunarchski, *Gas* by Georg Kaiser, *Four Short Plays* (British Drama League series): *Spectator Literary Supplement* 5 April 1924.

D.20   *Fifth of November* by Howard Peacey, *The Prince* by Gwen John, *First Blood* by Allan Monkhouse, *Tolstoi's Dramas* Trans. by N.H. Dole: *Sp* 28 June 1924.

D.21   *Crossings: A Fairy Play* by Walter de la Mare: *Sp* 15 November 1924.

D.22 * *Mrs. Dalloway* by Virginia Woolf: *SRL* 16 May 1925.

D.23   *Messages* by Ramon Fernandez: *NA* 27 August 1927.

D.24   *Camera Obscura* by William Bolitho: *News Chronicle* 17 June 1931.

D.25   *Seven Pillars of Wisdom* by T.E. Lawrence: *Sp* 2 August 1935.

D.26   *Ships* by Hendrik van Loon: *Sp* 20 December 1935.

D.27   *Uffa Fox's Second Book* by Uffa Fox: *Sp* 24 January 1936.

D.28   *Freak Ships* by Stanley Rogers, *The History of American Sailing Ships* by Howard I. Chapelle: *Sp* 24 July 1936.

D.29   *Flowering Nettle* by Harry Martinson: *O* 4 October 1936.

D.30   *American Sailing Craft* by Howard *The Anatomy of Neptune* by Brian Tunstall, *Ships that have Made History* by Gregory Robinson, *The Flower of England's Garland* by G.E. Manwaring, *Crimes of the High Seas* by David Masters: *Sp* 16 October 1936.

D.31   *The Blue Bed* by Glyn Jones: *O* 7 February 1937.

D.32   *Sailing and Cruising* by K. Adlard Coles, *The King's Britannica* by John Irving, *Clipper Ships of America and Great Britain* by Helen and Jacques la Grange: *NSN* 26 June 1937.

D.33   *The Letters of T.E. Lawrence* ed. David Garnett: *NSN* 10 December 1938.

D.34   *The Beauty of Sail* by Uffa Fox, *The Yachtsman's Week-end Book* John Irving and Douglas Service, *Thoughts on Yachts and Yachting* by Uffa Fox, *The Yachtsman's Annual and Who's Who: NSN* 7 January 1939.

D.35   *The Passing of the Aborigines* by Daisy Bates: *ST* 15 January 1939.

D.36   *On Sailing the Sea:* a Collection of the Seagoing Writings of Hilaire Belloc and W.N. Roughead: *NSN* 10 February 1940.

D.37   *Wind Aloft, Wind Alow* by Marin-Marie: *ST* 18 November 1945.

D.38   *West Country Stories* by A.L. Rowse: *TLS* 8 December 1945.

D.39   *The Buttercup Field and Other Stories* by Gwyn Jones: *TLS* 30 December 1945.

D.40   *Prospects of the Industrial Areas of Great Britain* by M.P. Fogarty, *Quarterly Review* January 1946.

D.41   *Time in the East* by Evan John, *Jungle Pilot* by Barry Sutton: *ST* 28 April 1946.

D.42   *Sailing through Life* by John Scott Hughes: *ST* 31 August 1947.

D.43   *The Ashley Book of Knots* by Clifford Ashley: *ST* 16 November 1947.

D.44   *Sailing Around the World* by Captain Joshua Slocum: *T&T* 17 April 1948.

D.45   *Nuremberg Diary* by G.M. Gilbert: *ST* 1 August 1948.

D.46   *The Kon-Tiki Expedition* by Thor Heyerdahl: *O* 2 April 1950.

D.47   *Humanities* by Desmond MacCarthy: *Sp* 2 October 1953.

D.48   *The Hill of Devi* by E.M. Forster: *Sp* 16 October 1953.

D.49   *A Writer's Diary* — extracts from the Diary of Virginia Woolf ed. Leonard Woolf: *Sp* 20 November 1953.

D.50   *Except the Lord* by Joyce Cary: *Sp* 18 December 1953.

D.51   *The Golden Horizon* ed. Cyril Connolly: *ST* 20 December 1953.

D.52   *The Strachey Family* by Charles R. Sanders: *Sp* 5 February 1954.

D.53   *Under Milk Wood* by Dylan Thomas: *ST* 7 March 1954.

D.54   *Katherine Mansfield* by Anthony Alpers: *ST* 25 April 1954.

D.55   *The Memoirs of a Buccaneer* by Louis le Golif: *ST* 12 May 1954.

D.56   *The Bloomsbury Group* by J.K. Johnstone: *Sp* 11 June 1954.

D.57   *The Fellowship of the Ring* by J.R.R. Tolkein: *Sp* 1 October 1954.

D.58   *The Power of Words* by Stuart Chase: *ST* 15 May 1955.

D.59   *Double Talk* by Harry Hodgkinson: *ST* 26 June 1955.

D.60   *Elinor Glyn* by Anthony Glyn: *ST* 24 July 1955.

D.61   *The Opposing Self* by Lionel Trilling: *ST* 7 August 1955.

D.62   *Adventures in the Skin Trade* by Dylan Thomas: *ST* 11 September 1955.

D.63   *A History of Welsh Literature* by Thomas Parry, *An Introduction to Welsh Poetry* by Gwyn Williams: *ST* January 1956.

D.64   *Gipsy Moth Circles the World* by Francis Chichester: *ST* 12 November 1967.

D.65   *John Strachey* by Hugh *ST* 6 May 1973.

Index

Works of Richard Hughes discussed

Poetry

History:

as Co-editor:

Films: